NEW
BREAKTHROUGH
ITALIAN

SECOND EDITION

Giovanni Carsaniga
Professor, Department of Italian,
University of Sydney, Australia

Brian Hill
General Editor
Professor of Modern Languages
Language Centre, University of Brighton

MACMILLAN

First published 1982 by Pan Books Ltd
First Macmillan edition published 1988
Reprinted six times
Second edition published 1997
MACMILLAN PRESS LTD
Houndmills, Basingstoke, Hampshire RG21 6XS
and London
Companies and representatives throughout the world

ISBN 0–333–64810–2 book
ISBN 0–333–64811–0 book and cassette pack
ISBN 0–333–64812–9 cassettes

A catalogue record for this book is available from the British Library.

This book is printed on paper suitable for recycling and made from fully managed and sustained forest sources.

9	8	7	6	5	4	3	2	1
05	04	03	02	01	00	99	98	97

Designed by D&J Hunter
Audio producer: Gerald Ramshaw, Max II
Actors: Giancarlo Ciccone, Giovanna Mogil-Price, Elena Jeronimidis
Printed in Great Britain by Jarrold Book Printing, Thetford, Norfolk

Acknowledgements

The task of collecting recordings in Italy at various times was made easy by the co-operation of many casual acquaintances, whom I must necessarily thank collectively. Managers and employees of public offices and utilities gave freely of their time. Shops and markets gave me permission to eavesdrop on the conversation between their staff and customers. Some collaborators deserve a special mention: Aldo Visco-Gilardi and the staff of Casa Valdese (Rome), Dr Giuseppe Deluca, the manager and staff of Ristorante Il Balanzone (Milano), Hostaria Il Buttero (Rome), Gran Caffè Adriano (Rome) and Royal Victoria Hotel (Pisa), the directors and staff of the Ente Provinciale del Turismo in Milan and Pisa, the station managers and staff of Domodossola, Pisa and Roma Termini railway stations, the manager and staff of the passenger terminal, Galilei Airport (Pisa). May I finally thank my wife, for her perceptive advice; and my mother who was just as keen to contribute to the 1995 recordings at the age of 90 as she was when I was preparing the first version of this course in 1981.

The following illustration sources are acknowledged:
Alitalia pp. 21, 75; Tiggy Ansell pp. 3 (foot), 4, 28, 74, 79, 97, 101, 106, 147 (top), 192, 209 (top), 231; Rita Artuso pp. 3 (top four), 197, 203, 209, 220, 221; David Bugler pp. 189, 190, 224; Giovanni Carsaniga pp. 8, 29, 36, 41, 59, 61, 64 (foot), 65, 67, 88, 91, 105, 107, 111, 112, 123, 156, 161, 175, 208; Corriere della Sera, Milan p. 176; Ferrovie dello Stato p. 133; David & Jenny Hunter pp. 16, 18, 42, 92 (top), 100, 101, 153, 179, 232; Istituto Poligrafico e Zecca dello Stato p. 69; Italian State Tourist Board (ENIT), London pp. i, 12, 25, 62, 80, 92 (foot), 128, 136, 137, 139, 142, 157, 160, 169, 187, 195, 218, 226, 229; J. Allan Cash Ltd pp. 60, 225; Rhône-Poulenc Rorer p. 213; Telecom Italia p. 37; Paul & Cynthia Tyler pp. 1, 7, 29, 72, 83, 104, 127, 136, 143, 147 (foot), 170. The publishers would like to thank Andrew and Elizabeth Norton for their help with illustrative material.

Every effort has been made to trace all copyright holders, but if any have been inadvertently overlooked the publishers will be pleased to make the necessary arrangements at the first opportunity.

Contents

HOW TO USE THIS COURSE

Since the Breakthrough series was introduced in 1982, several million people world-wide have used the courses to learn a variety of languages. This is a completely revised edition: there are new recordings, new activities and new ways of presenting the material. We have talked to hundreds of learners about their 'Breakthrough' experiences and we have acted on what we were told to ensure the new course is even more enjoyable and useful.

Following this course will help you understand, speak and read most of the Italian you are likely to need on holiday or on business trips. The course is based on recordings made in Italy of ordinary Italian people in everyday situations. Step by step you will learn first to understand what they are saying and then to speak in similar situations yourself.

General hints to help you use the course

- Have confidence in us! Real language is complex and you will find certain things in every unit which are not explained in detail. Don't worry about this. We will build up your knowledge slowly, selecting only what is most important at each stage.
- Try to study regularly, but in short periods: 20–30 minutes each day is usually better than 3½ hours once a week.
- To help you learn to speak, say the words and phrases out loud whenever possible.
- If you don't understand something, leave it for a while. Learning a language is a bit like doing a jigsaw or a crossword: there are many ways to tackle it and it all falls into place eventually.
- Don't be afraid to write in the book and add your own notes.
- Do review your work frequently. It helps to get somebody to test you – and they don't need to know Italian.
- Memorising the vocabulary is easier if you group words together, say, in subject areas (as in this book) and notice similarities between English and Italian words, or between related Italian words.
- If you can possibly learn with somebody else you will be able to help each other and practise the language together.
- Learning Italian may take more time than you thought. Just be patient and above all don't get angry with yourself.

Suggested study pattern

Each unit of the course consists of approximately sixteen pages in the book and fifteen minutes of recording. The first page of each unit will tell you what you are going to learn and will give some hints on language learning. You should follow the material at first in the order in which it is presented. As you progress with the course you may find that you evolve a method of study which suits you better – that's fine, but we suggest you keep to our pattern at least for the first two or three units or you may find you are not taking full advantage of all the possibilities offered by the material.

The book contains step-by-step instructions for working through the course: when to use the book on its own, when to use the recording on its own, when to use them both together and how to use them. On the recording our presenter will guide you through the various sections. Here is an outline of the pattern proposed:

Pronunciation notes

At the start of each unit there are some tips on pronunciation. One or two points are explained in the book, which are then picked up and practised on the recording. It is important to listen to, and imitate, the speakers on the recordings. Remember, though, that while we wish to encourage you to sound as Italian-like as possible, Italians are willing to make allowances and you may achieve effective communication even if your pronunciation is not perfect!

Conversations

Listen to each conversation, first without stopping the recording, and get a feel for the task ahead. Then go over it bit by bit in conjunction with the vocabulary and the notes. You should get into the habit of using the pause/stop and rewind buttons on your machine to give yourself time to think and to go over the conversation a number of times. Don't leave a conversation until you are confident that you have at least understood it. There are usually two or three conversations in each section, and three sets of conversations in a unit.

Italian speakers, like English speakers, sprinkle their talk with fillers – sounds or words which are not relevant to the meaning. We shall point out some of their speech quirks to you (though we have edited out the most obtrusive). Listen in particular for a longer final vowel – a typical Italian marker of hesitation.

Practice

This section contains a selection of listening, reading and speaking activities which focus your attention on the most important language in the unit. To do them you will need to work closely with the book and often use your machine – sometimes you are asked to write the answers to an exercise and then check them on the recording, at others to listen first and then fill in answers in the book. Again, use your pause/stop and rewind buttons to give yourself time to think and to answer questions.

You will also find practice exercises for speaking the main words and phrases which you have already heard and had explained. The book gives only an outline of the exercises, so you are just listening in to the recordings and responding. Usually you will be asked to take part in a conversation where you hear a question or statement in Italian, followed by a suggestion in English as to what to say. You then give your reply in Italian and listen to see if you were right. You will probably have to go over these spoken exercises a few times before you get them absolutely correct.

Grammar

At this stage in a unit things should begin to fall into place and you are ready for the grammar section. You can still learn a lot without studying this part, but most people quite enjoy finding out how the language they are using actually works and how it is put together. In Italian the endings of words are important to the meaning; there are easy rules to predict what these endings should be, and we explain the most important ones in easy stages. But don't worry if you get some endings wrong: your Italian listeners will still understand you in most cases.

Key words and phrases

This is a list of the most important words and phrases used in the unit. Pause at this section to see how much you can remember. Look first at the Italian and find the English equivalent. Then try it the other way round, from English into Italian. If you find there are some groups of words you have forgotten (don't worry – it happens to everybody!), turn back and have another look at the conversations and notes. These key words and phrases are likely to crop up later in the course so it's worth getting to grips with them before you leave a unit.

Did you know?

In this section you will be given some practical background information on customs, culture and life in Italian-speaking countries.

Answers

The answers to all the exercises can be found on the last page of each unit, if they have not already been given on the recording.

If you haven't learned languages using recordings before, just spend five minutes on Unit 1 getting used to the mechanics: try pausing the recording and see how long the rewind button needs to be pressed to recap on different length phrases and sections. Don't be shy – take every opportunity you can to speak Italian to Italian people and to listen to real Italian. Try listening to Italian broadcasts on the radio or watch satellite television. It's even a good idea to talk to yourself in Italian as much as possible. Try describing what you see as you are travelling around for instance. **Buona fortuna e buon lavoro!** (Good luck and happy working!)

At the back of the book

At the back of the book is a reference section which contains:

1 GREETINGS!

WHAT YOU WILL LEARN

▶ how to greet people
▶ how to say where you are from
▶ how to say where you live

BEFORE YOU BEGIN

The function of greetings is to make contact, not necessarily to understand everything that people say about themselves. Concentrate on the things we ask you to listen for and do not worry about the rest. At this stage you can master simple sentences, like the ones at the beginning of this course, without knowing the grammatical rules that generate them. Of course you might be able to understand the recordings more easily if you already knew the rules. But it would be pointless to explain them in a vacuum before you heard the recordings. Obviously you will have to go back to the recordings after reading the explanations in the notes and in the grammar section. In fact, every part of this course, book and recordings, is designed to be read or listened to more than once, until you have mastered it.

Pronunciation notes

Italian pronunciation is much more straightforward than English, since an Italian letter always corresponds to one sound (unlike English 'a' in far, fat and fate). So it has only five basic vowel sounds. When you see them written down in combination (as in **stai**, **tuo**, **grazie**, **piacere**, **vediamo**, etc.) pronounce each in the order in which it appears. In this unit we concentrate on words ending in *-o* (**giorno**, **bravo**, **molto**, **tanto**, etc.). The *-o* must be kept short and sharp, and NOT turned into an *-ow* glide, as in English.

CONVERSATIONS

▶ Rita and Renzo exchange greetings

LISTEN FOR...

▶ **buon giorno**	good day (morning, afternoon)
▶ **Come stai?/sta?**	How are you?/is he/she?
▶ **sì**	yes

Rita	Renzo buon giorno.
Renzo	Buon giorno.
Rita	Come stai?
Renzo	Eh, abbastanza bene.
Rita	Abbastanza bene?
Renzo	Sì.
Rita	Nipotino sta bene?
Renzo	Sta bene, sì.
Rita	Bravo.

▶ **buon giorno**   good day, but used also for good morning and good afternoon. From late afternoon on, say **buona sera** (good evening). Before retiring at night say **buona notte** (good night). All three are often written as one word: **buongiorno**, **buonasera**, **buonanotte**.

▶ **Come stai?**   How are you? (lit. How you stay?) The ending of Italian verbs indicates who they refer to. The ending *-i* on **stai** refers to 'you', so there is no separate word for 'you'.

The verb **stare** (to be, to stay) is used when referring to one's state of health. Note also: [**Il**] **nipotino sta bene?** (Is [the] little grandson well?) **Come stai?** should be answered by a reference to one's actual state of health: [**sto**] **bene** (I'm well), **abbastanza bene** (quite well), **non tanto bene** (not too well), etc.

▶ **sì**   yes

Bravo, a word meaning various things in different contexts (clever, brave, good), is frequently used as a way of showing you approve.

▶ Aldo is not feeling very well

LISTEN FOR...

▶ **ciao**	hello! (hi!), bye bye
▶ **grazie**	thanks
▶ **non tanto bene**	not too well

Aldo	Ciao Mauro, come stai?
Mauro	Bene, tu?
Aldo	Oggi non tanto bene. Come sta tuo padre?
Mauro	Bene, grazie.
Aldo	Be' mi fa piacere.

▶ **ciao**   hello! (hi)!, bye bye; used on meeting and parting. **Buon giorno** (**buona sera**, **buona notte**) is used both with close friends and total strangers, but **ciao** is only appropriate in an informal context, talking to people one would address in English by their first name.

tu   you (singular), **tuo**   your(s)
oggi   today

Greetings!   *Unit 1*

▶ **non tanto bene**   not too well. The opposite is **non tanto male** (not too bad).
   padre   father
▶ **bene, grazie**   well, thanks. Note the pronunciation of **grazie** (thanks, thank you),
   because you will be using this word all the time.
   be'   shortened from **bene** (well), as an opener at the beginning of a sentence.
   mi fa piacere   I'm glad to hear it (lit. to me it makes pleasure)

PRACTICE

1   This is a pronunciation exercise for words ending in **-o**. Repeat them listening to the recording until you are sure you are pronouncing a short, sharp o (NOT -ow).

Buongiorno Mauro!
Ciao Aldo.
Ciao Renzo.
Bravo!
Non tanto bene.
No, non è tuo.

2   Answer the greetings of the various people in the recording by replying as suggested by the presenter.

3   Fill in the gaps in the following sentences with the appropriate form of **stare: stai** or **sta**. Use **stai** when you are on first-name terms with someone, **sta** when you are inquiring about someone else.

a. Ciao Renzo, come _____?

b. Il nipotino come _____?

c. Tuo padre _____ bene?

d. Buongiorno Mauro, come _____?

ANSWERS P. 14   e. La signora Gilardi come _____?

▶ *Introducing oneself*

LISTEN FOR...

▶ **mi chiamo ...** }
   il mio nome è ... }   my name is ...

▶ **Lei come si chiama?**   What is your name?

▶ **vengo da ...**   I come from ...

Giovanni	Io mi chiamo Giovanni. Lei come si chiama?
Marcella	Marcella.
Giovanni	Marcella. Lei non è di Roma?
Marcella	Non sono di Roma, e vengo da Lecce.
Giovanni	E come mai è venuta da Lecce a Roma?
Marcella	Per studiare.

io   I. This is not usually necessary as the verb ending (**chiamo**) includes the notion of I (see note to '**Come stai?**' in the first Conversation, p. 2) but, like **Lei** further on, is used here for emphasis: 'Me, I'm called ...'

▶ **mi chiamo**   my name is (lit. myself I call)

▶ **Lei come si chiama?**   What is your name? **Lei** (you) is used in addressing people one does not know well (see *Grammar,* p. 10).

▶ **non è ...**   you are not ..., **non sono ...**   I am not .... **Non** always precedes the word it negates; **è** and **sono** are two forms of the verb **essere** (to be) (see p. 10); **è** is always written with an accent to distinguish it from **e** (and).

▶ **vengo da ...**   I come from ...
    come mai   why (lit. how ever); **Come mai è venuta da Lecce a Roma?** Why have you come from Lecce to Rome?
    per studiare   to study

◆ *More personal details*

▶ **il mio nome è ...**   my name is ...
▶ **Da dove viene?**   Where do you come from?
▶ **vivo a Roma da tanti anni**   I have been living in Rome for many years

Giovanni	Signorina, come si chiama?
Paola	Il mio nome è Paola Di Carlo.
Giovanni	Da dove viene?
Paola	Vivo a Roma da tanti anni, ma le mie origini sono abruzzesi.

▶ **Signorina**   Miss. This does not have to be followed by the person's name. Nor does **Signora**, traditionally used to address older or married women, but used for all women by feminists who object to two different forms of address being used for women when only one suits men of all ages or family status: **Signore** (or **Signor** if followed by the surname: **Signor Di Carlo**).

▶ **il mio nome è ...**   my name is ...; an alternative to **mi chiamo**. Here **è** means 'is', but it is used also to mean 'you are' when addressing people one does not know well (see *Grammar*, pp. 10–11).

▶ **Da dove viene?**   Where do you come from? (lit. From where (do you) come?) In the next conversation the same phrase is repeated adding **Lei: Da dove Lei viene?**

▶ **vivo a Roma da tanti anni**, etc.   I have been living in Rome for many years (lit. I live in Rome since many years) but my origins are from Abruzzo.

PRACTICE

4   Listen to the questions in the recording about yourself and other people, and answer them all in the negative. The questions are easy to understand, but you would not yet be able to ask them. The answers are all based on recorded material you are already familiar with. Here is an example:

Giancarlo   **Lei è di Milano?**
You   **No, non sono di Milano.**

---

5 Who comes from where and who lives or studies where? Listen to the questions and answers on the recording and, in the box below, pair up the names and locations. You will hear the words **chi?** who? and **abita** lives.

Names		Locations	
	Cesarina		Abruzzo
	Enrico		Bologna
	Enza		Milano
	Lorena		Lecce
	Marcella		Suzzara
			Lurago

ANSWERS P. 14

a. _____   _____

b. _____   _____

c. _____   _____

d. _____   _____

e. _____   _____

f. _____   _____

6 Some (NOT all!) adjectives indicating origin end in *-ese*. Paola comes from Abruzzo: she is **abruzzese**. Someone coming from England (or Britain: Italians are not very precise) is **inglese**. Note these adjectives do not begin with capital letters. See whether you can complete the following sentences:

a. Marcella viene da Lecce. È _____

b. Franco viene da Malta. È _____

c. Giorgio viene dal Piemonte. È _____

d. Giovanni viene da Milano. È _____

e. Cristoforo Colombo viene da Genova. È _____

ANSWERS P. 14

▶ A town in Abruzzo

LISTEN FOR...

▶ **grande/piccola**   large/small
▶ **Quanti?**   How many?
▶ **più o meno**   more or less

Giovanni	Come si chiama la città dell'Abruzzo da dove Lei viene?
Paola	Schiavi d'Abruzzo.
Giovanni	E che città è, grande, piccola?
Paola	No, è un piccolo paese di montagna.
Giovanni	Quanti abitanti?
Paola	Più o meno mille.
Giovanni	E cosa fanno gli abitanti in questo paese di montagna?
Paola	Sono agricoltori.

▶ **Come si chiama ...?** What is the name of ...? (as well as What is your name? see Conversations 2)

Che città è? What (sort of) city is (it)? Schiavi d'Abruzzo is the complete name of the town.

▶ **grande** large, **piccola** small. For the difference between **piccola**, referring to **città**, and **piccolo**, referring to **paese**, see the *Grammar*, p. 10.

paese di montagna mountain village

▶ **Quanti abitanti?** How many inhabitants? **Quanti giorni?** How many days? **Quante ore?** How many hours? The difference between **quanti** and **quante** will be explained in the *Grammar*, p. 24.

▶ **più o meno mille** more or less one thousand

Cosa fanno? What do they do ?

questo this

sono agricoltori they are farmers. **Sono** translates both 'I am' and 'they are'.

Long time no see

LISTEN FOR...

▶ **Come va?** How's it going? How are things?
▶ **molto bene** very well

Giovanni	Ciao Cini!
Cini	Ciao Giovanni!
Giovanni	Come va?
Cini	È parecchio che non ci vediamo.
Giovanni	E Franca come sta?
Cini	Franca sta molto bene.

▶ **Come va?** lit. How goes?; an alternative to **Come stai?** but not referring directly to a person: How's life?, How are things?

è parecchio che non ci vediamo long time no see (lit. it's a long time that we do not see each other)

▶ **molto bene** also **benissimo** (very well), **non molto bene, non tanto bene** (not so well)

Giovanni and his cousin Aldo

PRACTICE

7 You may have noticed the similarity between some Italian and English words: **studiare** to study, **abitante** inhabitant, **origine** origin, **agricoltore** agricultural worker, farmer. See whether you can make a few more links, all to do with geographical locations or areas.

villaggio _____

regione _____

capitale _____

provincia _____

valle _____

penisola _____

ANSWERS P. 14 promontorio _____

8 Unlike in English there is no difference in word order between Italian questions and statements (Are you tired?/You are tired); nor is a verb such as 'to do' used in questions (Does she live in Rome?). This exercise will help you to say the same phrase, first as a question, then as a statement. Listen to the sentences below and repeat them after Giancarlo and Giovanna.

Renzo sta bene
Il nipotino non sta bene
Paola vive a Roma
È una città grande
È un piccolo paese di montagna

9 On the recording you will hear four sentences using words from the unit but in different combinations. Listen to each sentence two or three times and write in the translation.

a. _____

_____

b. _____

_____

c. _____

_____

d. _____

ANSWERS P. 14 _____

GRAMMAR AND EXERCISES

Endings

In Italian the endings of most words (nouns such as **nipotino**, adjectives such as **piccolo**) change depending on:

number: whether the word refers to one (singular) or more than one (plural) person or thing as in: **abitante** (inhabitant), **abitanti** (inhabitants),

gender: in some cases the word refers to male (masculine) or female (feminine) individuals. But, regardless of sex, ALL Italian nouns MUST belong to one gender or the other. So you get **il villaggio** (the village) but **la città** (the city/town). Try to learn which gender nouns belong to as you go through the course.

This pattern of change is called inflexion. There are easy rules to predict most patterns of inflexion, as you will see throughout this course. Don't worry too much if you get some endings wrong: your Italian listeners will still be able to understand you in most cases. There are TWO main patterns for nouns and adjectives. The most common has <u>four</u> endings (see Table below).

Another <u>two</u>-endings pattern will be studied later. Words that 'go together' may have the same endings, but only if they belong to the same pattern (see Unit 3, p. 38).

Verbs

In English the verb remains largely the same apart from an -s in some cases (I stay, he/she stays) and a pronoun (I, he/she) shows who the verb refers to. In Italian what changes is the ending of the verb (**sto**, **sta**, **stiamo**, **state**, **stanno**)

and pronouns are mostly redundant.

Italian verbs fall into three main groups according to the ending of their *infinitive* (the dictionary entry word). Verbs ending in -*are*, like **abitare** (to live in), **chiamare** (to call), **stare** (to be, to stay), **studiare** (to study), **lavorare** (to work), belong to the first class or *conjugation*. Normally the endings of verbs belonging to the same conjugation are the same. Verb forms are specified as one of three *persons*: First (speaking), Second (spoken to) and Third (spoken of), both singular and plural (but see below How to say 'you' in Italian). There are also distinctions of *tense* (present, past, future, etc.). All verbs in this unit are in the present tense which refers to the time the conversation is taking place (see Table opposite).

In many languages the most commonly used verbs do not conform to regular patterns. One of them is the verb **essere** (to be):

sono	I am
sei	you (informal) are
è	he/she/it is <u>or</u> you (polite) are
siamo	we are
siete	you (plural) are
sono	they are

How to say 'you' in Italian (1)

Whenever you address someone by his/her first name, you use the second person singular: e.g. **Dove abiti?** (Where do you live?), **Come stai?** (How are you?). Otherwise, you use the so-called polite form, which amounts to using the third (he/she) person: **Dove abita?**, **Come sta?** More about that in Unit 2, p. 24.

	singular	plural		
masculine	-o	-i	**nipotino piccolo**	little grandson
			nipotini piccoli	little grandsons
feminine	-a	-e	**nipotina piccola**	little granddaughter
			nipotine piccole	little granddaughters

Infinitive	abitare	to live	studiare	to study
Singular 1 2 3	abito abiti abita	I live you live he/she/it lives <u>or</u> you (polite) live	studio studi studia	I study you study he/she/it studies <u>or</u> you (polite) study
Plural 1 2 3	abitiamo abitate abitano	we live you live they live	studiamo studiate studiano	we study you study they study

10 You are encouraging or complimenting various people. Write the correct form of **bravo** (good, well done), which behaves like **piccolo**, before their name. Where genders are mixed, as in **e.** below, use the masculine plural form.

a. _____Paola!

b. _____Renzo!

c. _____nipotini!

d. _____agricoltori!

e. _____Paola e Renzo!

f. _____signorine!

ANSWERS P. 14

11 Fill in the missing endings in the following sentences, taking the ending of the first verb as a model. You will easily guess what some of these people are studying.

a. Mi chiamo Paolo. Abit _____ a Roma e studi _____ architettura.

b. Franca sta a Ostia ma lavor _____ a Roma.

c. Si chiamano Renzo e Paola. Abit _____ a Milano e studi _____ matematica.

d. Si chiama Marcella. St _____ a Lecce e studi _____ arte.

e. Mi chiamo Mauro. St _____ a Lecce dove studi _____ agricoltura.

ANSWERS P. 14

12 Fill in the gaps in this conversation with the correct form of **essere** (to be):

a. Cesarina, Lei _____ di Roma?

b. No, non _____ di Roma.

_____ di Suzzara.

c. Suo padre _____ di Suzzara?

d. No, mio padre e mia madre _____ di Bologna.

e. Io e Renzo _____ di Milano.

ANSWERS P. 14

KEY WORDS
AND PHRASES

buon giorno	good day (morning, afternoon)
buona sera	good evening
buona notte	good night
Ciao!	Hi!, Hello!
Come stai? Come sta?	How are you?, How is he/she?
[sto] bene, molto bene, benissimo	I'm well, very well
non [sto] tanto bene, non [sto] molto bene	I'm not so well, not very well
grazie	thanks
Come va?	How's it going? How are things?
mi chiamo…, il mio nome è …	my name is …
Lei come si chiama?	What is your name?
Signore	Sir
Signor (+ surname)	Mr
Signora	Mrs
Signorina	Miss
vengo da …	I come from …
vivo a …	I live in …
piccolo	small
è un piccolo paese	it's a small town/village
grande	large
è una grande città	it's a large town/city
oggi	today
più	more
meno	less
sì	yes
no	no, non-, not
Quanto, quanta?	How much?
Quanti, quante?	How many?
mi fa piacere	I'm glad to hear it (lit. it gives me pleasure)

Regions

Italy is divided into 19 **regioni** (regions) which enjoy a certain degree of administrative autonomy from central government (see map on p. 14). Before 1861, several of them (Piemonte, Lombardia, Veneto, Toscana, Lazio, Campania) were either independent states or the seats of government of larger independent states. Earlier on in Italian history, political fragmentation was even greater: at some stage nearly all important Italian towns were capital cities in their own right, which explains their individual variety and unparalleled artistic richness. Regional dialects, much different from the standard language and from each other, are still in widespread use and often impart a characteristic flavour (**accento**) to people's speech. In fact, it is only since the advent of the mass media, particularly television in the 1950s, that Italian as a language has spread to all parts of Italian society, having been for centuries the written language of the cultivated élite. About a third of the present-day population grew up as native speakers of the regional dialects and still use them within their family and language community. Bear that in mind if you hear, while in Italy, something totally different from what you have been taught to expect in this course.

Common Italian names

Most Italians still bear a 'Christian' name hallowed in the Catholic tradition as the name of a saint. Giving a family name as a first name (like Shelley or Gordon) was attempted by a few, but never caught on (Garibaldi named his two sons Menotti and Ricciotti from the surnames of two other Risorgimento patriots). The giving of non-traditional names was discouraged in the past or even forbidden. Many common names have English equivalents, such as Adriano, Alberto, Alessandro, Anna, Bernardo, Carlo, Caterina, Cristina, Elena, Elisabetta, Emilia, Franco, Laura, Lorenzo, Marco, Maria, Riccardo, Susanna, Teresa, Vincenzo, etc. Some names are reminiscent of Italy's Roman past, like Marcello, Fabio, Tullio, with a feminine counterpart in **-a**. A few names ending in **-a** are masculine: Andrea and Nicola are always given to boys, never to girls (note the stress). Many names are endearment forms, for instance Peppe or Peppino from Giuseppe, Nino and Nina from various names (Giovanni > Giovannino; Anna > Annina). The real name of Cini in the dialogue is Gabriele but those who know him hardly ever use it. In stating their identity, many Italians adopt the bureaucratic convention of placing their surname before their name, e.g. Rossi Carlo.

Titles

Titles are used more frequently in Italian than in English. All university graduates, not only medical ones, are entitled to call themselves **dottore** (men) and **dottoressa** (women). All secondary and tertiary teachers are called **professore** (or **professoressa**). **Cavaliere** and **commendatore**, the two grades in the Italian honours system, are often given to men as courtesy titles, whether they are actually recipients of the honour or not. Titles in **-ore** drop the final **-e** when followed by a surname: **dottor Rossi, professor Bianchi**. **Don** and **Donna** followed by the first name are frequent courtesy titles in the South (from Latin DOMINUS lord, and DOMINA lady).

AND FINALLY...

13 The last exercise in this unit is only on your recording. You will practise the use of the polite and informal forms.

ANSWERS

EXERCISE 3
(a), (d) stai   **(b), (c), (e)** sta

EXERCISE 5
(a) Enrico: Abruzzo **(b)** Lorena: Bologna **(c)** Enza: Lecce
(d) Marcella: Milano **(e)** Suzzara: Cesarina **(f)** Lurago:
Marcella

EXERCISE 6
(a) leccese   **(b)** maltese   **(c)** piemontese   **(d)** milanese
(e) genovese

EXERCISE 7
village region capital province valley peninsula
promontory

EXERCISE 9
(a) Today I'm feeling more or less well   **(b)** My father's
origins are French but he lives in Rome   **(c)** Is [my, his,
etc.] grandson small?   **(d)** To study gives me pleasure

EXERCISE 10
(a) brava **(b)** bravo **(c), (d), (e)** bravi   **(f)** brave

EXERCISE 11
(a) abito, studio   **(b)** lavora   **(c)** abitano, studiano   **(d)** sta,
studia   **(e)** sto, studio

EXERCISE 12
(a), (c) è   **(b), (d)** sono   **(e)** siamo

2 COMING AND GOING

WHAT YOU WILL LEARN

▶ how to say where your home is
▶ how to talk about where you are going, and understand the reply
▶ how to understand simple train and flight announcements
▶ numbers 1–29

BEFORE YOU BEGIN

Do not judge your ability to understand Italian from your ability to say things in the language. At all stages in your language learning you will be able to understand much more than you can say. What you want to say can be kept simple and does not need to include all the grammar used by Italians when they talk to you.

POINTS TO REMEMBER FROM UNIT 1

Greeting words: **Buongiorno, come sta? Ciao, come stai? Come va?**
Saying who you are: **Mi chiamo ... Il mio nome è ...**
Two genders masculine and feminine, normally with different endings for the singular and the plural: **nipotino   nipotina   nipotini   nipotine; piccolo piccola piccoli   piccole**
-*are* verbs, e.g. **studiare: studio, studi, studia, studiamo, studiate, studiano**

Pronunciation notes

C is pronounced *k-* as in cat before -*a*, -*o*, and -*u*: **come, casa, acuto** but *ch-* as in cheese before -*e* and -*i*: **Lecce è una città, ciao.** *ch-* in Italian is always pronounced as in chemistry, never as in cheese: **chiamare; chiesa** church; **che** who, which, that; **qualche** some.

ECONOMY
SAF SOCIETA' AEROPORTO FIORENTINO
CARTA D'IMBARCO - BOARDING PASS
NOME DEL PASSEGGERO /NAME OF PASSENGER
HUNTER/RMISS
DA/FROM
FLORENCE   REMARKS
A/TO LONDON

VOLO/FLIGHT   CLASSE/CLASS DATA/DATE   ORA PARTENZA DEP. TIME
UK 925 Y 14APR
04 1635   09D   NO
USCITA/GATE   ORA IMBARCO   POSTO/SEAT
              BOARDING TIME

071   SD

► Giovanni talks to two travellers on a train

LISTEN FOR...

► **Dove va**	Where are you going?
► **vado a ...**	I am going to ...
► **torno a ...**	I'm returning to ...
► **rientriamo di nuovo in ...**	we are going back again to ...

1º Viaggiatore	Va a Pisa, no?
Giovanni	Si, vado a Pisa.
Viaggiatore	Dopo Pisa dove va?
Giovanni	Vado forse a Siena, a ... a Firenze, e poi torno a Milano. E Lei va soltanto a Roma?
Viaggiatore	Soltanto a Roma, e domani sera rientriamo di nuovo in Alessandria.
Giovanni	*(to another passenger)* E Lei dove va?
2º Viaggiatore	Vado a Roma.

viaggiatore   traveller, **viaggiare**   to travel

Va a Pisa, no?   You're going to Pisa, aren't you?

► **vado**   I go/I'm going; **va** (you go/you're going): the Italian present tense translates both English forms. The forms of **andare** (to go) cannot be predicted from the infinitive: you will find them in the *Grammar* on p. 24.

  dopo   after

► **Dove va?**   Where are you going?

  forse   perhaps

► **e poi torno a Milano**   and then I'm returning to Milan: from the verb **tornare** to return, to go back (also **ritornare**).

  soltanto   only

  domani sera   tomorrow evening

► **rientriamo di nuovo in Alessandria**   we're going back again to Alessandria

A Neapolitan lady living in Rome speaks about her house in Naples

LISTEN FOR...

▶ **Di dov'è Lei?**   Where are you from?
▶ **c'è ...; ci sono ...**   there is ...; there are ...
▶ **ogni tanto**   every now and then
▶ **Che bello!**   How nice!

Aldo	Di dov'è Lei?
Signora	Ci ho la casa dove sta la chiesa di San Gennaro, il protettore di Napoli. A via Duomo.
Aldo	A via Duomo?
Signora	La tengo mobiliata. Ogni tanto mi faccio la mia bella passeggiatina per la riviera di Santa Lucia.
Aldo	Che bello!
Signora	Ci sono dei ristoranti, alberghi. C'è il 'San Domenico', uno dei primi. I primi alberghi stanno sulla riviera di Santa Lucia.
Aldo	Bello, sì.

▶ **Di dov'è Lei?**   Where are you from? **Dov'è** is shortened from **dove è**.
   A similar question is **Dove abita?**   Where do you live?
  ci ho   I have (lit. there I have). This use of **ci** will be further explained in Unit 3, p. 36.
  la casa   the house, my house
  la chiesa   the church
  il protettore   protector, patron saint
  via Duomo   Cathedral Street
  la tengo mobiliata   I keep it furnished. You might also need **i mobili** ([the] furniture; considered as mobile items). **La** refers to **la casa** (the house); more about this in Unit 5, p. 70.

▶ **ogni tanto**   every now and then (lit. every so much); **ogni**   every, each (invariable)
  mi faccio la mia bella passeggiatina   I take my lovely little walk; **passeggiare** (to walk, to stroll), **la passeggiata** (the walk), **la passeggiatina** (the little walk)
  la riviera di Santa Lucia   Santa Lucia seaside promenade in Naples; **per** and **su** before **la riviera** both correspond to 'on'; **per** indicates movement, **su** (**sulla** = **su** + **la**) indicates location.

▶ **Che bello!**   How nice!

▶ **c'è** (= **ci è**)   there is, **ci sono**   there are. Further explanations in Unit 3, p. 36.
  dei ristoranti   some restaurants (this use of **del**, **dei** will be explained later);
    alberghi   hotels. The singular is **il ristorante**, **l'albergo** (see *Grammar*, p. 24).
    uno dei primi   one of the first/best; **i primi alberghi**   the best hotels
    stanno from **stare** (to be, to stay)   are

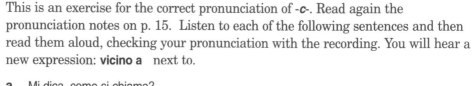

1

This is an exercise for the correct pronunciation of *-c-*. Read again the pronunciation notes on p. 15. Listen to each of the following sentences and then read them aloud, checking your pronunciation with the recording. You will hear a new expression: **vicino a** next to.

a. Mi dica, come si chiama?

b. Mi chiamo Cesare e vengo da Lecce.

c. Dove ha la casa?

d. Ci ho la casa in piazza Comunale, vicino alla chiesa di Santa Chiara.

e. Come dice? Non capisco.

The last example is most useful in case you fail to understand what people are saying to you: What did you say? (lit. How are you saying?) I don't understand.

2

Listen to Giovanni on the recording. He is asking a student a few things about her home town. You do not need to understand every word. Tick the right answers.

a. The student comes from   (i) Viterbo   (ii) Latina

b. Her home town is   (i) large   (ii) small   (iii) medium sized

c. It is   (i) more agricultural than industrial   (ii) more industrial than agricultural

ANSWERS P. 28

3

For this exercise, during which you will be giving information about yourself, listen to the recording and follow the presenter's instructions. You will need another word: **anche** also.

Marciana Alta

Announcements recorded in an Italian railway station

LISTEN FOR...

▶ **è in partenza** is departing
▶ **è in arrivo** is arriving
▶ **ore** hours, o'clock
▶ the numbers: **zero** zero, **due** two, **tre** three, **cinque** five,
   nove nine, **tredici** thirteen, **venti** twenty
   For the complete list of numbers 1–29 see the Practice section p. 20.

Altoparlante	Treno locale per Treglia, Varzo, Iselle, Briga, è in partenza dal binario numero cinque. Treno espresso per Milano centrale, Venezia, delle ore nove, è pronto sul binario numero tre.

Altoparlante	Treno interregionale ventitré zero nove proveniente da Firenze delle ore tredici e venti è in arrivo al binario due. Interregionale ventitré zero nove proveniente da Firenze delle ore tredici e venti è in arrivo al binario due.

altoparlante loudspeaker
treno locale local train, stopping train
Treglia, etc. places where the train stops.
▶ **è in partenza** is departing. On train timetables in stations look for **partenze** (departures) and **arrivi** (arrivals).
dal = da + il from the; similarly **sul = su + il** (on the). Further explanations in Unit 4, p. 54.
binario numero cinque platform number five. Check other numbers in Practice overleaf. **Binario** actually means binary (i.e. pair of) rails.
treno espresso fast train

Milano centrale Milan Central (station)
▶ **ore** hours, o'clock
è pronto is ready, waiting
interregionale interregional
proveniente da coming from
▶ **è in arrivo** is arriving (lit. is in arrival); **arrivo** could also be a form of **arrivare** (I arrive).

PRACTICE

4

Repeat the numbers from zero to 29 after the speaker.

0 **zero** 1 **uno** 2 **due** 3 **tre** 4 **quattro** 5 **cinque** 6 **sei** 7 **sette** 8 **otto**
9 **nove** 10 **dieci** 11 **undici** 12 **dodici** 13 **tredici** 14 **quattordici** 15 **quindici**
16 **sedici** 17 **diciassette** 18 **diciotto** 19 **diciannove** 20 **venti** 21 **ventuno**
22 **ventidue** 23 **ventitré** 24 **ventiquattro** 25 **venticinque** 26 **ventisei**
27 **ventisette** 28 **ventotto** 29 **ventinove**

NOTE THAT

(a) from 11 to 16 the part of the word indicating single figures comes before the ending **-dici** -*teen* (e.g. **tredici** 3 + 10); but from 17 onwards **dici-** comes first (**diciassette** 10 + 7; **diciotto** 10 + 8; **diciannove** 10 + 9: in English that happens from 21 onwards).

(b) the ending of **venti** (twenty) drops before **-uno** and **-otto**: **ventuno**, **ventotto** (this rule applies generally: see Unit 3, p. 38).

5

Listen to the recorded train announcements. Write the platform number from the box below next to the origin or destination announced for the trains.

(a) ROMA

(b) EMPOLI, PONTEDERA, PISA

(c) MILANO, BOLOGNA

(d) BOLOGNA, VERONA, BRENNERO

(e) SIENA, EMPOLI

(f) PRATO, PISTOIA

ANSWERS P. 28

| 1 | 2 | 4 | 7 | 11 | 18 |

6

Listen again to the same train announcement. This time for every platform number specify the type of train (**locale**, **intercity**, **interregionale**, **rapido**) and tick whether it is arriving or leaving.

Tipo di treno	Binario	In arrivo	In partenza
	1		
	2		
	4		
	7		
	11		
	18		

ANSWERS P. 28

CONVERSATIONS 3

Airport announcements

LISTEN FOR...

▶ **imbarco** boarding
▶ **uscita** (airport) exit, boarding gate

Altoparlante	ATI arrivo volo tre sette quattro da Alghero.

Altoparlante ATI arrivo volo tre sette quattro da Alghero.
ATI partenza per Milano volo tre quattro zero. Imbarco all'uscita sei.
British Airways partenza per Londra volo BA cinque due nove, imbarco dall'uscita numero sei. Volo BA cinque due nove per Londra, uscita numero sei.
Chiamata finale per il volo BA cinque due nove per Londra. Imbarco immediato uscita numero sei.

ATI initials of Aero Trasporti Italiani, an Italian internal airline
volo flight, from **volare** (to fly)
▶ **imbarco** boarding. Like its English translation the Italian word reflects a maritime origin: to get onto a **barca** (boat) as boarding refers to the boards on a ship's deck.
▶ **uscita** exit (**uscire** to go out), airport gate. The opposite is **entrata** entrance, entry (**entrare** to go in, to enter).
chiamata finale per final call for
immediato immediate

Weighing a suitcase at the check-in

LISTEN FOR...

▶ **ho questa valigia**   I have this suitcase
▶ **Quanti chili pesa?**   How many kilos does it weigh?
▶ **non lo so**   I don't know

Impiegata	Buon giorno.
Giovanni	Vado a Londra e … ho questa valigia.
Impiegata	Benissimo. Quanti chili pesa?
Giovanni	Non lo so.
Impiegata	Pesa venti chili. Allora, il peso consentito è di venti chili.
Giovanni	Non c'è eccedenza.
Impiegata	Non c'è eccedenza.

impiegata   female employee
▶ **ho questa valigia**   I have this suitcase; **borsa**   bag, purse
   benissimo   very well
▶ **Quanti chili pesa?**   How many kilos does it weigh? **Questo** (this) and **quanto** (how much) change their endings like **piccolo** (p. 10), see *Grammar*, p. 24.
   un chilo one kilo
▶ **non lo so**   I don't know (lit.[I] not it know). There is no equivalent of 'to do' in Italian negative sentences: **pesa venti chili**   it weighs 20 kilos, **non pesa venti chili**   it does not weigh 20 kilos.
   allora   occasionally equivalent to 'then', but mostly a filler with no specific meaning.
   il peso consentito   the luggage allowance (lit. the weight allowed, **consentire**   to allow). **Il peso è di** (or simply **è**) **venti chili**   The weight is 20 kilos.

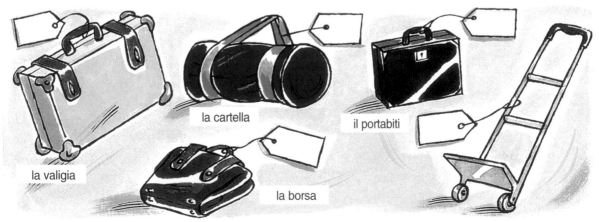

la cartella

il portabiti

la valigia

la borsa

il carrello portavaligie

ANSWERS P. 28

PRACTICE

7 Look at the monitor below announcing the arrivals and departures of flights at Pisa airport, then answer the following questions.

	AEROPORTO *GALILEO GALILEI* : PISA					
	A R R I V I		E	P A R T E N Z E		
VOLO	PROVENIENZA	ARRIVO	PARTENZA	DESTINAZIONE		AEREO
BM 368	LONDRA	06 25	07 00	ROMA		A 320
BM 374	ALGHERO	07 55	08 25	MILANO		A 320
BM 340	ROMA	09 50	10 20	MILANO		BA 1-11
AZ 257	LONDRA	10 45	11 15	ROMA		B 737
AZ 243	LONDRA	11 25	12 30	LONDRA		B 737
AS 015	VENEZIA	12 15	12 45	CAGLIARI		F 100
AS 016	CAGLIARI	12 55	13 25	VENEZIA		F 100
AT 142	PALERMO	13 20	13 50	PALERMO		B 737
AT 105	MILANO	14 30	15 00	MILANO		B 737
AT 305	NAPOLI	15 20				B 767

a. Da dove arriva il volo per Milano delle ore 10.20?

b. Quanti voli arrivano da Londra?

c. Quanti voli sono in partenza per Milano?

d. Da dove arriva il volo delle ore 15.20?

e. Da dove arriva il volo AT 142?

ANSWERS P. 28 **f.** Dopo Pisa dove va il volo AS 016?

8 A baggage handler will tell you the weight of the pieces of luggage on the opposite page. Write the weight of each on its label in figures.

9 Write down which of the objects above weighs …

a. un chilo _____

b. dodici chili _____

c. sei chili _____

d. due chili _____

ANSWERS P. 28 **e.** quattro chil _____

GRAMMAR AND EXERCISES

Questo (this), *quanto* (how much)

These words change their ending like **piccolo** (p. 10): **questo treno** this train, **questi treni** these trains, **questa valigia** this suitcase, **queste valige** these suitcases, **Quanto tempo?** How much time?, **Quanti chili?** How many kilos?, **Quanta valuta estera?** How much foreign currency?, **Quante ore?** How many hours?

Quanto can also be used in statements: **non so quanti chili pesa** I don't know how many kilos it weighs (**so,** from **sapere,** to know).

Translation of 'the' in the singular

In Italian there are different words for 'the' (known as the definite article), depending, as usual, on whether the noun is masculine or feminine, singular or plural. In this unit you will study the singular forms (plural forms in Unit 4, p. 54).

Lo is used before masculine nouns beginning with **s-** followed by another consonant: **lo studente** the student, **lo spuntino** the snack; also before a small number of nouns beginning with **gn-**, **ps-**, **x-** and **z-**. The most common of these you are likely to come across are **lo psicologo** psychologist, **lo zero** zero, **lo zio** uncle, **lo zucchero** sugar.
Il is used before all other masculine nouns beginning with a consonant: **il treno** the train, **il rapido** the fast train.
L' is used before all masculine and feminine nouns beginning with a vowel: **l'aereo** the aircraft, **l'entrata** entrance, **l'uscita** exit.
La is used before feminine nouns beginning with a consonant: **la valigia** the suitcase, **la bilancia** scales (weighing).

It is important to remember the gender of Italian nouns, because often the meaning changes with the gender: **lo scalo** the landing stage, **volo senza scalo** non-stop flight (lit. flight without stage); but **la scala** the staircase.

Present tense of *andare*, *venire*

Andare (to go) and **venire** (to come) have an irregular pattern:

andare

vado	I go
vai	you (sing) go
va	he/she/it goes <u>or</u> you (polite) go
andiamo	we go
andate	you (pl) go
vanno	they go

venire

vengo	I come
vieni	you (sing) come
viene	he/she comes <u>or</u> you (polite) come
veniamo	we come
venite	you (pl) come
vengono	they come

How to say 'you' in Italian (2)

Look at the following questions: **Dove vai? Dove va? Dove andate?**

They all translate 'Where are you going?' but they mean three different kinds of 'you'. You use **Dove vai?** when talking to someone (a child, a friend, a relation) you would address by his/her first name. Use **Dove va?** (the polite form) in all other cases, when talking to one person. Use **Dove andate?** when talking to more than one person, whether friends or strangers. The different ways of saying 'you' apply to all verbs.

10 Write the correct translation of 'the' before the following singular nouns. Treat nouns ending in *-o* as masculine, in *-a* as feminine (applicable to this exercise but NOT always true!).

a. _____ espresso

b. _____ uscita

c. _____ imbarco

d. _____ numero

e. _____ partenza

f. _____ arrivo

g. _____ telefono

h. _____ borsa

ANSWERS P. 28

11 Use the polite form when you ask the questions about travelling suggested by the presenter on the recording. You will need to use **dove** (where), forms of **andare** (to go), and towards the end, new words, **quando** meaning when; and **soltanto** meaning only.

12 This exercise allows you to practise some of the most important words and expressions used so far. Follow the instructions on the recording.

Sienna

KEY WORDS
AND PHRASES

Di dov'è Lei?, Da dove viene?	Where are you from?
Dov'è?	Where is he/she/it?, Where are you? (polite)
c'è ...	there is ...
ci sono ...	there are ...
(negative: **non c'è**, pl **non ci sono**)	
ogni tanto	every now and then
Che bello!	How nice!
Dove va?	Where are you going?
vado a ...	I am going to ...
torno a ...	I'm returning to ...
è in partenza per ...	is departing for ...
è in arrivo da ...	is arriving from ...
rientriamo di nuovo in ... (or **a ...**)	we go back again to ...
ore	hours, o'clock
imbarco	boarding
uscita	exit, boarding gate (airport)
ho questa valigia	I have this suitcase
Quanti chili pesa?	How many kilos does it weigh?
non lo so	I don't know
non capisco	I don't understand

0	**zero**	15	**quindici**
1	**uno**	16	**sedici**
2	**due**	17	**diciassette**
3	**tre**	18	**diciotto**
4	**quattro**	19	**diciannove**
5	**cinque**	20	**venti**
6	**sei**	21	**ventuno**
7	**sette**	22	**ventidue**
8	**otto**	23	**ventitré**
9	**nove**	24	**ventiquattro**
10	**dieci**	25	**venticinque**
11	**undici**	26	**ventisei**
12	**dodici**	27	**ventisette**
13	**tredici**	28	**ventotto**
14	**quattordici**	29	**ventinove**

DID YOU KNOW?

Italian railways

The Italian railway system **Ferrovie dello Stato** (FS) is largely nationalized, with only a few surviving privately owned narrow-gauge suburban lines. It is generally acknowledged to be one of the most efficiently run public services in the country (though Italians complain about commuter trains) and good value for money. If you do not travel to Italy by rail you may find it convenient to use railways once you are there. Ask about discounts for return trips, for students and family groups. A **biglietto chilometrico** allowing one or more specified persons unlimited travel up to 30,000 kms is worth considering. Reduced fares often apply to special occasions (such as International Trade Fairs or Festivals), package tours and rail-drive combinations. Special reduced tickets valid for the whole network may be available to people coming from outside Europe.

It is worth using express trains called Eurocity (on international routes) and Intercity, paying a surcharge (**supplemento**) where applicable and booking seats in advance. You can also book sleepers in special sleeping carriages (**vagone letto**) and *couchettes*, ordinary carriages where seats turn into sleeping berths at night. Avoid international trains between Northern Europe and Southern Italy at peak holiday times: they <u>will</u> be overcrowded and late. Porters are increasingly difficult to find and station trolleys hard to come by: luggage with wheels or a collapsible trolley can be very useful. Make sure *before* you book your ticket that your journey is not going to be affected by strikes. Information is usually available from electronic panels and prominently displayed noticeboards, often including the sequence of carriages in the train. Through coaches are clearly labelled: look out for them.

People in uniform

You may be surprised at the variety of uniformed officers you will see while in Italy. Apart from railway officials (if you travel by train) your papers will be checked at the frontier by a plain-clothes police inspector, usually accompanied by a railway police officer (**Polfer** or **Polizia ferroviaria**) or a **carabiniere** in navy-blue uniform with red collar badges. **Carabinieri** are a special corps of the Italian Army performing police duties: in recent years they have acquired a reputation for efficiency greater than that of the grey-uniformed state police (**Pubblica Sicurezza**). Customs and Excise Officers wear battle green with bright yellow collar badges, giving them the soubriquet of **Fiamme gialle** (yellow flames). In towns you will see **Vigili Urbani,** members of the local traffic police force, and a number of private security guards often stationed outside banks. All uniformed police carry arms.

'Italian spoken here'

Even today no more than two thirds of the Italian population (some 40 million people) are native speakers of Italian. Many speak as their first language one of the various local dialects and learn Italian at school. A few old people in remote areas may use only their dialect. Italian is also one of the official languages of Switzerland, is a common trade language in the countries bordering the Adriatic sea and parts of Northern Africa, and is widespread among people of Italian origin in the United States, South America and Australia. An Italian dialect, easily understood by Italians, is spoken in Corsica besides French. Conversely a variety of non-Italian languages is spoken in Italy: French and German dialects in the Alpine regions; and small pockets of Albanian, Franco-Provençal and Greek in Southern Italy and Sicily.

AND FINALLY...

13 Imagine you are on holiday and want to go somewhere by train. You see a railway official at the local station and ask him some questions. You will need a new and important phrase: **per piacere** please.

ANSWERS

EXERCISE 2

(a) ii **(b)** iii (media) **(c)** ii

EXERCISE 5

(a) 2 **(b)** 4 **(c)** 18 **(d)** 1 **(e)** 7 **(f)** 11

EXERCISE 6

binario 1: interregionale, in partenza; binario 2: rapido, in partenza; binario 4: locale, in partenza; binario 7: locale, in arrivo; binario 11: locale, in partenza; binario 18: intercity, in arrivo

EXERCISE 7

(a) Roma **(b), (c)** tre **(d)** Napoli **(e)** Palermo
(f) a Venezia

EXERCISE 8

(a) 12k **(b)** 6k **(c)** 2k **(d)** 4k **(e)** 1k

EXERCISE 9

(a) il carrello portavaligie **(b)** la valigia **(c)** la borsa
(d) la cartella **(e)** il portabiti

EXERCISE 10

(a) l'espresso **(b)** l'uscita **(c)** l'imbarco **(d)** il numero
(e) la partenza **(f)** l'arrivo **(g)** il telefono **(h)** la borsa

3 BOOKING A ROOM

WHAT YOU WILL LEARN

▶ how to tell other people about your profession or occupation
▶ how to book a room in a hotel
▶ how to ask for basic information
▶ numbers 30–999,999
▶ about tourist accommodation in Italy

BEFORE YOU BEGIN

Try to be aware at all times of what you are saying and why you believe it's the right way of saying it. If you then discover you were wrong, you will know why and will be able to avoid repeating the same mistake.

POINTS TO REMEMBER FROM UNIT 2

The singular articles: **il treno**, **lo studente**, **l'aereo**, **l'uscita**, **la valigia**
The verbs **andare** (to go): **vado**, **vai**, **va**, **andiamo**, **andate**, **vanno**
venire (to come): **vengo**, **vieni**, **viene**, **veniamo**, **venite**, **vengono**
Numbers 1–29 (see p. 20)
Saying you don't know or don't understand: **non lo so**, **non capisco** (from the verb **capire**).

Pronunciation notes

G is pronounced **g-** as in gap before **-a**, **-o**, and **-u**: **albergo** hotel, **gusto** taste; but **j-** as in jest before **-e** and **-i**: **valigie** suitcases, **oggi** today.
To form a hard **g** sound before **-e** and **-i**, add **-h-**: **Alghero** (a town in Sardinia), **alberghi**. To form a soft **-j-** sound before **-a**, **-o**, **-u**, add **-i-**: **valigia**, **orologio** clock, **giù** down, **giusto** right.
The spelling **-gn-**, as in **bagno** bath, **Bologna** a town in northern Italy, **signora**, **signorina**, has no equivalent sound in English, though it resembles the sound **-ni-** in onion.

Giovanni and a lady discuss the work they do

LISTEN FOR...

▶ **io sono un insegnante**	I am a teacher
▶ **E Lei?**	And you?, What about you?
▶ **E suo marito?**	What about your husband?

Giovanni	Io sono un insegnante. Sono professore d'italiano. Insegno l'italiano all'estero. E Lei?
Signora	Io sono una segretaria. Lavoro in una ditta di Milano.
Giovanni	E suo marito?
Signora	Mio marito è un commerciante.

▶ **io sono un insegnante** I'm a teacher (from **insegnare** to teach). To state your profession or occupation you either say: (**io**) **sono un insegnante**, **sono una segretaria** (I'm a secretary), **sono un medico** (I'm a doctor) or, more simply, **sono insegnante**, **sono segretaria**, **sono medico**. **Insegnante** defines teachers of all categories, both male and female; **professore** is a secondary or tertiary male teacher (a female teacher is called **professoressa**).

all'estero abroad

▶ **E Lei?** And you?, What about you? Remember that **e** without an accent means 'and' (**è** = is). **Lei** also means 'she': it is used instead of the informal 'you' because in the past it was customary to address not the person directly but his/her ceremonial titles (as in English 'your Grace', 'your Lord-/Ladyship', etc.) Such titles in Italian are all feminine (**grazia**, **signoria**, etc.) To make it clear that **Lei** means 'you' and not 'she', the capital L is often (but not always) used in writing.

▶ **E suo marito?** What about your husband? Just as **Lei** in formal address means 'you', **suo** means 'your': see *Grammar*, p. 39).

lavoro I work, from **lavorare** to work; **il lavoro** work

ditta firm

commerciante business person, dealer (**il commercio**, commerce)

A member of a group of beekeepers tells Giovanni where they are going

LISTEN FOR...

▶ **da quanti anni ...**   [for] how many years ...

Giovanni	Io sono un turista inglese che va a Pisa.
Signore	Noi andiamo a Roma ad un congresso, un congresso di apicultura.
Giovanni	E Lei è un apicultore?
Signore	Sì, eh, sono un vecchio apicultore, ecco ...
Giovanni	Da quanti anni fa l'apicultore?
Signore	Eh, trentacinque anni adesso.

▶ **io sono ...**, **noi andiamo ...**   As in the previous conversation (**Io sono un insegnante ... e Lei?**) the use of the pronoun **io** gives emphasis. **Noi** means 'we'. As noted earlier, personal pronouns are not normally necessary, since Italian verbs have specific endings for person, number and tense.

il turista (m), **la turista** (f)   tourist

che   who

congresso   conference, congress

apicultura   beekeeping, **apicultore**   beekeeper, **ape** (f)   bee

vecchio   old

ecco   an end-of-sentence filler, something like 'there you are'.

▶ **Da quanti anni fa l'apicultore?**   How many years have you been a beekeeper? (lit. From/since how many years you do the beekeeper?), **quanto**, **quanta** (how much), **quanti**, **quante** (how many). Another way of stating one's occupation or trade, particularly if it involves some form of manual work, is to use, as here, the verb

fare (to do, to make) (for its forms see *Grammar*, p. 39): **Che cosa fa?** What do you do?, **Che lavoro fa?** What work do you do? What's your line of work? **faccio l'apicultore** I'm a beekeeper, **faccio la segretaria** I'm a secretary. Note that in this case the name of the profession or trade must be preceded by 'the'. For more occupations see Practice 3.

▶ **trentacinque**   thirty-five. See Practice exercise 3 p. 32.

adesso   now, by now

PRACTICE

1 This is an exercise for the correct pronunciation of *g-* and *-gn-* introduced on p. 29. Listen to the following sentences on your recording and repeat them.

La signora Gerace fa l'insegnante.
Paola insegna geografia a Bologna.
Signorina, le mie valigie sono all'albergo.
Per piacere, una camera con bagno.
Ho la casa giusto dov'è la chiesa di San Gennaro.

2 Here are the words you need to count from thirty onwards. Repeat them in the gaps on the recording.

30 **trenta**,　40 **quaranta**,　50 **cinquanta**,　60 **sessanta**,　70 **settanta**,　80 **ottanta**, 90 **novanta**,　100 **cento**,　200 **duecento**,　300 **trecento**,　400 **quattrocento**, 500 **cinquecento**,　1000 **mille**,　2000 **duemila**,　3000 **tremila**,　4000 **quattromila**, 15 000 **quindicimila**. See *Grammar*, p. 38.

3 For each of the various people illustrated below, choose the appropriate profession or occupation from those in the box. You may have to make one or two simple guesses. Then listen to the recording to check your answers. You'll hear **faccio** (from **fare**, to do) and two new words, **suonare**, to play an instrument; **precisamente** meaning precisely.

1 _____　2 _____　3 _____　4 _____

5 _____　6 _____　7 _____　8 _____

| commerciante　musicista　portiere　segretaria　studente |
| turista　insegnante　dottoressa |

▶ Asking for a room

LISTEN FOR...

▶ **vorrei una camera**	I'd like a room
▶ **un attimo**	just a moment
▶ **ne abbiamo una**	we have one (lit. of it we have one)
▶ **molte grazie**	many thanks
▶ **senz'altro**	absolutely, of course

Giovanni	Buona sera, signorina.
Receptionist	Buona sera.
Giovanni	Senta, io vorrei una camera doppia questa sera per cinque giorni. Lei ne ha una?
Receptionist	Devo controllare. Un attimo. Sì, ne abbiamo una disponibile al secondo piano. Le va bene?
Giovanni	Mi va bene senz'altro. Molte grazie.

Senta 'Listen' in Italian is not at all rude: it's merely a sentence opener, warning the listener that you are about to say something.

▶ **vorrei una camera** I'd like a room. **Vorrei** is the conditional ('would' form) of **volere** (to want) (see p. 118), but you don't have to use it. You can ask for a room simply by saying: **una camera, per piacere**. Other options: **una camera doppia** (double), **a due letti** (twin-bedded), **singola** (single), **a un letto** (with one bed), **con letto matrimoniale** (with a double bed), **con bagno** (with bathroom), **con doccia** (with shower). Italian Renaissance scientists noted that the scene outside a dark room (**camera oscura**) through a pinhole in the shutters was projected on the opposite wall. The word **camera** was borrowed in English to name the device based on this optical principle (in Italian **macchina fotografica**).

Lei ne ha una? Have you got one? (lit. You of it have one?)

devo controllare I must check

▶ **un attimo** just a moment. Also: **un momento, un momentino, un attimino**. The ending *-ino, -ina* is used to indicate smallness or shortness (remember **nipotino, una bella passeggiatina**). **Camerino** (small room) is sometimes used to mean 'the small room', i.e. the toilet, normally called **gabinetto** (see Unit 7, p. 93).

▶ **ne abbiamo una disponibile** we have one available; the receptionist might also say **ne abbiamo una libera** we have one free.

piano floor. You don't need to be told that **secondo** means...

Le va bene? Is that all right for you? (lit. To you goes well?); **Mi va bene.** It's all right for me.

▶ **senz'altro** (shortened from **senza altro**, lit. without other) absolutely: an expression used to indicate definite agreement. —**Vieni oggi alle cinque?** —**Senz'altro!** 'Will you be coming to-day at five?' 'Most certainly.'

▶ **molte grazie** many thanks

▶ *Making a firm booking*

Giovanni	Signorina, allora la prendo.
Receptionist	Benissimo. Allora per questa camera il prezzo è di duecentotrentamila lire a notte, con la prima colazione compresa. È d'accordo?
Giovanni	Senz'altro. Duecentotrentamila. Va bene.

▶ **allora la prendo**   then I'll take it. Note the use of the present tense to indicate future action. For **la** meaning 'it', see Unit 5, *Grammar*, pp. 70–71. **Allora** is often used as a filler when one is thinking what to say next. **Prendo** is from **prendere** (to take).
il prezzo   the price
a notte   per night; **Per quante notti?**   For how many nights?
con   with   (opposite: **senza** without): **con bagno**   with bathroom (or with bath), **con doccia**   with shower

▶ **con la prima colazione compresa**   (with lit. first collation), breakfast included. Lunch is often called **seconda colazione** but is more usually known as **pranzo**.
È d'accordo?   Agreed?, Are you in agreement? (lit. of agreement)

PRACTICE

4   Answer the questions on the recording as suggested by the presenter. You will be practising the use of **ne**, as in **ne ha uno** (it has one of them). There is a new word: **appartamento**, meaning apartment.

5   Listen to the conversation on the recording. You do not have to understand every word: only what is necessary to tick the correct answer to the following questions. You will hear a new phrase: **una doppia uso singola** meaning a double room to be used as a single.

a.   Giovanni needs   (i) a single room   (ii) a double room
b.   Where is the single room he is being offered?   (i) on the first floor   (ii) on the third floor
c.   The room Giovanni eventually takes costs   (i) 220,000 lire a night
(ii) 180,000 lire a night

ANSWERS P. 42

6 Here is a registration form such as you may be asked to fill in when booking in at an Italian hotel.

COGNOME
NOME
LUOGO E DATA DI NASCITA
NAZIONALITÀ
PASSAPORTO N°
ALTRO DOCUMENTO D'IDENTITÀ (SPECIFICARE)   N°
ABITANTE A   PROVINCIA
IN   N°   CAP
DATA D'INGRESSO IN ITALIA
DATA

What you have learned so far, and what you can easily guess, should enable you to answer the following questions.

a. Which should you fill in first? (i) your first name (ii) your family name
b. Which should you fill in first? (i) your place of birth (ii) your date of birth
c. Is your passport the only proof of identity allowed? (i) yes (ii) no
d. What would you write after **abitante a**? (i) the town where you live (ii) the street where you live
e. The two dates at the end would be the same (i) if you filled in the form on the last day of your stay in Italy (ii) if you filled in the form on the first day of your stay in Italy.

ANSWERS P. 42

Are there any department stores nearby?

LISTEN FOR...

▶ c'è ...	there is .../is there ...?
▶ ci sono ...	there are .../are there ...?
▶ qui vicino	near by

| **Giovanni** | Signora, ci sono dei grandi magazzini qui vicino? |
| **Signora** | Vicino a piazza Duomo c'è ... la Rinascente, e in via Torino c'è sia la STANDA che la UPIM. |

▶ **c'è** there is (shortened for **ci è**), **ci sono** there are, which we have already come across in Unit 2, are among the most common expressions in Italian. Note that the word order is the same in both question and answer. **Ci** (there) can be used also in conjunction with other verbs: **ci andiamo** (we are going there), **ci lavoro** (I work there). When used with **avere**, as in **ci ho la casa a via Duomo** (p. 17), it has no English equivalent.

grande magazzino department store (lit. large store), pl **grandi magazzini**

▶ **qui vicino** near by

piazza Duomo (also **piazza del Duomo**) Cathedral Square

sia la STANDA che la UPIM both STANDA and UPIM (well-known chains of department stores, as well as la Rinascente); **sia ... che ...** both ... and ...

sia oggi che domani both today and tomorrow

Is there a telephone?

LISTEN FOR...

▶ C'è il telefono?	Is there a telephone?
▶ di fronte	opposite
▶ prego	don't mention it, you're welcome

Giovanni	Signorina, c'è il telefono?
Cassiera	No, c'è una cabina di fronte che va colla scheda.
Giovanni	Grazie.
Cassiera	Prego.

cassiera cashier; **cassa** till, cash desk

▶ **C'è il telefono?** Is there a (lit. the) phone? The question may also be phrased: **C'è un telefono?**

cabina booth

▶ **di fronte** opposite (lit. of front)

che va colla scheda requiring a phonecard (lit. which goes with the card).

▶ **Prego** (lit. I pray): the customary polite rejoinder to **grazie** (thank you). It may also mean 'please', when inviting people to come in or sit down.

7 Listen to the phone numbers given in the recording, and transcribe them against the name of each hotel given below, but NOT in the same order.

Albergo:	Numero telefonico:
a. CAPITOL	_____
b. ROMA	_____
c. ARISTON	_____
d. LA PACE	_____
e. CALIFORNIA	_____

Tutti scelgono la scheda perché è più comoda e la trovi dappertutto.

ANSWERS P. 42

8

FINESTRA LETTO

ARMADIO TELEFONO

SEDIA VALIGIA

Look at this room and describe it using **c'è** or **ci sono**, as appropriate. Check back to the Grammar section in Unit 1 on plural forms and follow the presenter's instructions on your recording.

9 Listen to the recording and tick the right answer to the following questions (you do not have to understand every word).

a. What expression does Giovanni use to say 'please'?   (i) **per piacere** (ii) **per favore**   (iii) **prego**

b. What is the hotel's phone number?   (i) 231 5362   (ii) 321 5632 (iii) 321 5362

c. What code should be used when calling from outside Rome?   (i) 06 (ii) 07   (iii) 60

GRAMMAR AND EXERCISES

Numbers 31 to 999,999

Basically you make up the numbers as you do in English, e.g.

n o v e / c e n t o / n o v a n t a / n o v e / m i l a / n o v e / c e n t o / n o v a n t a / n o v e
nine / hundred [and] ninety / nine / thousand/ nine / hundred [and] ninety / nine

Note that the final vowel -*a* of the tens drops before -*uno* and -*otto* (**quarantuno, quarantotto**). As in English all numbers from 200 to 900 are made up by a number from **due** to **nove** and the word **cento** (hundred) (**duecento** two hundred, **trecento** three hundred etc.). Figures from **mille** to **duemila** are never counted as multiples of one hundred: twelve hundred is **mille duecento**; nineteen hundred and ninety eight is **mille novecento novantotto**. The thousands after **mille** use the plural form -*mila*: **duemila** 2000, **ventitrémila** 23,000, etc.

When written in figures, numbers over 999 have a full point or a space where English has a comma: **15.000**.

Two-ending pattern

	Singular -e	Plural -i
masculine/ feminine	**il/la negoziante**	**i/le negozianti**

Nouns and adjectives belonging to this group have only *two* endings (-*e* singular and -*i* plural) for both genders. Some, like **lo studente** (the student) are masculine; some, like **l'ape** (the bee) are feminine; and others, like **negoziante** (shop-keeper) (and *all* adjectives ending in -*e*), can be either masculine or feminine. Since the other group has *four* separate masculine and feminine endings (-*o*, -*a*, -*i*, -*e*) when adjectives 'agree' with nouns belonging to a different group, they may end up with different endings. An honest (male) shopkeeper is **un onesto negoziante**; the same compliment paid to the female equivalent would be **una onesta negoziante**. See also the examples in the next section.

Translation of 'a', 'an' (indefinite article)

Masculine nouns beginning in **s** + another consonant, *gn*-, *ps*-, *z*-	**uno**	**uno studente** **uno specchio** (a mirror)
Masculine nouns beginning in any other consonant or vowel	**un**	**un treno** **un albergo** **un ristorante,** **un aperitivo** (aperitif)
Feminine nouns beginning in a vowel	**un'**	**un'albicocca** (an apricot) **un'ora**
feminine nouns beginning in a consonant	**una**	**una guida** (a guide) **una camera**

Other examples:

uno studente australiano, uno specialista di elettronica, uno psicologo eminente
un turista inglese, un segretario privato, un bravo insegnante
un'onesta negoziante, un'università (university) **americana**
una turista inglese, una segretaria privata, una brava insegnante, una strana storia (a strange story)

How to translate 'my', 'mine', 'your(s)', 'his' and 'her(s)'

Mio, **tuo** and **suo** indicate possession or belonging: **la mia camera** my room, **il tuo passaporto** your passport, **la sua valigia** his/her/your suitcase. Note that:

(a) they agree in gender and number with the things possessed (whether the suitcase is his or hers, you say **sua** because it agrees with **valigia**);

(b) they tend to be omitted in Italian when it is obvious to whom something pertains or belongs: **vado in camera** I'm going to my room;

(c) they are normally preceded by articles when followed by a noun: **la mia bella passeggiata** my nice little walk; **una mia bella passeggiata** a nice little walk of mine; otherwise they can be used without the article: — **Questa valigia è di Giorgio?** — **No, è mia.**

(d) **suo**, **sua** may also mean your(s) when using the polite **Lei** form. For their plural forms see p. 134.

Present tense of fare (to do)

Fare

faccio	I do
fai	you do
fa	he/she/it does <u>or</u> you (polite) do
facciamo	we do
fate	you do
fanno	they do

10 Answer affirmatively the questions in your recording, using the appropriate translation of 'his, her, my' preceded by the article. In the first two questions **suo**, **sua** are used in the polite form, and mean 'yours'.

Model: — **Questa valigia è sua?** — **Sì, è mia.**

Follow the instructions given by the presenter.

11 Fill in the gaps with the correct form of the indefinite article (**un**, **uno**, **una**, **un'**).

a. _____ turista australiana

b. _____ studente di architettura

c. _____ dottoressa inglese

d. _____ passeggiatina sulla riviera di Chiaia

e. _____ bravo insegnante

f. _____ insegnante brava

ANSWERS P. 42

12 In the following conversation, the traveller's part has been omitted. His/her replies are jumbled, *together with extra inappropriate replies*, in the box after the dialogue. Choose the correct ones and write them in the appropriate places.

— Buongiorno. Dica.

a. _____

— Come la vuole, singola, doppia?

b. _____

— Un momento che controllo... Sì, ne abbiamo due singole, una con bagno e una con doccia.

c. _____

— Senz'altro. Per quante notti?

d. _____

— Il prezzo è di 185 mila lire per notte.

e. _____

— Numero 205 al secondo piano.

> (i) Singola.   (ii) Vorrei quella col bagno.
> (iii) Va bene. Dov'è la camera?   (iv) Cinque.
> (v) Tre. Quanto costa?   (vi) Buongiorno. Ha una camera?   (vii) C'è la doccia?

ANSWERS P. 42

KEY WORDS
AND PHRASES

C'è il telefono?	Is there a telephone? (lit. the telephone)
Che cosa fa?	What do you do?
con la prima colazione compresa	breakfast included
da quanti anni …	[for] how many years …
di fronte	opposite (lit. of front)
E Lei?	What about you?
io sono un insegnante	I am a teacher
segretario -a	secretary, receptionist
impiegato -a	employee, clerk
dottore (m) dottoressa (f)	doctor, GP
portiere (m) portiera (f)	door-person, concierge
musicista (m/f)	musician
turista (m/f)	tourist
commerciante (m/f)	trader, dealer, business person
marito	husband
moglie (f)	wife
figlio	son
figlia	daughter
fratello	brother
sorella	sister
zio	uncle
zia	aunt
cugino -a	cousin
genitori	parents
nonno	grandfather
nonna	grandmother
un attimo	just a moment
vorrei una camera	I'd like a room
singola	single
doppia	double
a due letti	twin-bedded
con un letto matrimoniale	with a double bed
con bagno	with bathroom
con doccia	with shower
ne abbiamo una	we have one
la prendo	I'll take it
molte grazie	many thanks
prego	don't mention it, you're welcome
va bene	OK
mi va bene	that's OK for me, that suits me

DID YOU KNOW?

Tourist accommodation

The terms **albergo** and **hotel** (pronounced in Italian without the **h**) are interchangeable. Less luxurious types of establishment are called **pensione** (guest house), and **locanda** or **alloggio**, roughly corresponding to simple bed-and-breakfast type accommodation. The term **ostello** is reserved for youth hostels (also called **albergo della gioventù**). In many Italian towns you can find **alberghi** and **pensioni**, often of a quite respectable standard, occupying only part of a block of flats, with the reception and the rooms on one of the upper floors of the building.

In recent years many Italian farmers have entered the tourist market by offering accommodation on their farms. **Agroturismo**, agricultural tourism, is good value for money and is becoming increasingly popular with holidaymakers who are no longer prepared to put up with crowded and possibly polluted beaches.

A particularly useful type of establishment, without a counterpart in English-speaking countries, is the **albergo diurno**, or simply **diurno**, day-time hotel. As its name suggests it does not have overnight accommodation, nor does it provide food, but it does offer many services available in hotels, such as showers, baths, toilets, hairdressers, manicure, laundry and valet service, etc.

Hoteliers are required by law to display in every room, usually behind the door, the cost of accommodation, plus the IVA (**Imposta sul Valore Aggiunto**, Value-Added Tax) and **tassa di soggiorno** (local tourist tax) percentages. The cost often varies according to the season, and may be discounted. Unless it is specified as being **per persona** it refers to the charge for the room, which may be occupied by more than one person. Breakfast is seldom included, though the habit of making an inclusive charge is spreading. Anyway it is often better and cheaper to have breakfast in a nearby café (and you will be taught how to order it in the next unit). Full board is called **pensione completa**, and half board **mezza pensione**. Not all hotels have a restaurant. In those which do, the standard of accommodation is no reliable guide as to the standard of catering. Some unassuming **alberghi** in small out of the way hill towns are capable of producing heavenly food and superb wines.

Tourists travelling with caravans, motor homes or tents will find a bewildering variety of campsites of all sizes and standards. It is difficult to generalize, but on the whole, those recommended by the main motoring organizations are usually reliable, though it is possible to find quite satisfactory campsites that have not been included in any list or noted on any map. Because of the high density of urban settlement, particularly at the seaside, town sites may be cramped, noisy, dusty and overlooked by tower blocks. 'Wild' camping is difficult and unadvisable, unless you have made friends with the landowners and/or they have given you permission to park or set up your tent on their land. The Italian word **campeggio** tends to be superseded by the international word 'camping'.

AND FINALLY...

13 In this exercise you will be asked to book a room in a hotel using the phrases you have learned in this unit. Follow the instructions on the recording.

Venice

ANSWERS

EXERCISE 5

(a) i   **(b)** i   **(c)** ii

EXERCISE 6

(a) ii   **(b)** i   **(c)** ii   **(d)** i   **(e)** ii if you guessed that the **in-** in **ingresso** points to an entry date

EXERCISE 7

(a) Capitol 495 97597   **(b)** Roma 226 9873
(c) Ariston 242 559   **(d)** La Pace 502 2668
(e) California 890 7263

EXERCISE 9

(a) ii   **(b)** iii   **(c)** i **il prefisso è zero sei**

EXERCISE 11

(a) una   **(b)** uno   **(c)** una   **(d)** una   **(e)** un   **(f)** un'

EXERCISE 12

(a) vi   **(b)** i   **(c)** ii   **(d)** v   **(e)** iii

4

'WHAT WILL YOU HAVE?'

WHAT YOU WILL LEARN

▶ about ID papers and credit cards
▶ how to inquire about methods of payment
▶ how to ask how much something costs
▶ how to order breakfast, drinks and snacks

BEFORE YOU BEGIN

Learning a new language may appear to you largely as a question of memorizing words and grammar rules. In fact, it is more like learning to play tennis or bowls: you don't get to play well simply by memorizing the vocabulary of the game and its rules. Once you have done that you still need practice to acquire the necessary skills. Memory is strengthened through practice.

POINTS TO REMEMBER FROM UNIT 3

Saying what you do, and asking about the other person's occupation: **Io sono un turista, e Lei? Faccio il negoziante, e Lei che cosa fa?**

Is there?/There is; Are there?/There are: **C'è il telefono? Sì, c'è un telefono in ogni camera; Quanti letti ci sono? Ci sono due letti nella camera.**

Booking a room: **una camera singola/doppia con/senza bagno per … giorni**

Endings ▶

When nouns and adjectives from different groups 'agree' or go together, they may not have the same endings: e.g. **grande camera, grandi camere, piccolo ristorante, nuove assistenti** (new female assistants).

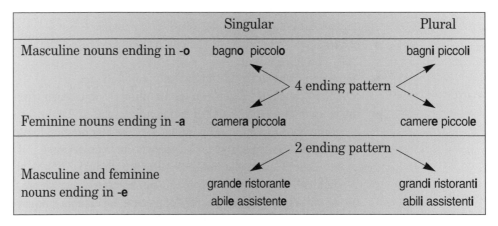

	Singular	Plural
Masculine nouns ending in **-o**	bagno piccolo	bagni piccoli
	4 ending pattern	
Feminine nouns ending in **-a**	camera piccola	camere piccole
	2 ending pattern	
Masculine and feminine nouns ending in **-e**	grande ristorante abile assistente	grandi ristoranti abili assistenti

Pronunciation notes

In Standard English, initial consonants are pronounced with a small puff of breath. Hold a small piece of paper by one end and place the other before your lips while saying: two cups of tea. You will see the paper move as you say *c-* and *t-*. That should not happen when pronouncing initial Italian consonants. In this unit you will be concentrating on initial *c-* and *t-* as in **carta** and **tutto**.

CONVERSATIONS *1*

The hotel receptionist gives Giovanni the hotel's address and telephone number, and asks him for his identity papers

LISTEN FOR...

▶ l'indirizzo è ...	the address is ...
▶ se chiama di fuori Pisa	if you call from outside Pisa
▶ con comodo	at your convenience
▶ mi fa un favore se ...	you'll do me a favour if ...
▶ lo stesso	all the same

Albergatore	L'indirizzo è Albergo Vittoria, Lungarno Pacinotti numero dodici. Il telefono ... eh, se chiama di fuori Pisa, zero cinquanta, due trentatré otto due. E poi con comodo quando scendono mi fa un favore se mi portano i loro passaporti, o carte d'identità. Qualsiasi documento va bene.
Giovanni	Abbiamo carte d'identità. Va bene lo stesso?
Albergatore	Va bene lo stesso, sì sì.
Giovanni	Molte grazie.
Albergatore	Prego.

albergatore   hotel-keeper, hotel employee: related to **albergo** (hotel)

▶ **l'indirizzo è ...**   the address is ... In Italian addresses the number always comes *after* the street name. **Lungarno** in Pisa and Florence are river walks (lit. 'along the Arno').

▶ **se chiama di fuori Pisa**   if you call from outside Pisa. **Se** = if: **se ha una camera ...** if you have a room ...

▶ **e poi con comodo**   and then at your convenience

quando scendono   when you (polite plural) come down (from **scendere**)

▶ **mi fa un favore se ...**   you('ll) do me a favour if ... This useful phrase may be completed in any number of ways: ... **se mi portano i loro passaporti** (... if you bring me your passports); ... **se mi porta la colazione** (... if you bring me breakfast); ... **se mi cambia cinquecento dollari** (... if you change me five hundred dollars). The simpler expression **per piacere** or **per favore** is much more common: **mi porta un caffè, per favore; Per piacere, mi cambia cinquecento dollari?**

carta d'identità   ID card (all Italians are supposed to have one). Other types of card: **carte da gioco** (playing cards), **carta da visita** (visiting card), **carta di credito** (credit card). Note that in all these phrases the main word (**carta**) comes first: this is typical of Italian word order.

qualsiasi documento   any document, any paper. More about **qualsiasi** in the notes to Conversations 2, 'Methods of payment'.

▶ **lo stesso**   all the same (lit. the same), **va bene lo stesso**   that's OK all the same

Giovanni asks Signor Silvestri, a bank manager, about changing foreign currency and using credit cards

LISTEN FOR...	
▶ **Posso cambiare ...?**	May/Can I change ...? I can change ...
▶ **tutti i tipi di ...**	all kinds of ...
▶ **prelevare con carte di credito**	make a withdrawal by credit card

Giovanni	Mi dica, posso cambiare valute straniere?
Sig. Silvestri	Certo, certamente. Può cambiare quasi tutti i tipi di valuta straniera.
Giovanni	E anche travellers cheques?
Sig. Silvestri	Anche travellers cheques. E prelevare anche con carte di credito. Noi accettiamo le carte di credito del nostro circuito, quindi Mastercard, carte VISA, American Express.
Giovanni	Diners?
Sig. Silvestri	Diners, Diners Club.

mi dica   tell me, a common phrase opener, like **senta**; from **dire** (to say).

▶ **Posso cambiare ...?**   May/Can I change ...? The reply is: **può cambiare** ... All the present tense forms of **potere** are given in the *Grammar*, p. 55. This verb translates can, may, to be able to: **Dove posso pagare?** (Where can I pay?), **Posso entrare?** (May I come in?), **non posso venire oggi** (I am not able to come today).

certo, certamente both mean certainly

quasi   nearly, almost

▶ **tutti i tipi di valuta straniera**   all kinds of foreign currency. **Tutto -*a*, -*i*, -*e*** behaves much like 'all' in English: if 'the' is used, it comes between **tutto** and the noun: **tutto il tempo** all the time, **tutte le camere hanno un telefono** (all the rooms have a telephone).

anche   also, too

▶ **prelevare**   to withdraw (cash), to make a withdrawal; **con carte di credito** by credit card(s). In other contexts **carta** usually means paper: **carta igienica** (toilet paper), **carta da scrivere** (writing paper), and by extension chart, map, charter: **carta di navigazione** (navigation chart), **carta geografica** (map), **la carta dei diritti umani** (human rights charter).

noi accettiamo   we accept, from **accettare** (to accept), **Accetta carte di credito?** Do you accept credit cards?

del nostro circuito   of our circuit/network

quindi   therefore, that is

PRACTICE

1 This is a pronunciation exercise for words beginning in *c-* and *t-*. Avoid puffs of breath when articulating these sounds.

Tutti i turisti oggi hanno carte di credito.
Tutte le camere sono con bagno?
No, tutte hanno la doccia.
Dov'è il telefono?
Il telefono è in camera. C'è il telefono in tutte le camere.
Che carta di credito ha?
Ho una carta di credito VISA.

2 Half of the conversation is missing. Pair the tourist's phrases with the other person's replies jumbled in the list below. NOTE: there are more replies than needed and some are not valid.

Per il pagamento che cosa accetta?

a. _____

Non ho lire. Accetta una carta di credito?

b. _____

American Express.

c. _____

Ho dei travellers cheques. Va bene?

d. _____

   i   Accettiamo qualsiasi carta.

   ii Certamente. Travellers cheques va benissimo.

  iii Non accettiamo American Express. Accettiamo solo VISA e Mastercard.

  iv Quasi tutti i turisti hanno American Express.

   v Sì, che carta di credito ha?

ANSWERS P. 58   vi Soltanto lire italiane. Non accettiamo valuta straniera.

3 You are at a bank to withdraw some money. Answer the teller following the presenter's prompts on your recording.

▶ Methods of payment

	LISTEN FOR...
▶ **Accetta travellers cheques?**	Do you take travellers cheques?
▶ **qualsiasi tipo di ...**	any kind of ...
▶ **va benissimo**	OK, super

Giovanni	E per il pagamento Lei accetta travellers cheques e anche carte di credito?
Albergatore	Sì, sì, qualsiasi tipo di pagamento.
Giovanni	Io ho una carta di credito VISA.
Albergatore	VISA va benissimo.
Giovanni	VISA va benissimo.
Albergatore	Sì, sì, va bene, sì sì.
Giovanni	Allora ...
Albergatore	VISA, o anche American Express, o Eurocard. Qualsiasi carta.
Giovanni	Va bene.
Albergatore	Grazie.

il pagamento   payment, related to **pagare** (to pay). Several words ending in -*mento* correspond to English words ending in -*ment*: **complemento, elemento, filamento, momento, monumento, parlamento, supplemento, temperamento**, etc.

▶ **Accetta travellers cheques?**   Do you accept/take travellers cheques?

▶ **qualsiasi tipo di** any type of. Further on: **qualsiasi carta**   any card. Note that **qualsiasi** cannot be used in questions. Have you any ID papers? is **Ha dei documenti?** (see *Grammar*, p. 54). But, if you ask **Che documento vuole?** Which document do you want? and the questioner is prepared to accept any ID whatever, the answer will be: **Qualsiasi documento**.

▶ **va benissimo** an even stronger expression than **va bene** (OK); the ending -*issimo*, -*issima* may replace the ending of some descriptive words (adverbs and adjectives) to mean very: **benissimo** (very well), **una città bellissima** (a very beautiful town).

allora ...   You will find in these conversations words like **allora, be'** (**bene**), **dunque, ecco, senta, diciamo**, which are mere sentence openers or stopgaps, like well, really, sort of, I mean, right, OK in English, and are therefore difficult or impossible to translate.

Giovanni asks a bookseller how much a travel guide costs

LISTEN FOR...

▶ **ha delle guide di Roma?**   have you got some/any guidebooks of Rome?
▶ **cose da guardare**   things to see
▶ **Quanto costa questa guida?**   How much does this guidebook cost?

Giovanni	Signorina, ha delle guide di Roma da consigliarmi?
Libraia	Sì, senz'altro. Abbiamo la Guida di Roma del Touring Club, ripartita per strade, piazze, dà le indicazioni dei principali monumenti ...
Giovanni	Chiese.
Libraia	Chiese, principali cose da guardare.
Giovanni	E quanto costa questa guida?
Libraia	Questa guida costa settantottomila lire.
Giovanni	Settantottomila lire.
Libraia	Sì.

libraio, **libraia**   bookseller; **libro** book; **libreria** bookshop (NOT library)

▶ **Ha delle guide di Roma da consigliarmi?**   Can you suggest a travel guide of Rome? (lit. Have you any guides of Rome to advise to me?). You could simply ask: **Ha delle guide di Roma?** or even **Ha una guida di Roma?** The initial *h-* of **ha** (you have, he/she/it has) is not pronounced. **Dei**, **degli**, **delle** are used to mean some/any: **delle guide di Roma**, **dei monumenti**. There will be a fuller explanation of these points in the *Grammar*, p. 54.

abbiamo   we have

Touring Club Italiano is a sort of Italian National Geographic Society. It offers its membership guidebooks, maps, periodical publications and discounted travel.

ripartita per   divided by

la strada (**le strade**)   street(s); **la piazza** (**le piazze**)   square(s), **il monumento** (**i monumenti**)   monument(s), **la chiesa** (**le chiese**)   church(es)

dà le indicazioni   gives indications; **do**, **dai**, **dà** (with an accent, to distinguish it from the preposition **da**), **diamo**, **date**, **danno** are the forms of the present tense of **dare** (to give).

▶ **principali cose da guardare**   principal things to see. **Guardare** (to look at, to watch, e.g. **guardare un programma alla televisione** to watch a programme on TV). Related words: **guardiano -a** (warden, watchperson); **la guardia** (watchperson, police officer); **cane da guardia** (watchdog).

▶ **Quanto costa questa guida?**   How much does this guidebook cost? A different word order is also possible: **Questa guida quanto costa?** Remember that endings change according to what follows: **Quanto costa questo libro** (book)?, **Quanto costano questi libri** (books)?, **Quanto costano queste guide?** Verbs change too: **costa** (it) costs, **costano** (they) cost. All expressions meaning how much? involve **quanto**: **Quanto è?** (often pronounced quant'è?), **Quanto fa?** or simply **Quanto?**

PRACTICE

4

Listen to a bank teller giving the day's exchange rates, **il cambio di oggi**, for the main currencies. Write the name of each currency (boxed below, but not in the same order as the recording!) next to each rate. You should be able to work out the English translation of the currencies. If you can't, never mind: the point of the exercise is numbers; and you'll find the translations later in the Answers (p. 58). You'll hear **virgola** comma, used in Italian in place of the decimal point.

> £ Sterlina inglese   DM Marco tedesco   Pt Peseta spagnola   Ffr Franco francese
> Fsv Franco svizzero $ Dollaro americano

	Lire 1584,50
	Lire 1043,46
	Lire 300,47
	Lire 2498,76
	Lire 9,70
	Lire 1237,50

ANSWERS P. 58

5

Match the objects below with their prices, given on your recording, and write each price on the appropriate tag. You will hear a new word **l'uno -a** meaning each.

a.   **Guida di Firenze**

b.   **Carta d'Italia**

c.   **Carta da lettere**

d.   **Carte da gioco**

e.   **Cartoline**

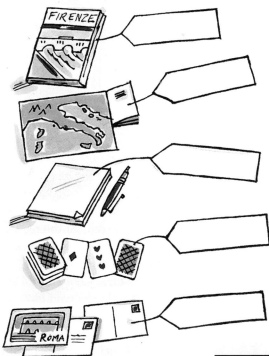

ANSWERS P. 58

6 This bill, from the Hotel 'La Terrazza in Collina' ('Terrace on the Hill'), is called **ricevuta fiscale** (statutory receipt). Customers are obliged by law to keep it since it is evidence that both they and the **esercizio** (a general word for business or concern) have complied with IVA (VAT) legislation. Look carefully at the bill and answer the following questions.

La Terrazza in Collina	RICEVUTA FISCALE
di Angelo Gerlini	LEGGE 30.12.1991 N. 413 - DM 30.03.1992
	PARTITA IVA N. 01108380473
Via del Lavoro, 36 66019 TORRICELLA PELIGNA (Chieti) Tel. - Fax [39] 0871 66 24	DATA 8/1/96 Nº

DATI IDENTIFICATIVI DEL CLIENTE
Giuseppe Corsi, Via Rossini 24, Pesaro

CAMERA Nº _18_

DATA	QUANTITA', NATURA E QUALITA' DEI SERVIZI	IMPORTO
6–8/1/96	Camera e prima colazione x 3	360 000
6/1/96	Ristorante	36 750
	Bar	10 000
7/1/96	Ristorante	42 800
	Bar	4 000
	Lavanderia	25 000
8/1/96	Telefono / Facsimile	17 250
	TOTALE [IVA inclusa]	499 800

a. What is the date of the receipt?   (i) 1 August 1996   (ii) 8 January 1996
b. How many rooms were booked?   (i) three for one day   (ii) one for three days
c. Was breakfast included?   (i) yes   (ii) no
d. Was any meal taken at the hotel restaurant?   (i) yes   (ii) no
e. How were drinks paid for?   (i) cash   (ii) by charging them to the account
f. Is the laundry charge more or less than the telephone/fax charge?   (i) more   (ii) less

ANSWERS P. 58   g. Was VAT included in the total?   (i) yes   (i) no

CONVERSATIONS

 What is there for breakfast?

LISTEN FOR...

▶ **Che cosa c'è per colazione?** What is there for breakfast?
▶ **qualche cos'altro** something else
▶ **si può fare ...** one can make ..., one can do ...

Giovanni	Mi dica che cosa c'è per colazione.
Cameriere	Eh, caffè col latte, oppure del té o del cioccolato con pane, burro e marmellata. Se poi vuole anche qualcos'altro si può fare delle uova à la coque, o omelette, o qualche cos'altro del genere.
Giovanni	Va bene, molte grazie.
Cameriere	Prego, niente.

cameriere waiter
▶ **che cosa** what: the standard way of asking a question. **Che cosa prende?** What will you have? (lit. What thing you take?), **Che cosa faccio?** What am I to do?, **Che cosa c'è ...** What is there ... **per colazione** (for breakfast),

... per pranzo (for lunch), **... per cena** (for dinner)? Often the initial **che** is omitted: **Cosa prende? Cosa c'è?**, etc.

caffè coffee, invariably black, made from ground coffee. If milk is wanted it has to be asked for: **caffè col** (= **con il**) **latte**, or **caffè e latte**, sometimes written **caffellatte**. Other types of coffee: **espresso**, **macchiato** (lit. spotted) with a spot of milk, **corretto** with a dash of your favourite spirit, **decaffeinato** decaffeinated. If you do not want a thimbleful of black treacly liquid, say '**un caffè lungo** (long) **per favore**' or, in Tuscany, '**alto**' (tall).

oppure or

del té some tea. Regrettably that often means a teabag and a cupful of warm water.

cioccolato (m), also **cioccolata** (f) chocolate, both drinking and confectionery

pane bread

burro butter

marmellata any jam, not just marmalade which is **marmellata d'arance** (**arancia** = orange).

se poi vuole anche ... if/then (you) also want ...

▶ **qualche cos'altro** (= **qualche cosa d'altro**) something else; also **qualcosa d'altro**

▶ **si può fare ...** one can make ... Useful also in questions: **Si può fare una frittata?** Can you (lit. one) make/do an omelette?

uova à la coque soft-boiled eggs

del genere like that (lit. of the kind)

prego, niente don't mention it. **Niente** (nothing) is often used as a negative before a noun, e.g. **niente uova** (no eggs), **niente latte nel mio té** (no milk in my tea).

Ordering a quick breakfast for two at the Caffè Adriano

LISTEN FOR...

▶ **cappuccini** cappuccinos
▶ **cornetti** croissants

Signora	Due cappuccini e due cornetti.
Cassiera	Cinquemila e due.
Signora	Quanto?
Cassiera	Cinque e due.

▶ **Cappuccino** (often shortened to **cappuccio**) **espresso** is coffee mixed with frothy steamed milk. There are two explanations for the name: the froth sits on top like a **cappuccio**, a hood or a cap; the liquid is brown in colour like the habit of a Capuchin monk.

▶ **cornetti** (lit. little horn) croissants

cinque e due note the short-style prices. At the time of writing, the basic unit of currency in Italy is effectively 1000 lire, and the smallest lower denomination is 100 lire. Single figures after the thousands mean hundreds: **due** does not mean two lire but 200. Often prices are further shortened by dividing the thousands by 1000. The final quote thus comes to **cinque e due**. **41.500 lire** would be **quarantuno e cinque**. The official adoption of this idea, often mooted by the Italian Treasury, seems likely to be superseded by the creation of a unified European currency.

Ordering aperitifs at the bar

LISTEN FOR...

▶ **Io prendo ... E Lei che cosa prende?** I'm having ... And what will you have?

Giovanni	Io prendo un Campari soda. E Lei che cosa prende, signor Gabrielli?
Gabrielli	Un Bitter Campari.
Giovanni	Signor Ranieri, che cosa prende Lei?
Ranieri	A me un analcoolico.
Giovanni	Senza alcool ...
Ranieri	Benissimo.
Giovanni	E io prendo un Campari soda.

▶ **io prendo ...** I'm having ... (lit. I take); **E lei che cosa prende?** And what will you have? Note that the order is flexible: in asking Signor Ranieri, Giovanni says: **Che cosa prende Lei?** Other things you could order: **sugo** or **succo di frutta** fruit juice (**ananas** pineapple, **albicocca** apricot, **arancia** orange, **limone** lemon, **mela** apple, **pera** pear, **pesca** peach, **pompelmo** grapefruit, **uva** grapes), **acqua minerale** mineral water (**liscia** still or **gasata** fizzy), **aranciata** orangeade, **birra** beer (**nazionale** locally produced and **estera** imported).

a me for me (lit. to me)

un analcoolico an alcohol-free aperitif. As Giovanni explains:
  senza alcool without alcohol.

7 For each of the following items choose the appropriate form, **quanto costa?** or **quanto costano?**

a _____ la colazione?

b Un té _____ ?

c _____ un cappuccino?

d Due analcoolici _____ ?

e Le uova à la coque _____ ?

f _____ un cioccolato?

ANSWERS P. 58 g Questi cornetti _____ ?

8 A couple are ordering breakfast. Listen to the conversation on the recording and write down the items each of them has ordered. Be careful: the words in the bubble include items neither of them has ordered! You will hear a useful new expression to recognize: **E da bere?** And to drink?

Uova à la coque, omelette, cappuccino, succo di arancio, caffellatte, marmellata, pane, cioccolata, cornetti, burro, té, caffè, decaffeinato, succo di mela.

ANSWERS P. 58

9 Match the questions to the replies.

Questions	Answers
a. Che cos'è un analcoolico?	i Il Duomo.
b. Quant'è il cambio della sterlina oggi?	ii 2584,36.
c. Ci sono le principali strade in questa guida?	iii Sì, mela, pesca, arancio, di tutti i tipi.
d. Quant'è?	iv Certo, e anche le principali chiese e i monumenti più importanti.
e. Come si chiama questo monumento?	v Settemila e sei.
f. Ha succhi di frutta?	vi È un aperitivo senza alcool.

ANSWERS P. 58

GRAMMAR AND EXERCISES

The article

(i) translation of the definite article 'the'
All the forms, singular (see p. 24) and plural, are tabled here for your convenience.

	Singular		Plural	
Masculine nouns beginning in a consonant	il	il treno il ristorante	i	i treni i ristoranti
Masculine nouns beginning in s + another consonant	lo	lo studente lo specchio	gli	gli studenti gli specchi
Masculine nouns beginning in a vowel	l'	l'albergo l'aperitivo		gli alberghi gli aperitivi
Feminine nouns beginning in a vowel		l'albicocca l'ora	le	le albicocche le ore
Feminine nouns beginning in a consonant	la	la guida la camera		le guide le camere

(ii) translation of 'some', 'any'
This is a combination of **di** and the definite article (as if one said [some] of the …):

	il	lo	la	l'	i	gli	le
di +	del	dello	della	dell'	dei	degli	delle

You use the form corresponding to the article you would normally use. Examples:

Noun with the article		Combination	Translation
Singular	Plural	di + article	
il treno	i treni	dei treni	some trains
lo studente	gli studenti	degli studenti	some students
l'albicocca	le albicocche	delle albicocche	some apricots

You can use this construction also with singular words indicating an indefinite quantity. **Ha del té?** Have you any tea? **Mi porta dello zucchero per favore** Bring me some sugar, please.

(iii) other combinations
This is for recognition only. Other prepositions combine with the article as **di** above. It is not possible to give translations for prepositions since what they mean depends on the context (see Unit 10, p. 150). The forms preceded by an asterisk tend not to be used in writing.

	il	lo	la	l'	i	gli	le
a +	al	allo	alla	all'	ai	agli	alle
da +	dal	dallo	dalla	dall'	dai	dagli	dalle
in +	nel	nello	nella	nell'	nei	negli	nelle
su +	sul	sullo	sulla	sull'	sui	sugli	sulle
con +	col	*collo	*colla	coll'	coi	*cogli	*colle

e.g. **allo studente** to the student, **agli studenti** to the students; **dalla montagna** from the mountain, **dalle montagne** from the mountains; **nella camera** in the room, **nelle camere** in the rooms; **sulla strada** on the road, **sulle strade** on the roads; caffè **col latte** coffee with milk.

Verbs

The verbs **potere** (to be able), **volere** (to want), **avere** (to have), all follow an irregular pattern (see the table on the opposite page).
Examples:
Posso entrare? May I come in?; **Vuoi** (informal)/**vuole** (polite) **prendere un aperitivo?** Would you like an aperitif?; **Abbiamo della marmellata di albicocche.** We have some apricot jam. Remember that the initial *h*- of some forms of **avere** is not pronounced. The traditional explanation for the initial *h*- (which is found only in a few words of foreign origin, such as **hotel**, **habitat**, **hippy**) is that it avoids confusing those forms of **avere** with **o** or, **ai** to the, **a** to, **anno** year.

	potere to be able, can, may	**volere** to want, will	**avere** to have
I	**posso**	**voglio**	**ho**
you	**puoi**	**vuoi**	**hai**
he/she/it <u>or</u> you (polite)	**può**	**vuole**	**ha**
we	**possiamo**	**vogliamo**	**abbiamo**
you (pl)	**potete**	**volete**	**avete**
they	**possono**	**vogliono**	**hanno**

10 Fit the missing forms (singular or plural) in the grid below. All the words included belong to either the four endings (-*o*, -*a* or -*i*, -*e*) or the two endings pattern (-*e* or -*i*) and have been used in one and/or the other form in the first four units.

Singular	Plural
la nipotina	**le** _____
l' _____	**gli abitanti**
il paese	**i** _____
l'agricoltore	**gli** _____
l' _____	**le uscite**
un chilo	**tre** _____
il _____	**i telefoni**
un _____	**dei treni interregionali**
una _____	**due camere doppie**
una brava segretaria	**delle** _____

ANSWERS P. 58

11 Fill in the appropriate form for 'the' (**il**, **lo**, **la**, **l'**, **i**, **gli**, **le**) in the following sentences.

a. _____cabine del telefono sono di fronte.

b. Come vuole _____cornetti? col burro o senza?

c. _____camere hanno tutte _____telefono.

d. _____appartamenti al terzo piano costano 300 mila lire per notte.

e. Ci sono _____strade e _____ monumenti principali in questa guida?

f. _____alberghi più importanti sono sulla riviera di Santa Lucia.

ANSWERS P. 58

12 Fill in the appropriate form for some/any: **del**, **dello**, **della**, **dell'**, **dei**, **degli**, **delle** in the following sentences.

a. Ha _____cornetti?

b. No, non abbiamo cornetti. Vuole _____ pane tostato (toast)?

c. Anche _____marmellata, per piacere. E _____succo di arancio.

d. Posso cambiare _____dollari e _____sterline?

e. Mi fa un piacere se mi porta _____latte freddo (cold).

f. Accetta _____carte di credito?

ANSWERS P. 58

KEY WORDS
AND PHRASES

con comodo	at your convenience
mi fa un favore se …	you'll do me a favour if …
lo stesso	all the same
posso cambiare	may I change?/I may change
… prelevare con carte di credito?	… make a withdrawal by credit card?
… fare colazione?	… have breakfast?
si può fare …	one can make …, one can do …
Accetta travellers cheques?	Do you take travellers cheques?
qualsiasi tipo di …	any kind of …
tutti i tipi di …	all kinds of …
va benissimo	OK, super
Ha delle guide di Roma?	Have you some/any guides of Rome?
cose da guardare	things to see
Quanto costa questa guida?	How much does this guide cost?
Che cosa c'è per colazione?	What is there for breakfast?
caffè (m)	coffee
espresso, cappuccino	espresso, cappuccino
latte (m)	milk
cornetti	croissants
pane (m)	bread
pane tostato	toast
sugo or succo di frutta	fruit juice
ananas	pineapple
albicocca	apricot
arancia	orange
limone	lemon
mela	apple
pera	pear
pesca	peach
pompelmo	grapefruit
uva	grape
aperitivo	aperitif
analcoolico	alcohol-free
acqua minerale	mineral water
liscia	still
gasata	fizzy
aranciata	orangeade
birra	beer
nazionale	locally produced
estera	imported
qualche cos'altro	something else

Paying your bills

Nearly all Italian hotels will accept one or more of the international credit cards. They will also accept **assegni di viaggio**, mostly called by their English name of **travellers cheques**, and foreign currency, but often at a less favourable rate of exchange than can be had through a bank. Don't be surprised if banks apply slightly different rates: that depends on their varying estimate of what the rate of exchange of the foreign currency bought today will be when they have to re-sell it in three or four days' time.

In large towns and, outside them, in important tourist areas, you can get all the cash you need from automated bank tellers (**Bancomat**, from the name of one particular service popularly given to all) using an international credit card or a Eurocheque card. Make sure the machine displays your card's logo before slotting it in.

In practically all bars, fast food outlets and food shops, money matters are dealt with by a **cassiere** (m) or **cassiera** (f), and not by the waiter or employee who has been attending you. Often you have to pay the cashier first, get a receipt and then go to the counter. This is a sensible hygienic precaution preventing food items and money from being handled by the same person. Listen for the phrase **prego, si accomodi alla cassa** please go to the cash till.

Drinks and snacks

The place to go when you feel thirsty or peckish is the ubiquitous bar, which you will find on almost every street corner. Bars come in all shapes, sizes and degrees of luxury, but most of them have a shortage of indoor seating, often inversely proportional to the pavement space they occupy. Most local customers have their drinks and snacks at or near the counter.

As there are no licensing laws in Italy, you are free to enjoy any drink you fancy, from milk to strong alcoholic concoctions, at any time of day and often of night.

Italian beer is a palatable but mostly undistinguished lager, with low alcoholic content, but foreign brews are widely available. A glass of **acqua minerale** (mineral water, sometimes not much more than good quality tap water in fancy bottles) may cost as much, and occasionally more, than a glass of wine. If you like your mineral water fizzy, ask for **acqua minerale gasata**, otherwise ask for **acqua minerale liscia** or **naturale**. If you like bitter lemon drinks you may wish to try **aranciata amara** bitter orange, or **chinotto**, made from citrus peel: these are normally drunk straight and not as mixers. There is a bewildering variety of **aperitivi**, of various degrees of bitterness, some made up by the barman (**aperitivo della casa**), others pre-mixed with soda, bearing familiar brand names. If you want then alcohol-free ask for an **analcoolico**.

Caffè consists of a few drops of scalding black liquid extracted from ground high-roast coffee by high-pressure steam through an espresso machine. If you want more than a few drops ask for **caffè lungo** (lit. long coffee). White coffee is called **cappuccino** if made on an espresso machine, or **caffè e latte** (**caffellatte**). Decaf is **caffè decaffeinato**. You will never be served instant coffee (**caffè liofilizzato** or **solubile**) except on trains.

Most bars have a mouthwatering selection of fresh cakes (**paste**), buns, biscuits and confectionery. Note that the word **pasta** may refer either to a single cake or to a quantity of **spaghetti**, **maccheroni**, **penne**, **linguine**, etc. Some cakes are filled with **crema** which is a sort of rich custard: the Italian for cream is **panna** (whipped cream **panna montata**). If your taste is for savoury snacks, you may choose between **panini**, soft rolls with a variety of fillings; **tosti**, toasted sandwiches; and **pizzette**, small pizzas reheated in a microwave oven.

AND FINALLY...

13 The Italian shop assistant gives you a price in its shortened form. Confirm that you have understood it correctly by giving its full form, and listen for the check.

```
        EDICOLA
   PARMESAN CRISTIANO
 C.PO S VIO 669/A VENEZIA
     P.I.02854160278

     11              22-04-1996
   12:59               CASSA 1
  REPARTO1              4.000
  TOT                   4.000
        FAT 49010575
```

```
       BAR TORINO
   DI DONADINI FRANCO
  S.MARCO 4591 VENEZIA
   PAR.IVA 02139650275

 REP.5              1.000
 REP.5              1.000
 CONTANTE    2      2.000

 OP. 1      N.SCONTR.    62
 RE
```

```
   OSTERIA AI ASSASSINI
 GALARDI G. & PILOT M.* SNC
   SAN MARCO 3695 VENEZIA
      P.I. 02416200273

 VINO 1/2LT         3.000
 BIBITA             2.000
 VARIE              4.000
 PASTA              9.000
 PASTA              9.000
 CARNE              8.000
 CARNE              8.000
 VINO DOC           2.000
 VINO DOC           2.000
 BISCOTTI           4.000
 TOTALE     10     51.000
 CONTANTE          51.000

 OP. 1      N.SCONTR.    14
 REG.001    24-04-96 19:14

    MF GZ 72014323
```

```
      CAFFE MAIOLI
   DI PICCINI & C. SAS
    VIA DEI BARDI 73/R.
   FIRENZE TEL.284108
    P.IVA  04660810484

 REPARTO 12         6.000

 TOTALE    1        6.000

 CASS. 1 13:49 CASSA    1
 28-04-96  SCONTR. N. 311
 ARRIVEDERCI E GRAZIE

    MF XT 13027562
```

```
   ROSTICCERIA
   GIULIANO
 VIA DE NERI 74
   TEL 2382723
   27-APR-96        05:22
 NETTO TARA PREZZO IMPORTO
   kg    g   L/kg    LIRE

 BIL 1
        3500x 2=     7.000
 BIL 1
        8000x 2=    16.000
 BIL 1
   Non Pesato       10.000
 BIL 1
        4500x 2=     9.000
 BIL 1
   Non Pesato        4.000
 BIL 1
   Non Pesato        2.000
                  ----------
 NC. 6 TOTALE L.    48.000
 OPER. 1 N. PROGR. 0003449
```

ANSWERS

EXERCISE 2

(a) vi **(b)** v **(c)** iii **(d)** ii

EXERCISE 4

$ US dollar 1584.50, DM German Mark 1043.46, Ffr French Franc 300.47, £ Pound sterling 2498.76, Pt Spanish Peseta 9.70, Fsv Swiss Franc 1237.50

EXERCISE 5

(a) 120.000 **(b)** 15.000 **(c)** 43.000 **(d)** 20.000
(e) 2.500

EXERCISE 6

(a) ii **(b)** ii **(c)** i **(d)** i **(e)** ii **(f)** i **(g)** i
The normal order of Italian dates is day/month/year, and it can be deduced from the dates of the booking: 6 to 8 of month 1.

EXERCISE 7

(a) (b) (c) (f) Quanto costa? **(d) (e) (g)** Quanto costano?

EXERCISE 8

Uomo: succo di arancio, pane, burro e marmellata, caffellatte.
Donna: succo di mela, due cornetti, té.

EXERCISE 9

(a) vi **(b)** ii **(c)** iv **(d)** v **(e)** i **(f)** iii

EXERCISE 10

le nipotine, l'abitante, i paesi, gli agricoltori, l'uscita, tre chili, il telefono, un treno interregionale, una camera doppia, delle brave segretarie.

EXERCISE 11

(a) le **(b)** i **(c)** le, il **(d)** gli **(e)** le, i **(f)** gli

EXERCISE 12

(a) dei **(b)** del **(c)** della, del **(d)** dei, delle **(e)** del
(f) delle

5 'HOW DO I GET THERE?'

WHAT YOU WILL LEARN

- ▶ how to ask where various places are
- ▶ how to ask the best way to get to these places
- ▶ how to understand simple street directions
- ▶ how to understand information about public transport

BEFORE YOU BEGIN

Seek every opportunity to expose yourself to spoken Italian. You may be living in an area where a TV and/or radio channel is devoted to broadcasts in non-English languages among which is Italian; or you may be able to receive radio broadcasts directly from Italy (the news is a good starting point because you already have some idea of what will be in it). Listening will improve your sound pattern recognition, i.e. your ability to isolate words out of continuous speech. You have to be able to single out the words you don't know before you can ask what they mean.

POINTS TO REMEMBER FROM UNIT 4

Verbs: **avere** (to have) (**ho, hai, ha, abbiamo, avete, hanno**), **potere** (may, can, to be able to) (**posso, puoi, può, possiamo, potete, possono**), **volere** (to want) (**voglio, vuoi, vuole, vogliamo, volete, vogliono**).

Questions: **quanto costa? posso ... ? si può fare? ha del burro, delle guide di Roma?**

'the': **il bagno, i bagnl, lo studente, gli studenti, l'aperitivo, gli aperitivi
la colazione, le colazioni, l'acqua minerale, le acque minerali.**

Pronunciation notes

The two letters **-sc-** are pronounced **-sk-** (as in scoot) before **-a, -o, -u** and **-h**: **scala** staircase, **scozzese** Scot, Scottish, **scusi** excuse me, **dischi** disks.

They are pronounced **-sh-** (as in shoot) before **-i** and **-e**: **esci** you go out, **esce** he/she/it goes out, **la Rinascente** (the name of the department store mentioned in Unit 3).

How do I get there?

LISTEN FOR...

▶ **scusi**	excuse me
▶ **Come faccio per andare ...?**	How do I go to ...?
▶ **sinistra**	left
▶ **dritto** or **diritto**	straight on

Giovanni	Buongiorno.
Impiegato	Buongiorno.
Giovanni	Scusi, come faccio per andare da qui in Vaticano?
Impiegato	Prende la prima qui a sinistra, va sempre dritto, sono cento metri.
Giovanni	Grazie.
Impiegato	Prego.

▶ **scusi** excuse me (lit. excuse). You may also say **mi scusi**. Use **scusi** when addressing strangers: the familiar form is **scusa**, from the verb **scusare** (to excuse). It is useful also to attract the attention of people, or to make way in a crowd.

▶ **Come faccio per andare ...?** How do I go to ...? After **come faccio per** you use the infinitive form of the verb: **Come faccio per pagare?** How do I pay?; **Come faccio per telefonare in Canadà?** How do I ring Canada?
da qui from here
in Vaticano to the Vatican (also: **al Vaticano**)

▶ **la prima qui a sinistra** the first (street) here on the left; **a destra** (on the right)

▶ **va sempre dritto** you continue straight on (lit. you go always straight); also **diritto**
sono cento metri it's (lit. they are) a hundred metres

Vatican City

● *It's very close*

Giovanni	Scusi, dov'è la Rinascente?
Signore	È proprio di fronte a Lei. Attraversa la strada.
Giovanni	Grazie.

     proprio   just, right
▶ **di fronte**   opposite; **di fronte a Lei** (opposite you); **di fronte all'albergo** (opposite the hotel); **di fronte alla stazione** (opposite the station)
▶ **attraversa** from **attraversare** (to cross, to traverse); **attraverso** across, through; **attraverso le montagne** (across the mountains)

● *Where is the bank?*

Giovanni	Scusi, dov'è la Banca Commerciale?
Signore	È a sinistra, venti metri avanti.

▶ **avanti**   forward
Also **Avanti!** Come in!, Move on!, Get on with it! Do not confuse **avanti** with **davanti** opposite, before (in space), in front: **davanti alla banca** (opposite the bank), **la stanza davanti** (the front room).
▶ **venti metri avanti** or **venti metri più avanti**   20 metres further on

PRACTICE

1

This exercise is about the pronunciation of the spelling **-sc-**. Read one by one the following sentences (one contains two new words which you will understand very easily) and check their pronunciation on your recording.

— Scusi, dov'è la Rinascente?
— Che cos'è la Scala?
— Questo telefono va colla scheda.
— Mi dica il suo luogo di nascita.

— È proprio di fronte all'uscita dell'albergo.
— La Scala di Milano è un famoso teatro.

— Sono scozzese.

2

Listen to the recorded conversation and answer the following questions:

a. The woman wishes to go   (i) to piazza del Duomo   (ii) to La Scala theatre.
b. The entrance to the Galleria is   (i) opposite   (ii) on the left.
c. The woman is told   (i) to turn left   (ii) to go straight through the Galleria.

ANSWERS P. 74

d. The place where she wants to go is   (i) on the right   (ii) on the left.

3

Thinking of Exercise 2, match the following questions with their answers:

a. — Scusi, dove posso telefonare?
b. — Scusi, posso cambiare qui questi travellers' cheques?
c. — Scusi, dove posso prendere la colazione?
d. — Scusi, come faccio per andare in banca?
e. — Scusi, dov'è piazza della Scala?

 i — Nel ristorante dell'albergo, al primo piano.
 ii — La cabina è lì a destra. Va colla scheda.
 iii — È vicino alla Galleria, proprio all'uscita della Galleria.
 iv — All'uscita dell'albergo, prenda la prima strada a destra e vada dritto per trecento metri.

ANSWERS P. 74

 v — No: può andare alla banca più vicina che è la Banca Commerciale.

'How do I get there?'   *Unit 5*

Turn left for the nearest bank

LISTEN FOR...

- ▶ **più vicina** nearest
- ▶ **quando esce** when you go out
- ▶ **marciapiede** pavement

Giovanni	Buon giorno, signora.
Signora	Buon giorno.
Giovanni	Mi sa dire dov'è la banca più vicina?
Signora	Guardi, quando esce qui dal negozio va a sinistra e quando arriva al semaforo attraversa la strada e sul marciapiede di fronte c'è il Banco di Napoli.
Giovanni	Molte grazie, signora.
Signora	Prego.

Either by bus or on foot

LISTEN FOR...

- ▶ **Mi sa dire come ...?** Can you tell me how to ...?
- ▶ **o ... oppure ...** either ... or ...

Giovanni	Signora, mi sa dire come andare da qui a piazza Cavour?
Signora	O prende il 492, oppure fa tutta Cola di Rienzo, via Cola di Rienzo, via Cicerone, e arriva a piazza Cavour.
Giovanni	Molte grazie, signora.
Signora	Prego, buongiorno.

▶ **più vicina** nearer, nearest. Most English *-er, -est* forms are translated into Italian by **più** followed by the adjective. **Il Banco di Napoli è più vicino della Banca Commerciale** Banco di Napoli is nearer than Banca Commerciale; but, in the absolute, **il Banco di Napoli è il più vicino** Banco di Napoli is the nearest, **la banca più vicina è il Banco di Napoli** the nearest bank is Banco di Napoli. Some banks have kept their old name **banco** (meaning counter).

▶ **quando esce** when you go out, from **uscire** to go out (remember **uscita** exit)? This verb has an irregular present: see *Grammar,* p. 70; **quando arriva al semaforo** when you get to the traffic lights (notice that **semaforo** is singular). More about **quando** in the next unit.

negozio shop

▶ **marciapiede** pavement, sidewalk (lit. march-on-foot); **a piedi** (on foot)

▶ **Mi sa dire come ...?** (lit. to me you know tell how?) Can you tell me how ...?, **Mi sa dire come telefonare negli Stati Uniti?** (Can you tell me how to ring the United States?), **Mi sa dire come andare in centro?** (Can you tell me how to go to the centre/downtown (lit. in centre)?

andare ... a piazza Cavour go to piazza Cavour. But also **andare in piazza Cavour**, **in Vaticano**, **in centro**. **Andare in ...** suggests that one is going to a location with definite boundaries, which one has to cross to go 'in' (a connotation missing from **andare a ...**); in the next conversation we find **andare sulla piazza**, 'on' the square, pictured as a surface with various tram and bus stops on it. There is no easy way of accounting for the use of these prepositions in Italian.

▶ **o prende ... oppure fa ...** either you take [bus No.] 492, or you do the whole [of **via**] **Cola di Rienzo**, etc.

... or by tram

LISTEN FOR...

▶ **Come devo fare?** What must I do?
▶ **si prende ...** one takes ...
▶ **si va ...** one goes ...
▶ **si scende ...** one gets off ...

Giovanni	Buongiorno. Per andare in via Francesco Sforza da qui come devo fare?
Signore	Sì, si va sulla sulla piazza, si prende il tram tredici, via Cappellari, tredici; si scende alla seconda fermata, corso di Porta Romana, angolo via Francesco Sforza.

▶ **Come devo fare?** What (lit. How) must I do? **Come devo fare per ...?** can be used as an alternative to **Come faccio per ...?** **Devo**, I must or have to, comes from **dovere** which has an irregular present tense: see *Grammar*, p. 70.

▶ **si va ...** one goes ...

▶ **si prende...** one takes ... **il tram** the tram, **l'autobus** the bus, **il tassì** the taxi, **il** (or **la**) **metro** (short for **la metropolitana**) the underground/subway. Private coaches and long-distance coaches are called **il pullman**. For more information on public transport, see *Did you know?*, p. 73.

▶ **si scende** (from **scendere** lit. to step down) one gets off. For this form with **si ...** see *Grammar*, p. 70.

fermata stop; from **fermare** (to stop)

angolo via Francesco Sforza 'telegraphic' style for **all'angolo di via F. S.** on the corner of F. S. street; also **sull'angolo**. In other contexts **angolo** means angle.

A **metro** *sign*

A bus stop

4

In the conversation on your recording Giancarlo is asking for directions. Listen to the conversation, then tick the correct answers. You will hear two new words: **modi** means, methods; **semplice** simple.

a. He wishes to go to (i) Stazione Termini (ii) via Farnese (iii) via Lépanto

b. He is told that (i) there is only one way of getting there (ii) there are two ways and this is the simpler of the two.

c. One should take the underground (i) line A (ii) line B (iii) line C

d. (i) There is a stop in via Farnese (ii) There is a stop in via Lépanto and via Farnese is on the corner.

ANSWERS P. 74

5

This is the continuation of the previous conversation. Listen to it, then tick the correct answers. You will need a new word **cinema** cinema, movie house.

a. (i) There is only one bus going there. (ii) There are several buses.

b. The nearest stop is bus No. (i) 70 (ii) 81 (iii) 180

c. One should get off (i) at piazza Cavour (ii) at the corner of via Caro

d. Via Farnese is (i) the first street left from the stop (ii) the first street right (iii) the street at the bottom of via Caro

ANSWERS P. 74

6

Number the various parts of the following conversation so that the new order makes sense. Note the useful expressions **ogni ora** (every hour) and **il modo più comodo** (the most convenient way).

a. — Sì. Ma se lei vuole può anche andare in metropolitana. C'è un treno ogni ora.

b. — Senta, come devo fare per andare all'aeroporto?

c. — Certo. La fermata è proprio a destra della stazione.

d. — Ma costa molto! Non c'è un autobus?

e. — Ferma anche davanti ai principali alberghi?

ANSWERS P. 74

f. — Il modo più semplice è di andare in tassì.

Taking the underground

LISTEN FOR...

▶ **in direzione Marelli**   bound for Marelli
▶ **la quarta fermata**   the fourth stop

Giovanni	Buongiorno. Come faccio per andare da qui a piazzale Lima?
Signore	Dunque, prende una metropolitana in direzione Marelli e scende alla quarta fermata.
Giovanni	Molte grazie.

piazzale Lima   name of an underground station; **piazzale** is a smaller public square.

dunque   here a sentence opener, but in other contexts, therefore.

▶ **direzione**   direction. Many Italian word ending in *-zione* have English equivalents in *-tion* (**animazione, meditazione, posizione, situazione, stazione, variazione** etc.): they are ALL feminine. **in direzione Marelli**   bound for Marelli (name of the terminus), going towards Marelli

▶ **alla quarta fermata**   at the fourth stop **fermare** (to stop); **Ferma a piazzale Lima?** (Does it stop at piazzale Lima?), **ferma a tutte le stazioni** (it stops at all stations). We have by now come across the first four ordinals (numerals indicating order): **primo** first, **secondo** second, **terzo** third, **quarto** fourth. They are four-ending adjectives (**primo, prima, primi, prime,** etc.). See a few more in Unit 7, p. 95.

Terminus for Termini

LISTEN FOR...

▶ **Che mezzo prendo?** What transport do I take?
▶ **il capolinea** the terminus

Giovanni	Senta, per andare da qui alla Stazione Termini che mezzo prendo?
Impiegato	Lì c'è il capolinea del 492 che transita per la Stazione Termini, se no il 64 sempre in quella direzione, per San Pietro.
Giovanni	Molte grazie.
Impiegato	Prego.

▶ **Che mezzo prendo?** What transport do I take?, **mezzo** (means of transport)
▶ **lì** there; also **là**. Using one or the other is a matter of choice, as in **qui/qua** (here).
▶ **il capolinea** the terminus, end of the line (lit. head [of the] line). Termini, the name of Rome's main railway station, is in fact the plural of the Latin word TERMINUS meaning boundary, end of the road.

transita per goes through; **transitare** (compare English transit) to go through
se no otherwise (lit. if not)
in quella direzione in that direction; for more details about **quello** -a see *Grammar*, p. 70.

Here is a young woman who cannot help with directions

LISTEN FOR...

▶ **mi dispiace** I'm sorry
▶ **non lo so** I don't know (it)

Giovanni	Come si fa per andare in piazza della Scala?
Signorina	Mi dispiace, non lo so perché non sono di Milano.

▶ **mi dispiace** I'm sorry (lit. me it displeases)
▶ **non lo so** I don't know (it); from **sapere** to know (**so** I know, **sai** you know, **sa** he/she/it knows)
   perché because

7-8 For these two exercises follow the instructions on your recording. You will be prompted to ask for directions. You will need two new words: **vedere** to see, **Vede?** Do you see? and **finché** until.

9 Look at this section from an imaginary town map. **Magazzini Generali** is the name of a department store, and **Ente del Turismo** is the Tourist Office. Complete the following sentences which describe what is shown in the map, inserting expressions from the box below. There are two extra expressions which do not fit anywhere!

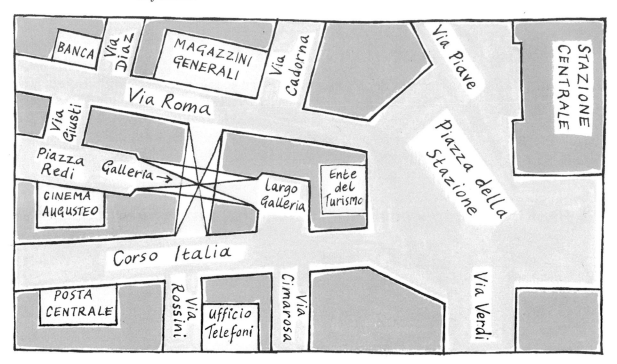

a. La banca è _____ di via Diaz e di via Roma.

b. I Magazzini Generali sono _____ alla Galleria.

c. Quando _____ dalla Posta Centrale, via Rossini è

_____ .

d. Per andare da piazza Redi a largo Galleria _____ la Galleria.

e. L'Ente del Turismo è _____ alla Stazione Centrale.

di fronte   esce   quasi davanti   la prima a destra   la seconda a sinistra
deve attraversare   all'angolo   la fermata dell'autobus

ANSWERS P. 74

10 Look again at the map and tick those among the following statements that appear to you to be true.

a. L'Ente del Turismo è in piazza della Stazione. ☐

b. La Galleria ha solo due uscite. ☐

c. La Posta Centrale è proprio di fronte alla Galleria in Corso Italia. ☐

d. Il cinema Augusteo è in via Giusti. ☐

e. Per andare dalla Stazione Centrale alla Posta Centrale si attraversa la piazza della Stazione e si prende Corso Italia. La Posta Centrale è dopo via Rossini, a sinistra. ☐

f. La banca è in via Rossini. ☐

g. I Magazzini Generali sono all'angolo di via Roma e via Cadorna. ☐

h. Per andare da via Rossini a via Roma si attraversa la Galleria. ☐

ANSWERS P. 74

GRAMMAR AND EXERCISES

Verbs

	dovere to have to, must	uscire to go out
I	devo	esco
you	devi	esci
he/she/it, you (polite)	deve	esce
we	dobbiamo	usciamo
you (pl)	dovete	uscite
they	devono	escono

More plurals

Bello means beautiful. **Quello** is a 'pointing' word meaning 'that'. Their ending, like that of the article, is determined by the beginning of the following word. See table below.

If no word follows, their endings are those of a normal four-ending adjective, agreeing with the thing qualified or pointed at: **Questo libro è molto bello!, ha una casa così bella, prendo due di quelle [albicocche], Che cosa sono quelli?** [unspecified objects considered masculine], etc.

Nouns ending in a consonant (like **tram**) and in a stressed vowel (like **tassì**, taxi) do not change in the plural (**i tram, gli autobus, i tassì**, etc.).

Words with a -*c*- or a -*g*- in the singular ending tend to keep the sound ('hard' or 'soft') of the consonant, and they adjust the spelling accordingly: **il banco** the counter, **i banchi**; **la banca** the bank, **le banche**; **l'ago** the needle, **gli aghi**; **la paga** the pay, **le paghe**; **l'ufficio** the office, **gli uffici**; **la valigia** suitcase, **le valigie**.

The exceptions are nouns and adjectives ending in unstressed -*ico*, whose hard -*c*- softens in the plural: **pubblico** public, **pubblici**; **traffico** traffic, **traffici**; **magnifico** magnificent, **magnifici**, etc. (you will be reminded of them in Unit 14).

Mi, si, lo, and other monosyllabic pronouns

You are already familiar with **mi chiamo** (my name is), **come si chiama?** (what is your [polite]/his/her/its name?). Here **mi** and **si** function as objects of the verb (see the definition of object in *Grammar summary*, p. 239), as if **mi chiamo** meant I call me (myself) and **si chiama** he/she calls him/her(self). **Mi** can also mean 'me' in phrases such as **mi dica** (tell me), **mi fa un favore se …** (you'll do me a favour if …), **mi scusi** (excuse me).

One of the uses of **si** is to translate one, as an impersonal subject: **si prende il tram numero 5** one takes tram number five; **si deve attraversare la Galleria** one must cross the arcade.

Another useful set of monosyllabic pronouns is **lo, la, li, le**: they agree in gender and number

article	article + noun	bello + noun	quello + noun
il	il ristorante	bel ristorante	quel ristorante
lo	lo specchio	bello specchio	quello specchio
la	la camera	bella camera	quella camera
l'	l'automobile	bell'automobile	quell'automobile
i	i ristoranti	bei ristoranti	quei ristoranti
gli	gli specchi	begli specchi	quegli specchi
le	le camere	belle camere	quelle camere

with what they refer to. We have already met them in phrases such as **non lo so** (I don't know it), **lo segno?** (do I write it down?) [unspecified 'it': masculine singular]. **Come la vuole [la camera]**, **singola, doppia?** How do you want it, single, double? **queste albicocche mi piacciono, le prendo** I like these apricots, I'll take them.

All these monosyllabic pronouns (there are others we haven't yet come across) precede verbs and do not have a stress of their own.

11 Choose from the box below the appropriate word to insert in each incomplete sentence below. You should use the plural form of the word you choose. In the process you should be able to guess the meaning of one new word!

a. In piazza Stazione ci sono gli _____ del turismo e di Telecom Italia.

b. Il Gorgonzola e il Parmigiano sono due

_____ italiani.

c. All'angolo di via Redi ci sono due _____ dove lei può cambiare valuta.

d. Queste _____ pesano diciannove chili. Non c'è eccedenza.

e. Che cosa prendete? — Due _____, per piacere.

formaggio   ufficio   valigia   analcoolico   banca

ANSWERS P. 74

12 Replace the verb between square brackets in the following sentences with the impersonal **si** form.
Model: **In questa banca [cambiare] valuta.** ▷ **In questa banca si cambia valuta.**

a. [Devo] _____ fare questo tipo di esercizio, di tanto in tanto!

b. Dove [posso] _____ cambiare delle sterline?

c. Per andare all'aeroporto non [prendo]

_____ l'autobus: [vado]

_____ più comodo in tassì.

d. Come [faccio] _____ a telefonare se non

[ho] _____ una scheda?

ANSWERS P. 74

13 Practise giving negative answers. You will need to use **lo, la, li, le,** as appropriate, in your answers. Follow the presenter's instructions on your recording.

KEY WORDS AND PHRASES

scusi	excuse me
Mi sa dire come …?	Can you tell me how to …?
Come faccio per andare …?	How do I get to …?
Come devo fare?	What must I do?
Che mezzo prendo?	What transport do I take?
destra	right
sinistra	left
lì, là	there
dritto	straight on
di fronte	opposite
all'angolo, sull'angolo	on the corner
avanti	further on
più vicina	nearest
attraversare	to cross
quando esce	when you go out
o … oppure …	either … or …
si prende …	one takes …
si va …	one goes …
si scende	one gets off
in direzione …	bound for …
primo -a	first
secondo -a	second
terzo -a	third
quarto -a	fourth
il capolinea	the terminus, end of the line
mi dispiace	I'm sorry
negozio	shop
semaforo	traffic lights
marciapiede	pavement, sidewalk
a piedi	on foot

Urban transport

Public transport in Italian towns is as efficient and convenient as that in the UK, but it is certainly cheaper. It mostly operates on the flat rate principle: you can go from one end of Rome or Milan to the other for less than half of what it costs to travel across central London. Taxis are often less easy to find. Stick to official taxi cabs, with taximeters, and steer rigorously clear of taxi touts at railway stations and air terminals.

Almost all Italian urban transport companies have done away with conductors. They have been replaced by electronic machines which merely stamp your ticket with the date and time of issue and the identification of your transport. That is called **convalida** (validation) or **obliterazione** (cancellation), two words you may see on notices displayed in the vehicle or printed on the ticket itself. You must therefore buy the ticket before you board your bus or tram. Tickets can be bought in some transport outlets (e.g. metro stations) and in tobacconists' shops, newspaper kiosks, and espresso bars during shop opening hours, after which it may be practically impossible to obtain them. On some routes you may find coin-operated ticket vending machines, for which you are supposed to have the appropriate coins or banknotes ready. In some towns, surface transport tickets are valid for one hour and 10 minutes from cancellation: within that time you may use as many trams and buses as you like. In Milan and Rome surface tickets are interchangeable with metro (underground railway) tickets, but on the underground they are valid only for one journey, however short.

You will see the following signs on most public transport vehicles:
SALITA way in, from the verb **salire** to go up, to climb on; **DISCESA** way out, from the verb **discendere** to step down. That is because train and tram platforms in Italy are not level with the floor of the vehicle, so getting into or out of it means going up, or down, two or three steps.

Some towns have private narrow-gauge railway systems linking them with the surrounding region, like the **Ferrovia Circumvesuviana** operating between Naples and the towns at the foot of Vesuvius; and the **Ferrovia Nord**, between Milan and the 'lake district' towns.

Street names

Italian street names are more obviously 'meaningful' than those popular in the English-speaking world. They are usually chosen from the names of other towns or regions; names of famous men and women from local, national or world history; and include a few historical dates (like **via Venti Settembre**, commemorating the fall of Rome to the Italian army on 20 September 1870). **Via** corresponds to street in English. **Strada** is also a general word for 'street' but it is not used with names. **Viale** (avenue) is wider than a **via** and usually tree-lined. **Vico** or **vicolo** is a narrow alleyway. **Corso** is the main street, usually of particular architectural, historical or commercial importance. **Piazza**, **piazzale** and **largo** all refer to squares of different sizes. In Venice small squares are called **campo** or **campiello**, and **rio terà** is a filled-in canal. The Italian words for these thoroughfares and squares are normally written with a small initial letter, their names with a capital initial, e.g. via Roma, piazza Cavour.

14 You will be guided by the presenter in this exercise where you ask for directions.

ANSWERS

EXERCISE 2

(a) ii **(b)** i **(c)** ii **(d)** i

EXERCISE 3

(a) ii **(b)** v **(c)** i **(d)** iv **(e)** iii

EXERCISE 4

(a) ii **(b)** ii **(c)** i **(d)** ii

EXERCISE 5

(a) ii **(b)** iii **(c)** i **(d)** iii

EXERCISE 6

1 (b), 2 (f), 3 (d), 4 (c), 5 (e), 6 (a)

EXERCISE 9

(a) all'angolo **(b)** di fronte **(c)** esce, la prima a destra
(d) deve attraversare **(e)** quasi davanti

EXERCISE 10

The true answers are **a, e, g** and **h**.

EXERCISE 11

(a) uffici **(b)** formaggi (cheeses) **(c)** banche
(d) valigie **(e)** analcoolici

EXERCISE 12

(a) si deve **(b)** si può **(c)** si prende, si va **(d)** si fa, si ha

6

TIMES AND TIMETABLES

WHAT YOU WILL LEARN

▶ how to ask when?
▶ how to find out about opening and closing times
▶ how to understand announcements concerning time and timetables
▶ days of the week and other expressions of time

BEFORE YOU BEGIN

Learning is helped by patterning. Try to fit the new things you learn into the old patterns you have already learned (for instance, new nouns and adjectives into the known four- or two-ending patterns). Observing the correspondences between English and Italian words (such as the similarity between words ending in -*tion* and in -*zione*), and noting the way words relate to one another (e.g. **libro** book; **libraio**, **libraia** bookseller; **libreria** bookshop) will help you to increase your vocabulary.

POINTS TO REMEMBER FROM UNIT 5
The verbs
dovere   must, ought to, to have to: **devo, devi, deve, dobbiamo, dovete, devono**
     uscire   to go out: **esco, esci, esce, usciamo, uscite, escono**
quello   that: **quel prezzo, quello scalo, quella scala; quei prezzi, quegli scali, quelle scale**
lo, la, li, le as objects (it, him, her, them): **il prezzo? non lo so; la fermata? sì, la vedo; quei libri? li prendo.**

Pronunciation notes

The two letters -*gl*- stand for one sound only, which has no equivalent in English. The tongue is placed as if one were to pronounce an initial *l*- (as in English lid) but it is flattened against the palate. This is a very common sound in Italian, occurring as it does in the plural article **gli** and the plural of **quello** (that) and **bello** (beautiful): **quegli autobus, dei begli alberghi.**

A traveller books a couchette at Rome Termini Railway Station

LISTEN FOR...

▶	**vorrei prenotare un posto**	I'd like to book a seat
▶	**mi dia**	give me
▶	**la cuccetta da quattro**	a berth in a 4-berth compartment
▶	**fumatori/non fumatori**	smokers/non-smokers

Viaggiatore	Vorrei prenotare un posto sul treno che parte da Sibari alle ventidue zero due e arriva a Roma alle sei e quindici. Per sabato. Scusi, la cuccetta cosa costa?
Impiegata	Eh, diciotto e cinque in uno scompartimento da sei, venticinque nello scompartimento da quattro.
Viaggiatore	Eh, mi dia ... allora la cuccetta da quattro.
Impiegata	Cuccetta da quattro. Sabato ventuno.
Viaggiatore	Sì.
Impiegata	Allora, seconda non fumatori, non fumatori va bene, sì?
Viaggiatore	No. Fumatori.
Impiegata	Fumatori Venticinquemila. [*counting out the change of a 50,000 lire note*] trenta, quaranta e cinquanta. Buongiorno e grazie.
Viaggiatore	Grazie.
Impiegata	Prego.

▶ **vorrei prenotare un posto** I'd like to book a seat. This expression may also be used when booking seats for theatre and concert performances (see Unit 14). **Vorrei** is the conditional ('would' form) of **volere**.

alle ventidue zero due at 22.02, i.e. two past ten p.m. In Italy the 24-hour clock is used in all timetables and official communications. Except when referring to one o'clock (**è l'una**) the article is always feminine plural because **ore** (hours) is understood. To tell the time you say: **sono le tre** it's (lit. they are) three o'clock, **sono le cinque e mezza** (it's half past five, etc.).

sabato Saturday

La cuccetta cosa costa? (**cosa = che cosa**) What does the sleeping berth cost? an alternative to **quanto costa?**

uno scompartimento da sei, da quattro a six-berth, four-berth compartment. **Da** is often used with quantities: **un'auto da sei posti** a six-seater car, **un fiasco da due litri** a two-litre flask.

▶ **mi dia** give me. This expression uses a different form of the verb (the subjunctive) instead of **mi dà** (which could also be used).

▶ **la cuccetta da quattro** a berth in a four-berth compartment (lit. the berth by four).

seconda (**classe**) second class: you will be offered second class tickets unless you specifically ask for **prima classe** (first class).

▶ **non fumatori** non-smokers; **fumare** (to smoke), **fumo** (smoke, fume)

trenta, **quaranta** ... the employee at the ticket office is counting the change. Except when acknowledging the money received, she always uses 'short' figures (one to one thousand).

Trains can be delayed, as these station announcements indicate

LISTEN FOR...

▶ **viaggia con 60 minuti circa di ritardo**   is approximately 60 minutes late
▶ **annuncio ritardo in arrivo**   late arrival announcement

Altoparlante	Treno diretto proveniente da Roma Termini, Milano Centrale, per Briga, Losanna, Ginevra, Berna, atteso alle ore 7.50, viaggia con 60 minuti circa di ritardo.
Altoparlante	Annuncio ritardo in arrivo. Treno Intercity settecento cinquanta quattro proveniente da Reggio Calabria Centrale delle ore tredici e cinquanta viaggia con circa un'ora e quaranta minuti di ritardo. Treno Intercity sette cinque quattro proveniente da Reggio Calabria delle ore tredici e cinquanta viaggia con circa un'ora e quaranta minuti di ritardo, causa protesta sindacale del servizio produzione di Reggio Calabria.

diretto   limited stop train (lit. direct)
proveniente da   coming from (from **provenire**, same pattern as **venire**)
Briga, etc., Briga, Lausanne, Geneva, Berne, in Switzerland
atteso   expected (from **attendere** to expect, same pattern as **prendere**)
▶ **viaggia con 60 minuti circa di ritardo**   is approximately 60 minutes late (lit. travels with 60 minutes approximately of delay). **Circa** (approximately) may be placed before or after the words to which it refers: **con circa 60 minuti di ritardo**; **circa tre ore** or **tre ore circa** (about three hours).
▶ **annuncio ritardo in arrivo**   (lit. announcement delay on arrival) delayed arrival announcement
causa protesta sindacale   because of industrial action (lit. cause protest trade union). In this and in many other announcements the prepositions are omitted (**annuncio di un ritardo in arrivo, a causa della protesta sindacale**).
servizio produzione   production department

 An airport announcement: the flight to London will be delayed

LISTEN FOR...

▶ **sarà ritardata**   will be delayed

Altoparlante	La partenza del volo BA 529 per Londra sarà ritardata di circa 30 minuti a causa condizioni meteorologiche sull'aeroporto di Pisa.

▶ **sarà ritardata**   will be delayed; **sarà** will be, (future of **essere**: see p. 150); **ritardata** (from **ritardare**   to delay, to be late):
lo sciopero ritarda tutti i treni   the strike is delaying all trains; **l'aereo ritarda, l'aereo è in ritardo** (the aircraft is late).
condizioni meteorologiche   weather (lit. meteorological) conditions. Italian officialese is rather fond of technical terms: most people would speak of **il tempo**, which in Italian means BOTH weather AND time. More about weather in Unit 12.

PRACTICE

1 This is a pronunciation exercise for words containing the sound *-gl-*. Listen to the following phrases on your recording and repeat them until you've got them right. There are new words: **biglietto** meaning ticket and **negozi** shops.

a. Voglio degli aperitivi.
b. Quegli autobus fermano in piazza degli Ungari.
c. Non si può fumare negli aerei internazionali.
d. I biglietti non si prendono negli autobus.
e. Ci sono dei bei negozi negli alberghi.

2 Practise converting times given in the 24-hour clock to times given in the 12-hour clock, a.m. (**di mattina**) or p.m. (**di pomeriggio**). You may use the expressions **un quarto** (a quarter), **e mezza** (and a half), **meno venti** (twenty to), **meno dieci** (ten to), **meno cinque** (five to), only in the 12-hour clock.

3 Number the following sentences so that they form a meaningful conversation between a prospective traveller and the booking office clerk.

a. Va bene, mi prenoti un posto su quel treno.
b. Allora, dopo le diciotto e trenta c'è un treno intercity che parte alle diciannove zero cinque.
c. Senta, vorrei sapere se ci sono dei treni che vanno a Firenze dopo le sei e mezza.
d. Di sera.
e. E dopo?
f. Di mattina o di sera?
g. No, non fumatori. Seconda classe.
h. Fumatori?
i. Alle venti e quindici, ma deve prenotare il posto.

ANSWERS P. 90

CONImagesVERSATIONS

When are meals served?

LISTEN FOR...

▶ gli orari dei pasti	meal times
▶ tra le otto e le nove e trenta	between 8 and 9.30
▶ un po' presto	a little early
▶ un pochino anticipato	a tiny bit in advance

Giovanni	Può dirmi, per favore, gli orari dei pasti?
Albergatrice	Certo. La colazione la serviamo tra le otto e le nove e trenta. Il pranzo alle tredici, e la cena un po' presto, alle diciannove, un orario un pochino anticipato per le abitudini italiane.
Giovanni	Ah, a me va bene. Grazie.
Albergatrice	D'accordo.

albergatrice (f), **albergatore** (m)   hotelier

▶ **Può dirmi ... ?**   Can you (polite) tell me ...? **Può dirmi l'ora, per favore?** (Can you tell me the time (lit. the hour), please?)

▶ **gli orari dei pasti**   meal times; **orario** (related to **ora**, hour, time, timetable); **pasto** meal. Here they are called **colazione** (breakfast), **pranzo** (lunch), **cena** (dinner): but see *Did you know?*, p. 89 for a fuller explanation.

▶ **tra le otto e le nove e trenta**   between 8 and 9.30

▶ **un po'** short for **un poco** (a little), **un pochino** (**poco** + diminutive suffix *-ino*) a tiny bit. One of the most common expressions in the language: **un po' presto** (a little early), **un po' tardi** (a little late), **un po' stanco** (a little tired), etc. If followed by a noun it takes **di**: **un po' di zucchero** (a little sugar), **un po' di tempo** a (little time), **un po' di vino** (a little wine).

anticipato   advanced in time, early

per le abitudini italiane   for Italian habits

How far away is the famous Chartreuse of Pavia?

LISTEN FOR...

▶ **Quant'è lontano/-a ...?**	How far is it to ...?
▶ **sono venti minuti di autobus**	it's twenty minutes by bus
▶ **all'ora e alla mezz'ora**	on the hour and on the half hour
▶ **è chiusa**	it's closed
▶ **è aperta**	it's open

Giovanni	Signorina, quant'è lontana la Certosa di Pavia?
Signorina	La Certosa di Pavia non è molto lontana. Sono venti minuti di autobus da qui. E gli autobus sono frequentissimi, con la frequenza di ogni mezz'ora, all'ora e alla mezz'ora, in partenza da Piazza Castello.
Giovanni	Piazza Castello è vicina a qui?
Signorina	Dieci minuti a piedi. Allora, piazza Castello, ogni mezz'ora, ci sono i pullman che vanno a Pavia e fermano vicino alla Certosa. La Certosa è chiusa il lunedì, mentre è aperta in giorno normale dalle 10 alle 12.30, dalle 14 alle 17.

▶ **Quant'è lontana ...?** (short for **Quanto è lontana**) How far is ...? Note that **lontano -a** preceded by a form of **essere** agrees with what is being talked about, in this case **la Certosa**: **Quant'è lontano il supermercato?** How far is the supermarket?, **Quanto sono lontani i negozi?** How far are the shops?

▶ **sono venti minuti di autobus** (lit. they are twenty minutes of bus) it's twenty minutes by bus. Note that here **sono**, the third person plural form of **essere**, is used because it refers to **minuti**; but **è un minuto a piedi** (it's one minute on foot). Remember: **è l'una** (it's one o'clock), but **sono le due**.

frequentissimi very frequent; **frequenza** frequency

▶ **ogni mezz'ora** every half hour; **ogni ora** (every hour), **ogni due ore** (every two hours)

▶ **all'ora e alla mezz'ora** on the hour and on the half hour. Other similar expressions: **ai venti** (twenty minutes past the hour), **ai quaranta** (forty minutes past the hour), etc.; **ogni ora** (every hour); **ogni tre quarti d'ora** (every three quarters of an hour).

il lunedì on Mondays (lit. the Monday); also **ogni lunedì** (every Monday). For a full list of the days of the week and other expressions of time see the panel opposite.

▶ **è chiusa** it's closed from **chiudere** (to close)

▶ **è aperta** it's open from **aprire** (to open)

in giorno normale on a normal day (i.e. a working day, not a holiday)

dalle 10 alle 12.30 from 10 to 12.30

Days of the week and times of day

The names of days are spelled with a small initial letter: **lunedì** (Monday), **martedì** (Tuesday), **mercoledì** (Wednesday), **giovedì** (Thursday), **venerdì** (Friday), **sabato** (Saturday), **domenica** (Sunday). **Dì** is an old alternative to **giorno** (day). The days ending in -*dì* do not have a separate plural form. All are masculine except **domenica**.

Note the following useful expressions, taking **lunedì** as an example: **lunedì** (this Monday); **il lunedì** or **di lunedì** (on Monday) (in general); **ogni lunedì**, **tutti i lunedì** (every Monday); **lunedì prossimo** (next Monday) (counting from today); **il lunedì dopo**, or **il lunedì seguente** (next Monday), the following Monday (counting from any other date).

Workdays are called **giorni feriali**, and Sundays and other holidays **giorni festivi**.

The day is divided into: **mattina** (morning);
pomeriggio (afternoon); **sera** (evening) (until bed-time); **notte** (night, bed-time). To indicate one of these times, you have the choice between the word preceded by the article (**il mattino/la mattina**, **il pomeriggio**, **la sera**) or by di (**di mattino**, **di mattina**, **di pomeriggio**, **di sera**): **il/di pomeriggio riposo per un'ora** I rest for an hour in the afternoon, **la/di notte dormo** at night I sleep. Midday is **mezzogiorno**, midnight **mezzanotte**. You refer to today using **questo, -a: questa mattina** (this morning) and **questa sera** (this evening, tonight) are often shortened to **stamattina** and **stasera**; **questo pomeriggio**, etc.

The days immediately after **oggi** (today) are **domani** (tomorrow) and **dopodomani** (the day after tomorrow). They may combine with any time of day, as in **domani mattina** (tomorrow morning), **domani pomeriggio** (tomorrow afternoon), **dopodomani sera** (the day after tomorrow in the evening) etc.

PRACTICE

4

ANSWERS P. 90

Listen to the conversation between Giovanni and a clerk at the Rome Transport Information Office. You do not need to understand every word to answer the following questions about **un giro turistico** (tour of the town) organized by **l'Azienda** (the Company), with couriers giving **le spiegazioni in inglese** (English commentary).
a. How many monuments can be seen during the tour?   (i) 7   (ii) 47   (iii) 40
b. How long does the tour last?   (i) 2 hours   (ii) 3 hours   (iii) 3½ hours
c. How much does the ticket cost?   (i) 15,000 lire   (ii) 5,000 lire   (iii) 25,000 lire
d. Where does the bus leave from?   (i) piazza Quida   (ii) piazza dei Cinquecento

5

You have been staying in your boarding house for a week and by now know all about meal times. Answer the questions of another guest who has just arrived.

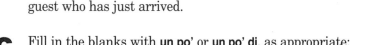

6   Fill in the blanks with **un po'** or **un po' di**, as appropriate:

a.   In questo albergo si serve la cena _____ presto.

b.   Mi porta _____ latte, per piacere?

c.   Centomila lire per una guida? Costa _____ molto!

d.   Vorrei _____ colazione: solo un cappuccino e un cornetto.

ANSWERS P. 90   e.   La piazza del Duomo è _____ lontana. Deve prendere un autobus.

CONVERSATIONS 3

 Bank and shop opening times

LISTEN FOR...

▶ **Quali sono ... ?** Which/What are ...?
▶ **Quando ... ?** When ...?
▶ **mattina** morning
▶ **pomeriggio** afternoon
▶ **lunedì** Monday
▶ **sabato** Saturday
▶ **domenica** Sunday

Giovanni	Quali sono gli orari di apertura delle banche?
Signorina 1	Le banche qui a Milano sono aperte dalle 8,30 alle ... euh ... 13.
Giovanni	Dalle 8,30 alle 13. E i negozi quando sono aperti?
Signorina 1	Dalle 9 alle 12,30, 15,30 – 19,30 circa, con piccole variazioni.
Giovanni	C'è un giorno di riposo alla settimana?
Signorina 1	Il lunedì mattina i negozi sono chiusi per il riposo, poi la domenica è chiuso tutto il giorno.
Signorina 2	Il lunedì hanno orari diversi, perché, appunto, la mattina i negozi di generi alimentari sono aperti, mentre sono chiusi gli altri negozi. E il contrario: il pomeriggio i negozi di generi alimentari sono chiusi, sono aperti invece i supermercati e poi tutti gli altri negozi. Cioè, lunedì hanno le loro chiusure, mattina o pomeriggio; mentre il sabato hanno una regolare apertura: 9 – 12.30, 15 – 19.30. Domenica chiusi, chiaramente.

▶ **pomeriggio** afternoon
invece instead, on the other hand
supermercati supermarkets
poi then
cioè that is
▶ **sabato** Saturday
chiaramente clearly, of course

▶ **Quali sono ...?** Which/What are ...?
orari di apertura opening times. The past participle of **aprire** (the form that combines with 'to have', as in 'I have opened') is **aperto** (opened, open); from which aperture (opening or, if photography is your hobby, aperture). Similarly, the past participle of **chiudere** (to close) is **chiuso**, from which **chiusura** (closure, closing time): **le loro chiusure** their closing times.

▶ **Quando ...?** When ...? Further explanations in the *Grammar*, p. 87.

piccole variazioni small variations

giorno di riposo (early) closing day (lit. day of rest); **riposare** to rest

settimana week, from **sette**, the number of days in a week

▶ **lunedì** Monday
▶ **mattina** (also **mattino**) morning
▶ **domenica** Sunday

appunto precisely, in fact, as a matter of fact, often used as a stopgap word

generi alimentari officialese for food (lit. alimentary kinds)

mentre while

gli altri negozi the other shops

contrario opposite, contrary

Plans for a holiday abroad

LISTEN FOR...

▶ **sabato prossimo**   next Saturday
▶ **ho intenzione di ...**   I intend to ...
▶ **il mattino dopo**   the morning after
▶ **andiamo in automobile**   we are going by car
▶ **Chi viene con voi?**   Who is going with you?

Giovanni Dimmi un poco che cosa fai ... euh ... sabato prossimo?
Aldo   Sabato ho intenzione di partire per ... euh ... fare una
settimana di vacanza. La sera partiamo da Milano, poi ci fermiamo a Venezia e ... euh ...
dormiamo la notte lì. Ripartendo il mattino dopo, arriviamo a Vienna, e ... euh ... dopo
qualche giorno di permanenza a Vienna, tappa a Budapest ... euh ... per tre giorni, e poi
direttamente da Budapest ancora a Venezia.
Giovanni Come andate, andate in treno o ...
Aldo   Andiamo in automobile.
Giovanni E chi viene con voi?
Aldo   Viene con ... euh ... con me viene Floriana e un'altra coppia di amici, Paolo e Marcella.

dimmi un poco tell me (a little); **dire** (to tell)

▶ **sabato prossimo** next Saturday. **Prossimo** means next from today. Next meaning 'following' is **dopo** (invariable). See **il mattino dopo** below.

▶ **ho intenzione di partire** I intend (lit. I have intention) to leave; a useful phrase which you can combine with other verbs, e.g. **ho intenzione di fare colazione** (I intend to have breakfast), **ho intenzione di prendere il treno** (I intend to take the train), **Che intenzioni hai?** What are you going to do? (lit. what intentions do you have?)

per fare una settimana di vacanza to take (lit. make) a week's holiday

ci fermiamo we stop. For **ci**, see *Grammar*, p. 86.

dormiamo we sleep, from **dormire**: see *Grammar*, p. 86; in this context, 'we'll spend the night there'.

ripartendo leaving again. Often *ri-* in Italian has the same function as *re-* in English: **ridire** (to retell); **rifare** (to redo, to remake); **ripagare** (to repay), etc.

▶ **il mattino dopo** the morning after

qualche giorno di permanenza a few days' stay

tappa stop, stage in a journey

direttamente directly

ancora once again

▶ **andiamo in automobile** we are going by car; **andiamo in aereo** we go by air (lit. in aircraft).

▶ **Chi viene con voi?** Who is going with you? **Chi** who, whoever, is used in questions: **Chi è?** (Who is he/she/it?), **Chi parla?** (Who's speaking?, on the phone), **Chi lo dice?** (Who says so?)

un'altra coppia another couple

amici friends

7

Listen to the conversation on the recording about museum opening times in Milan. Tick those statements below you think are true. You'll hear the word **alcuni** some, and **intervallo** meaning interval, break.

a. All museums are closed at lunch-time.

b. Some museums close between 12.30 and 2.30.

c. The Brera Museum opens (i) between 8 a.m. and 2 p.m.
   (ii) between 9 a.m. and 2 p.m.

d. The Pinacoteca Ambrosiana can be visited during lunch-time when other museums are closed.

ANSWERS P. 90

8 This is a page from the Lake Maggiore passenger boat service timetable. Study it carefully when answering the following questions:

NAVIGAZIONE LAGO MAGGIORE (Arona–Locarno)　　　　(Dal 5-IV al 27-IX)　　170

170 ARONA ...p.	...	...	...	...	705	...	735	805	830	845	935	1000	1000	1025	...	...	...	1100	...	...	1215	1235	1320	...	...
Angera	...	...	...	...	710	...	740	810	835	850	940	1005	1005	1030	...	...	...	1105	...	...	1220	1240	1335	...	...
Meina	...	...	...	...	X	...	X	X	X	900	...	...	③	...	...	...	...	♦15	...	...	...	...	...	...	...
Ispra	...	...	...	...	...	...	...	...	...	...	...	②	...	...	...	...	...	...	...	...	...	...	...	...	...
Lesa	...	...	...	...	...	...	...	...	...	920	...	...	...	...	...	...	...	★25	...	...	...	...	...	...	...
Belgirate	...	...	...	...	...	...	...	...	...	925	...	...	...	...	...	...	...	1130	...	...	...	...	Scolastica	...	...
STRESA ......a.	X	...	...	...	...	...	...	...	...	950	...	1045	1045	...	...	...	▲	1155	▲	...	1415	...	...	...	▲
STRESA ......p.	640	...	715	830	920	△55	905	930	1020	955	1040	1050	1050	1100	1120	...	1140	1205	1240	1320	...	...	...	1400	1420
Isola Bella	645	...	725	840	...	1000	910	935	1025	1000	1045	...	...	1105	1125	...	...	1210	1245	1325	...	...	...	1405	1425
Isola Superiore ...	650	...	730	...	...	1005	915	940	1030	1005	1050	...	...	1110	1130	...	1145	1215	1250	1330	...	...	...	1410	1430
BAVENO	655	...	740	...	...	1015	925	950	1040	1015	1100	1055	...	...	1140	...	1150	1225	...	1340	...	...	...	1420	...
Feriolo	...	...	...	...	...	...	...	...	...	...	...	...	...	...	...	...	...	...	...	...	...	Crociera Arona a. 1515	...	...	...
Isola Madre	X	...	750	...	...	...	935	1000	1050	1025	1109	②	...	...	1150	...	1200	1235	...	1350	...	...	...	1430	1440
Suna	...	...	...	dal 28-VI	...	...	...	...	...	...	...	...	...	...	...	...	...	...	...	...	...	...	...	...	...
PALLANZA	710	...	755	...	...	...	940	...	...	1030	...	1101	...	...	1155	...	...	1240	...	1355	...	...	...	1435	...
Villa Taranto	...	...	△805	...	...	...	959	...	...	1040	...	...	...	...	1205	...	...	1250	...	1405	...	...	...	1445	...
INTRA ......a.	725	...	815	...	...	...	959	...	...	1050	...	1105	1110	...	1215	...	...	1259	...	1414	...	...	...	1455	...
INTRA ......p.	740	...	820	...	...	...	1000	...	...	1100	...	1106	1115	...	1220	...	...	1300	...	1420	...	1415	...	1500	...
LAVENO ......a.	800	...	840	...	929	...	1015	...	...	1120	...	...	③	...	1240	...	...	1320	...	1440	...	...	...	1520	...
LAVENO ......p.	...	...	...	...	930	...	...	...	...	...	...	...	...	...	...	...	...	...	...	...	...	...	...	...	...
Ghiffa	...	...	...	...	938	...	...	...	...	...	...	...	...	...	...	...	...	...	...	...	...	◇21	...	...	...
Porto Valtr.	...	...	...	...	945	...	...	...	...	...	...	035	...	...	...	...	...	...	...	...	...	◇28	...	...	...
Oggebbio	...	...	...	...	952	...	...	...	...	...	...	...	...	...	...	...	...	...	...	...	...	◇35	...	...	...
Cannero	...	749	...	...	958	959	1051	...	...	...	...	...	...	...	1240	...	...	...	...	...	...	1442	...	...	...
LUINO ......a.	...	756	...	...	...	1005	...	...	...	...	1125	1200	②	...	1246	...	...	...	...	...	...	1449	...	...	...
LUINO ......p.	...	757	...	...	1006	...	...	...	...	...	1130	1210	1245	...	1247	...	1400	...	1415	...	...	1450	...	...	...
Maccagno	...	802	...	...	1012	...	...	...	...	...	...	...	1252	...	②	...	②	...	...	...	...	1456	...	...	...
CANNOBIO ...a.	...	815	...	...	1020	1100	...	...	...	...	1229	1310	...	...	1300	...	1419	...	...	...	...	1503	...	...	...
CANNOBIO ...p.	...	...	...	...	...	...	...	...	...	...	1230	...	1240	...	...	...	1420	...	...	...	...	...	...	...	...
BRISSAGO ...a.	...	...	...	...	...	...	...	...	...	...	1145	1250	...	1300	...	...	1440	...	...	...	...	...	...	...	...
BRISSAGO ...p.	...	...	...	...	905	1010	...	1130	...	...	1150	1300	...	1310	...	1340	1445	...	...	...	...	1520	...	...	...
Isole Brissago	...	...	...	...	920	1012	...	1135	...	...	...	①	...	1325	...	1355	...	...	...	...	...	1535	...	...	...
Porto Ronco	...	...	...	...	915	①	...	1140	...	...	...	...	...	1320	...	1350	1455	...	...	...	...	1530	...	...	...
Ranzo	...	...	...	...	935	...	...	...	...	...	②	...	...	⑤	...	⑥	...	...	1500	...	...	1550	...	...	...
Gerra	...	...	...	...	940	...	...	...	...	...	...	...	...	...	...	...	...	...	1505	...	...	1555	...	...	...
Ascona	...	...	...	...	...	1017	...	1200	...	...	1157	...	...	1340	...	1405	1510	...	②	...	...	1605	...	...	...
S. Nazzaro	...	...	...	...	950	1022	...	1215	...	...	...	...	...	...	...	1420	②	...	1515	...	...	...	...	...	...
Vira	X	...	X	...	...	1026	...	...	...	...	...	...	...	...	⑤	...	1430	...	1525	...	...	...	...	...	...
Magadino	630	...	730	830	930	1028	1130	...	1230	...	...	...	...	1330	⑤	1430	1435	...	1530	...	...	...	...	...	...
LOCARNO ...a.	650	...	750	850	950	1005	1035	1150	1230	1250	...	1205	1330	1350	1400	1450	1450	1530	...	1550	...	...	...	1625	...

△ Carciano.　▲ Festiva, fino al 27-VI, giornaliera dal 28-VI.　③ Non si effettua il mercoledì.　⑤ Si effettua la domenica.　★ Ferma nei festivi.　◇ Ferma dal 28-VI.　② Si effettua il mercoledì.　① Sospeso mercoledì e domenica.　⑥ Sospesa la domenica.　△ Ferma nei giorni di scuola.　⑤ Ferma il martedì.

a. Supposing you are in Angera for the weekend and wish to meet a friend in Baveno at 11 a.m., what is the latest time you can leave?

b. At what time does the Sunday service to Locarno leave Brissago?

c. Supposing you wish to travel from Angera to Meina on a Monday; is there any service you can use between 8.50 and lunch-time?

d. You are in Stresa and wish to visit the famous botanical gardens at Villa Taranto on a Sunday. Which is the earliest boat you can take?

e. Does the 2 p.m. boat from Stresa to Laveno stop at Suna?

f. How long does the 10 a.m. boat from Arona to Locarno stop at Luino on Fridays?

ANSWERS P. 90 **g.** How long is the shortest journey from Cannero to Cannobio?

9 The printer scrambled the programme of your week's holiday in northern Italy. Listen to the explanation of the programme on your recording, and match the various visits and activities with the day reserved for them. Write the letter for each item in the scrambled programme into the correct day's box. Remember that **libero** means 'free'.

a. Escursione ai laghi di Como e Maggiore.

b. Libero.

c. Partenza da Londra Gatwick per Milano Malpensa, ore 14.10. Arrivo alle 15.45 e sistemazione in albergo. Sera libera.

d. Mattino: escursione a Bergamo. Ore 19.30: partenza da Milano Malpensa per Gatwick.

e. Visita guidata dei musei della città. Sera: opera al Teatro alla Scala.

f. Mattino: visita della città in pullman. Pomeriggio libero. Sera: cena in un ristorante caratteristico.

ANSWERS P. 90 **g.** Escursione alla Certosa di Pavia. Visita della città di Pavia.

lunedì	
martedì	
mercoledì	
giovedì	
venerdì	
sabato	
domenica	

Reflexive form

In English 'to stop' may mean either (1) that someone/something stops, or (2) that he/she/it stops something else: as in (1) the car stops, or (2) the driver stops the car. In case (1) when the subject is a person, Italian verbs normally take a 'reflexive' object, i.e. a pronoun, like 'myself', 'yourself', etc. referring back to the subject. Remember that 'my name is' translates into Italian as **mi chiamo**, lit. 'I call myself'. Similarly, I stop is **mi fermo**, lit. 'I stop myself' (but I stop the car is **fermo l'automobile**). The complete range of forms is as follows:

	chiamarsi to be called	fermarsi to stop
I	mi chiamo	mi fermo
you	ti chiami	ti fermi
he/she/it or you (polite)	si chiama	si ferma
we	ci chiamiamo	ci fermiamo
you (pl)	vi chiamate	vi fermate
they	si chiamano	si fermano

Mi (me), **ti** (you), **si** (him/her/itself, themselves), **ci** (us) and **vi** (you pl) come before the verb (one exception is the infinitive where they replace the *-e* of the ending: **devo fermarmi** I must stop). Reflexive forms are much more frequent in Italian than in English.

Other common expressions are:
mi trovo   I am (lit. I find myself)
Si trova bene in quell'albergo?   Are you comfortable in that hotel?
Sì, mi trovo benissimo.   Yes, very.
mi trattengo   I stay (lit. I detain myself)
Quanto si trattiene?   How long are you staying?
Mi trattengo cinque giorni   I'll stay five days

Verbs in *-ere* and *-ire*

The conjugation of these verbs is very similar to that of verbs ending in *-are* (see **chiamare** and **fermare** on the left): as one might expect the changes occur in endings containing an *-a-*.

	prendere to take	dormire to sleep
I	prendo	dormo
you	prendi	dormi
he/she/it or you (polite)	prende	dorme
we	prendiamo	dormiamo
you (pl)	prendete	dormite
they	prendono	dormono

Apprendere (to learn), **comprendere** (to understand), **sorprendere** (to surprise) follow the same pattern as **prendere**.

Partire (to leave, to depart) follows the same pattern as **dormire**. Some verbs in *-ire*, however, follow a slightly different pattern: see Unit 8, pp. 118–19.

Qu- for question

These two initial letters characterize a number of Italian question words, much in the same way as *wh-* characterizes the English group who? which? where? when? what?

Quale   what, which, which one (related to **qualità**, quality):
Quale camera vuole?   Which room do you want?
A quali ore?   At what times? **Qual'è?**   Which one is it? **Quali sono i musei più importanti?**   Which are the most important museums?

Quanto -a   how much; **quanti-e**   how many.
As an adjective: **Quanto tempo ha?**   How much time have you got?, **Quanta pizza vuole?**   How much pizza do you want?, **Quanti chili pesa?**   How many kilos does it weigh?, **Quante camere vuole?**   How many rooms do you want?

As an adverb: when **quanto** is followed by a verb it does not change its ending: **Quanto pesa? Quanto costa?**

When it refers to an adjective indicating a dimension (time, length, distance or size) you translate it simply as 'how': **Quanto è distante?** How far is it?, **Quanto sono pesanti?**   How heavy are they?, **Quant'è grande?**   How big is it?

Quando   when (not to be confused with **quanto**, in spite of the fact that some southern Italian speakers find it difficult to pronounce them differently).
Quando apre il museo? When does the museum open?
Quando parte il treno? When does the train leave?

10 Fill in the gaps in the following exchanges with the appropriate forms of **trovarsi** in the box below.

a. _____ bene in questo albergo? — Oh,

sì, _____ benissimo.

b. Dove _____ il supermercato più vicino?

Mi dispiace, non lo so.

c. Mi può dire dove _____ i grandi

magazzini? — In via Roma.

d. Dove _____ questo pomeriggio? — Al

Gran Caffè Adriano.

e. E dove _____ questo caffè? — In piazza

Cavour.

ANSWERS P. 90

si trovano	ti trovi	si trova	si trova
	ci troviamo	mi trovo	

11 Assuming that now is the morning of **giovedì 18**, how would you indicate the following times using **questo -a, domani, dopodomani, mattina, pomeriggio** and **sera**:

a. venerdì 19, ore 19.30 _____

b. sabato 20, ore 10 _____

c. venerdì 19, ore 9.30 _____

d. giovedì 18, ore 15 _____

e. sabato 20, ore 20 _____

f. venerdì 19, ore 14.30 _____

ANSWERS P. 90

12 Fill in the gaps in the following questions with the appropriate *qu*- word: **quale, quanto, quando**

a. _____ arriva il treno? — Alle 12.10.

b. A _____ binario arriva? — Al binario 6.

c. _____ valigie ha? — Ho due valigie.

d. _____ pesano queste valigie? —
Pesano venti chili.

e. Mi può dire _____ parte l'autobus? —
Parte alle nove.

f. _____ autobus devo prendere per
andare in centro? — Deve prendere il numero 63.

g. _____ è lontano il centro della città? —
Dieci minuti di autobus.

h. _____ mezzi posso prendere per andare
in centro? — Può prendere l'autobus e la
metropolitana.

ANSWERS P. 90

KEY WORDS AND PHRASES

vorrei prenotare un posto	I'd like to book a seat
mi dia	give me (polite)
una cuccetta da quattro	a berth in a four-berth compartment
fumatori	smokers
non fumatori	non-smokers
annuncio ritardo in arrivo	late arrival announcement
viaggia con 60 minuti circa di ritardo	is approximately 60 minutes late
sarà ritardata	will be delayed
all'ora e alla mezz'ora	on the hour and on the half hour
è chiusa	it's closed
è aperta	it's open
Quali sono …?	Which/What are …?
Quando …?	When …?
Quant'è lontano/-a?	How far is it?
sono venti minuti di autobus	it's 20 minutes by bus
gli orari dei pasti	meal times
tra le otto e le nove e trenta	between 8 and 9.30
un po' presto	a little early
un pochino anticipato	a tiny bit in advance
mattino, mattina	morning
pomeriggio	afternoon
il mattino/la mattina dopo	the morning after
lunedì	Monday
martedì	Tuesday
mercoledì	Wednesday
giovedì	Thursday
venerdì	Friday
sabato	Saturday
domenica	Sunday
sabato prossimo	next Saturday
il sabato dopo	the following Saturday
andiamo in automobile	we go by car
ho intenzione di	I intend to
ho intenzione di partire	I intend to leave
Chi viene con voi?	Who is going with you?

41 prenotazioni VL posti e cuccette

Meal, business and leisure times

The names of the meals are affected by social class, occasion and local habits. Two of them, **colazione** and **pranzo**, are 'floating' meal times. Picture the sequence of **prima colazione**, **colazione**, **pranzo**, **cena**, as being able to slide one notch up and down a three-point scale: morning, noon, evening. If **prima colazione** corresponds to morning then **cena** lapses; conversely those who call the evening meal **cena** will not use **prima colazione**, and will speak of breakfast simply as **colazione**. The same speaker may use different terms according to the situation: a formal meal with separate courses, for instance, is always called **pranzo** whatever the time, just like dinner in English. A business working lunch tends to be called **colazione**. Other words for occasional meals are: **spuntino** (snack), and **merenda** (picnic or afternoon snack given to children).

Meal times tend to be later in the South than in the North. The midday meal can start as late as 1.30 or 2 p.m. in the South. The evening meal ranges from 7 p.m. in the North to 9 p.m. in the South. As a consequence concerts, theatrical performances and cinema shows tend to begin fairly late: about 8.30 p.m. for theatres and concerts and 10.20 for last screenings. It is not uncommon for theatre or concert-goers to dine out after the performance: there will be many restaurants still open for what everybody will call a **cena**.

Italian shops and offices fall into two groups. A growing minority is moving to **orario continuo**, with no lunch-break; and no doubt this trend will continue. The majority, however, still go by **orario spezzato** (lit. broken timetable) which allows for a lunch-time closure, generally from 12.30 to 3 p.m. In southern Italy, shops may re-open as late as 4 or 4.30 in the afternoon and stay open until 8 p.m. One of the consequences of the **orario spezzato** is two additional **ore di punta**, rush hours, when those people who do not crowd nearby food outlets specializing in **panini** (rolls) and sandwiches, called **paninoteche**, a name modelled on **biblioteche** (libraries) or **discoteche** (discos), go home for lunch and return to work after the interval.

Workdays and holidays

The names of the week days derive in both English and Italian from the names of kindred gods in the Germanic and Latin mythologies. However, Saturn, a Latin god, was adopted in English as the patron of Saturday, and replaced in **sabato** by the Sabbath. The Sun in Sunday gave way to the Christian God (**domenica**, from DIES DOMINICA the Lord's day in Latin).

The main religious holidays in Italy are: **Capodanno**, New Year's Day (lit. head of year); **Epifania** or **Befana**, Twelfth Night or January 6; **Pasqua**, Easter; **Pasquetta**, **lunedì in Albis** or **lunedì dell'angelo**, Easter Monday; **Ognissanti** or **Tutti i santi**, All Saints' Day on November 1, **Immacolata Concezione**, the festival of the Immaculate Conception of the Virgin Mary on December 8; **Natale**, Christmas; **Santo Stefano**, St Stephen's day or Boxing Day.

Ferragosto is the August bank holiday on August 15 when the whole country comes to a standstill, including the bumper-to-bumper car queues on the motorways. Other non-religious holidays are: **Anniversario della Liberazione**, to celebrate the freedom from fascist rule at the end of World War II, on April 25; **Festa della Repubblica**, to celebrate the proclamation of the Republic of Italy in 1946, on the first Sunday in June; **Festa del lavoro** or May Day.

There are also several local and regional holidays, often centering on the festivity of the Patron Saint of the town or a particular church; and many internationally famous historical pageants, like the **Festa dei Ceri** (May 15), when heavy decorative structures symbolising church candles (**ceri**) are paraded in Gubbio; **il Palio**, the horse race in Siena run twice a year, on July 2 and August 16; or the **Partita a scacchi**, the chess game played with live chessmen in the main square of Marostica (September 9–10).

Whenever a public holiday falls on a Friday or a Tuesday, firms and public offices often grant their employees a long weekend or 'bridging holiday' called **il ponte**.

13 For this exercise, look at the clock faces below. You will be asked five questions about what time it is. Say the five times in the order shown on the clock faces using the 12-hour clock; then listen to the correct answers on your recording.

ANSWERS

EXERCISE 3
1 (c), 2 (f), 3 (d), 4 (b), 5 (e), 6 (i), 7 (a), 8 (h), 9 (g)

EXERCISE 4
(a) ii   (b) iii   (c) i   (d) ii

EXERCISE 6
(a) un po'   (b) un po' di   (c) un po'   (d) un po' di
(e) un po'

EXERCISE 7
(b), (c) ii and (d) are true.

EXERCISE 8
(a) 8.50 because the 10 a.m. service from Angera stops at Baveno only on Wednesday.   (b) 13.10
(c) No, because the 11.05 stops at Meina only on Tuesdays.   (d) 9.05 because the 7.15 stops there only on schooldays (**giorni di scuola**).   (e) no
(f) 10 minutes   (g) 9 minutes
Si effettua is officialese for 'runs'.

EXERCISE 9
lunedì (e)   martedì (d)   mercoledì (c)   giovedì (f)
venerdì (a)   sabato (b)   domenica (g)

EXERCISE 10
(a) ti trovi, mi trovo   (b) si trova   (c) si trovano
(d) ci troviamo   (e) si trova

EXERCISE 11
(a) domani sera   (b) dopodomani mattina   (c) domani mattina   (d) questo pomeriggio   (e) dopodomani sera
(f) domani pomeriggio

EXERCISE 12
(a), (e) quando   (b), (f) quale   (c) quante   (d), (g) quanto
(h) quali

7

MORE
OR LESS

BEFORE YOU BEGIN

Correct pronunciation is essential both for clear understanding and to make yourself understood. Although the Italians will probably understand you even if you say 'ill telly phono' or 'law toe buzz', it is essential that you try to achieve as good a pronunciation as you can. The point is that, if you associate a mental picture of the spelling of those words with the wrong sounds, you will not be able to understand the Italians when they say 'il **telefono**' and 'l'**autobus**'.

POINTS TO REMEMBER FROM UNIT 6

telling the time: **è l'una e mezza; le quattro meno venti = le quindici e quaranta; sono le tre del pomeriggio, le sei di sera**

days of the week: **lunedì, martedì, mercoledì, giovedì, venerdì, sabato, domenica;** and **oggi, domani, dopodomani.**

question words: **quando? quanto -a, -i, -e? quale -i?**

Pronunciation notes

The spelling *qu-* corresponds to the initial sound in 'question'. It sounds the same as *-cu-* in words like **cuccetta** couchette, **cupola** dome, **acuto** acute; but, whereas *-cu-* is followed by a consonant (except in **cuocere** to cook, **cuoco** cook, **cuoio** leather and **cuore** heart), *-qu-* is always followed by a vowel: **quasi** almost; **acqua** water; **questione** question, matter; **acquistare** to acquire, to purchase.

▶ *A customer asks the baker for wholemeal bread*

LISTEN FOR...

▶ **un pane**	a loaf
▶ **se non ti dispiace**	if you don't mind
▶ **intero o mezzo?**	whole or a half?

Cliente	Un pane integrale, se non ti dispiace.
Fornaio	Intero o mezzo?
Cliente	Intero.
Fornaio	Intero. Desidera altro, signora?
Cliente	No.
Fornaio	(*to his assistant*) Paolo, mi dai diecimila lire, per favore?
Paolo	Eh?
Fornaio	Mi dai diecimila lire, per favore? ... Ecco, cinquanta di resto alla signora. Buongiorno, signora.

cliente   customer

fornaio   baker, **forno** (oven)

▶ **un pane** lit. a bread, is one way to ask for a whole loaf. Some loaves, however, are very large, in which case one may ask the baker to cut **un pezzo** (a piece) of it.
integrale   wholemeal (speaking of bread and flour); in other contexts, integral

▶ **se non ti dispiace**   if you don't mind. The woman is a habitual customer who uses the colloquial **ti** instead of the formal **le** for 'you' (**se non le dispiace**): see also *Grammar*, p. 102. It is less usual for shopkeepers to do the same when talking to regular customers, but it does happen.

▶ **Intero o mezzo?**   Whole or a half? **Intero** may also be spelled **intiero**.

Desidera altro?   Do you want (wish) anything else? from **desiderare** (to wish, to desire)

Mi dai 10.000 lire per favore?   (Can/Will you) give me 10,000 lire, please? In Italian you simply use the present tense to convey can/will you in this type of sentence. The baker addresses his assistant by his first name, so he uses the **tu** form. The polite form would be the 3rd person: **mi dà** (conventionally spelled with an accent).

ecco cinquanta di resto   here's 50 (lira) change Besides being a stopgap word, **ecco** is used when showing or pointing to something: **ecco il pane** (here's the bread), **ecco i panini** (here are the rolls), **ecco la focaccia** (here's the focaccia).

Buying bread: Aldo changes his mind

<table>
<tr><td colspan="2">LISTEN FOR...</td></tr>
<tr><td>▶ avrei bisogno di ...</td><td>I'd need ...</td></tr>
<tr><td>▶ Posso sostituire ...?</td><td>May I replace ...?</td></tr>
<tr><td>▶ basta</td><td>enough</td></tr>
</table>

Aldo	Avrei bisogno di due rosette, per favore.
Commesso	Sì.
Aldo	Di un panino integrale.
Commesso	Sì.
Aldo	Un bastone.
Commesso	Un bastone quale?
Aldo	Un bastoncino di quelli.
Commesso	Poi?
Aldo	E un pezzetto di pane casareccio.
Commesso	Va bene così?
Aldo	Posso sostituire le rosette?
Commesso	Sì.
Aldo	Allora, ehm, al posto delle rosette, per favore, prenderei un pane integrale rotondo.
Commesso	Sì. Uno rotondo. Poi?
Aldo	Un pezzo di pizza bianca. No, un pezzettino più piccolo.
Commesso	Che altro?
Aldo	Basta, grazie.

▶ **avrei bisogno di ...** I'd need ... (lit I would have need of) The 'would' form is often used in polite requests. You could also say **ho bisogno: ho bisogno di un chilo di pane integrale** I need a kilo of wholemeal bread.

due rosette: like *-ino*, *-etto* or *-etta* is an ending often indicating small size: **rosetta** (small rose), **pizzetta** (small pizza), **casetta** (small house), **pezzetto** (small piece). Also **pezzettino** (very small piece). A useful word ending in *-etto* is **gabinetto** (toilet) (oddly it means also ministerial cabinet: a throwback to the French word cabinet, small cabin, 'room for private business').

un bastone a French bread stick, **un bastoncino** (a small bread stick.) *-cino* is a variant of the *-ino* ending, indicating small size: as in **nipote** ▷ **nipotino, pane** ▷ **panino, filone** (another word for bread stick) ▷ **filoncino, panettone** (the Italian Christmas cake) ▷ **panettoncino, bottone** (button) ▷ **bottoncino.**

Un bastone quale? French bread, which one?, **uno di quelli** one of those (a phrase used when pointing)

pane casareccio home-made bread (from **casa** home), usually wholemeal

Va bene così? OK like that? **Così** is used when indicating size or quantity by gesture: **un bottone piccolo così** (a button small like this), **basta così** (that's enough). It is also translated as 'such a' or 'so' before an adjective: **una casa così bella** (such a beautiful house), **è così dolce** (it's so sweet).

▶ **Posso sostituire** ...? May I replace ...?

al posto di ... in place of ... **Posto**, translated in Unit 6 as 'seat', can also mean place: **un posto bellissimo** a most beautiful place, **mettere le cose a posto** (to put things in their place, to tidy up).

prenderei I'd rather have (lit. I would take)

rotondo round

poi? anything else? (lit. then?)

che altro? what else?, anything else?

▶ **basta** enough, that's all; **bastare** (to be enough); **questo pezzetto mi basta** (this small piece will do me, is enough for me; **Bastano diecimila lire?** Would 10,000 lire be enough?

PRACTICE

1 In this exercise you will practise the sound *-qu-*. Listen to the following phrases on your recording and repeat them until you can pronounce them correctly.

– Quale guida vuole acquistare?
– Non so decidere. Quanto costa questa guida?
– Quasi quanto quell'altra. Quarantacinquemila quattrocento lire.
– Quando è stata pubblicata?
– Nel novantaquattro. È una pubblicazione di qualità.

2 Giovanni asks the owner of a baker's in Milan what types of bread she has for sale. Listen to the recording and tick the ones she mentions from the following list (you may find that different names are used in another region). There are some types this baker does not stock.

a. banane (banana-shaped rolls)
b. ferrarese (Ferrara-type bread)
c. focaccia (focaccia, flat leavened bread seasoned with olive oil)
d. fogliette (a type of roll)
e. francese, francesini (French-type bread)
f. grissini (bread sticks)
g. michette (round bread rolls)
h. pane all'olio (bread made with olive oil)
i. pane di pasta dura (crusty bread)
j. pane integrale (wholemeal bread)
k. pizzetta (small pizza): rossa (red, i.e. with tomato and cheese); bianca (white, i.e. only with cheese)
l. rosette (like michette but hollow)
m. tartine (sliced white)

ANSWERS P. 106

3 Write in the gaps the appropriate form for 'will you give me … if you don't mind; i.e.: informal **mi dai** … **se non ti dispiace**; formal **mi dà** … **se non le dispiace**.

a. Paolo _____ cinquantamila lire,

_____ ?

b. Signorina, _____ la guida di Verdesi

_____ ?

c. — Ha del té? — Certo, signore. Abbiamo té di Ceylon, té verde dalla Cina, Earl Grey,

tutto quello che vuole. — Allora _____ un pacchetto di

Earl Grey, _____ ?

d. Senti, Rosanna, _____ un pezzetto di focaccia

ANSWERS P. 106   _____ ?

At the bookshop Giovanni asks for something less expensive

LISTEN FOR...

▶ **meno costoso** — less expensive
▶ **un decimo** — one tenth
▶ **venti per cento** — twenty per cent
▶ **intermedia** — intermediate, middle

Giovanni	Avrebbe qualche cosa di meno costoso?
Libraia	Qualche cosa di meno costoso potrebbe essere, senz'altro andiamo da un estremo all'altro, 'La guida di Roma e i suoi dintorni' pubblicata da Verdesi per lire seimila.
Giovanni	Ah, un decimo … della somma di prima.
Libraia	Un decimo. Ora questa qui è una guida più sommaria, ha un numero di pagine decisamente inferiore; sarà un venti per cento, venticinque per cento dell'altra. È arricchita però di qualche illustrazione che all'altra manca … Direi più scorrevole di lettura.
Giovanni	Hm hm. E come guide intermedie?
Libraia	Come guide intermedie, 'Vedere e capire Roma' di Armando Ravaglioli può essere considerata intermedia da un punto di vista senz'altro del prezzo perché costa quarantottomila lire.

Avrebbe …? Would you have …?, from **avere**. For a full explanation of this form see Unit 8, p. 118.

▶ **meno costoso** less expensive; also **meno caro**, **più economico**

potrebbe essere could be

senz'altro a stopgap expression in this context that is not particularly significant (but see Unit 3, p. 33).

andiamo da un estremo all'altro we go from one extreme to the other, from one end of the range to the other

dintorni surroundings, environs; **intorno** around, **intorno alla casa** (around the house)

pubblicata da published by, **pubblicare** (to publish). **Verdesi** is the name of a publisher.

▶ **un decimo** one tenth. The first four ordinals were listed in Unit 5, p. 66. To complete the first 10: **quinto** fifth, **sesto** sixth, **settimo** seventh, **ottavo** eighth, **nono** ninth: all agree with the noun e.g. **terzo piano** (third floor), **settima sinfonia** (seventh symphony). Fractions are expressed, as in English, by a number and an ordinal (third or above): **due terzi** two thirds, **quattro quinti** four fifths, etc. One half is **la metà**. Twice as much is **il doppio** (the double).

della somma di prima of the earlier amount. **Somma** also means sum, **sommare** (to add), **sommario** (summary). **Più di prima** more than before, **meno di prima** (less than before).

pagina page

decisamente inferiore decidedly smaller. **Inferiore** can mean inferior, but it's often used to mean smaller, lesser. Similarly, **superiore** can mean larger, greater as well as superior.

▶ **venti per cento** twenty per cent; **percentuale** (f) percentage. The indefinite article **un** before numbers may be translated with about: **un tre o quattro persone** about three or four people.

è arricchita però ... it is enriched, however, by some illustrations which the other one lacks (**mancare** to lack, to be missing).

direi I'd say, from **dire** (to say, to tell, see below)

più scorrevole di lettura of easier reading (lit. more flowing of reading). **Lettura** (reading) is a noun (compare English 'lecture', usually a reading from a prepared text); **leggere** (to read).

▶ **intermedia** intermediate, middle

vedere e capire to see and to understand

da un punto di vista del prezzo in terms of price (lit. from the point of view of price)

▶ The Manager of the Gran Caffè Adriano describes the venue

LISTEN FOR...	
▶ molto più a basso livello	at a much lower level (less sophisticated)
▶ molto meno elegante	much less elegant
▶ uno dei più eleganti	one of the most elegant
▶ belle giornate	beautiful days
▶ bellissima piazza	most beautiful square

Giovanni Da quanto tempo il Gran Caffè Adriano si è aperto?

Sig. Ramenghi Il Gran Caffè Adriano in questa nuova veste che Lei ha visto è aperto dal luglio del 1994.

Giovanni Ah, soltanto dal novantaquattro.

Sig. Ramenghi Sì, in questa veste nuova. Perché prima era una gestione molto più a basso livello, diciamo.

Giovanni Molto meno elegante.

Sig. Ramenghi Molto meno elegante. È stato portato a questo livello, ristrutturando tutto, rifacendo tutto. Abbiamo addirittura laboratori per poter fare noi la gastronomia, la pasticceria, la gelateria. E adesso in questo momento è uno dei bar più eleganti di Roma, diciamo. I tavolini esterni sul marciapiede che danno la possibilità nelle belle giornate come oggi ai clienti di sedersi e poter degustare qualcosa vedendo il passaggio di questa bellissima piazza che è piazza Cavour.

Da quanto tempo ... si è aperto? How long has ... been open? (lit. From how much time ... itself is open?). **Si** can be omitted, and in fact does not appear in the reply: **è aperto dal luglio del 1994** it has been open since July 1994 (lit. is open from the July of the 1994). **Gran = grande** (grand, big, large)

nuova veste new look (lit. dress)

prima before, previously

era was (from **essere**)

gestione (f) management, style of management; **gestore** (manager)

▶ **molto più a basso livello** at a much lower level/less sophisticated (lit. much more at lower level). You could also say **a livello molto più basso**. The opposite is **ad alto livello** (the **-d** is inserted to avoid two successive **a**-s).

▶ **molto meno elegante** much less elegant

è stato portato a questo livello it has been brought (up) to this level

ristrutturando tutto, rifacendo tutto rebuilding and refurbishing everything, from **ristrutturare** (to restructure) and

rifare (from the ancient **rifa[c]ere**) to redo, to remake. When you see **-ando** (for verbs in **-are**) and **-endo** (for the rest), translate it by *-ing* (but mind you, the reverse is NOT always the case). **Vedere** to see, **vedendo** (seeing).

addirittura even

laboratori workshops where food, cakes and ice cream are made. **Laboratorio** also means a scientific laboratory, and abstract terms like **gastronomia**, **pasticceria**, **gelateria** instead of **la cucina, i dolci e i gelati**, suggests high quality.

▶ **uno dei più eleganti** one of the most elegant

tavolini (lit. little tables) **esterni** outside tables

▶ **belle giornate** beautiful days

sedersi to sit down (lit. to sit oneself)

degustare to taste, to sample, **degustazione** (f) (tasting)

qualcosa a shortened form of **qualche cosa** (something)

il passaggio a typically Italian concept meaning the people strolling along ('passing by') to see and be seen; **passare** (to pass), **passante** (passer-by). A similar word with a similar meaning is **passeggio**, from **passeggiare** (to stroll, related to **passare**).

▶ **bellissima piazza** most beautiful square. The ending **-issimo**, **-issima** (see Unit 4, p. 47) is used when 'very' or 'most' can be used in English (e.g. **comodo** comfortable, **comodissimo** most comfortable).

4 Fill in the missing words in the following sentences using the words or phrases in the box below. As usual, there are more of them than you need.

a. Il Vocabolario Illustrato in due volumi è _____ dei tre libri.

b. Il Vocabolario Scolastico costa soltanto _____ del Vocabolario Illustrato.

c. Il Dizionario Bilingue può essere considerato _____ dal punto di vista del prezzo.

d. Il Vocabolario Scolastico italiano costa _____ del Dizionario Bilingue.

e. Per gli studenti il Vocabolario Illustrato costa sole 243.000 lire, con lo sconto del

_____ .

f. Il Dizionario Bilingue costa _____ del Vocabolario Illustrato.

ANSWERS P. 106

| un terzo   un quarto   dieci per cento   il più costoso   intermedio   la metà |
| molto meno   il meno costoso   sei per cento |

5 You will be expressing your appreciation of the renovation of Albergo Vittoria. Follow the instructions on your recording.

6 You do not wish to pay as much as you are being asked. Follow the instructions on your recording. You'll need a new word: **troppo** meaning too much.

A student describes her home town

> ### LISTEN FOR...
>
> ▶ **molto più piccola di**   much smaller than
> ▶ **non glie lo so dire**   I can't tell you
> ▶ **mi dicono che ...**   they tell me that ...
> ▶ **il centro storico**   the old (part of the) town

Giovanni	Mi parli un po' di Lecce. Che città è?
Marcella	Ah, è una piccola cittadina, tranquilla, molto più piccola di Roma.
Giovanni	Quanti abitanti avrà più o meno?
Marcella	Oh questo non lo so. Non glie lo so dire.
Giovanni	Mi dicono che sia molto bella proprio per l'architettura.
Marcella	È la città del barocco, diciamo. Nel Sud. Ci sono molte chiese. Cioè, il centro storico è quasi tutto barocco. E niente. Poi non è certo trafficata come qui a Roma, ma è molto tranquilla.

mi parli un po' di ...   tell me about ... There are various 'fillers' in this dialogue: **un po'** a little, **diciamo** let's say, shall we say (almost as frequent as 'I mean' in English),

niente   nothing (something like 'that's it', 'I've nothing to add'). Another frequent mark of hesitation is the lengthening of final vowels: listen to **la** and **chiese** in Marcella's last lines.

piccola cittadina: cittadina already means small town. The use of logically unnecessary words, like the 'fillers' mentioned above, is a normal feature of language.

▶ **molto più piccola di ...**   much smaller than ... Comparisons are normally expressed in Italian by using **più** or **meno** before an adjective; and only in a few cases by using modified forms (a bit like the *-er* form in English). Here **di** is the equivalent of 'than': **meno grande di ...** less large than ..., **più tranquilla di ...** quieter 'than' ... There is more on comparisons in the *Grammar*, p. 102.

avrà   future of **avere**. The future in Italian often indicates a possibility: may have.

▶ **non glie lo so dire**   I can't tell you (lit. not to you it I know tell)

▶ **mi dicono che ...**   they tell me that ... So far the verb **dire** has been introduced mostly in the polite form **dica**, **mi dica**, tell me, used as a conversation opener. The forms of the present tense are: **dico**, **dici**, **dice**, **diciamo**, **dite**, **dicono**. **Sia** is a form of the subjunctive of **essere**. Don't worry about the subjunctive: it would be equally acceptable to say **mi dicono che è ...** Giovanni, like many middle-aged people, uses the subjunctive more often than younger speakers. Language use changes with the passing of time.

proprio per l'architettura   especially for (its) architecture

barocco   baroque

nel Sud   in the South. Southern Italy is also called **il mezzogiorno** (lit. noon, when the position of the Sun marks south in the northern hemisphere), **il meridione** (from Latin MERIDIEM, noon). The preposition **a** is more often used with names of towns: **vado a Roma**, **abita a Milano**; **in**, sometimes combined with the article, with names of areas, regions, counties or nations: **vado in Italia**, **abito in Toscana**, **il barocco nel Sud** (southern baroque).

> **il centro storico** the old (part of the) town (lit. the historic centre)
> **trafficata** congested with traffic. Note the structure of the comparison: **non è**
> **trafficata come Roma** it is not as congested as Rome; **questa guida non è certo**
> **costosa come quella** this guidebook is certainly not as dear as that one.

Another student speaks about her home town

LISTEN FOR...

▶ **Dove si trova ...?** where is ...?
▶ **a sessanta chilometri di distanza da ...** sixty kilometres from ...

Giovanni	E lei è di Roma?
Laura	No. Di Latina.
Giovanni	Dove si trova Latina?
Laura	Latina si trova a sessanta chilometri di distanza qui da Roma verso sud.
Giovanni	È una cittadina grande, piccola, media?
Laura	È una città media, non so, più di centomila abitanti.
Giovanni	È una città agricola, industriale ...
Laura	No, è più industriale ... che agricola. Però anche un po' agricola.

> **Dove si trova Latina?** Where is Latina? Remember the use of **mi trovo** explained in Unit 6.

> **a sessanta chilometri di distanza da ...** sixty kilometres from ...(lit. of distance from); **verso sud** towards the south. In English it's simply '60 km south of Rome'. Use **a ... da ...** for distances (and times taken to cover them) from somewhere: **a 100 chilometri da Firenze** 100 kms from Florence, **a dieci minuti dall'albergo** ten minutes from the hotel.

> **più industriale che agricola** more industrial than agricultural. Note that, when 'than' is between two words of the same type (two adjectives, two verbs etc.), its translation is **che**. **È meglio prevenire che curare** Prevention is better than cure (lit. to prevent is better than to cure; **prevenire, curare**: both verbs); otherwise its translation is **di**: **questa cura è peggiore della malattia** this treatment is worse than the disease (**peggiore**, adjective; **malattia**, noun).

PRACTICE

7 Your Italian friend asks you about Brighton. Answer, following the instructions in your recording.

8 A bakery is called **Forno** (after the oven) or **Fornaio** (after the baker). A third name for baker is included among the shop signs below. Relate each Italian shop name to its English translation by writing the roman numeral next to it. By combining some judicious guessing with a process of elimination you should be able to understand all of them.

a.	ALIMENTARI	i.	Baker's
b.	ARTICOLI REGALO	ii.	Off-licence, wine shop
c.	BOTTIGLIERIA	iii.	Patisserie, confectioner's
d.	FARMACIA	iv.	Chemist's
e.	GELATERIA	v.	Fruiterer's (usually greengrocer's in the UK)
f.	FRUTTERIA	vi.	General food store, grocery
g.	PANIFICIO	vii.	Gift shop, souvenir shop
h.	PASTICCERIA	viii.	Ice-cream parlour
i.	POLLERIA	ix.	Perfumery
j.	PROFUMERIA	x.	Poulterer's
k.	SUPERMERCATO	xi.	Supermarket

ANSWERS P. 106

9 Now that you know the name of various types of shop you can answer the questions on your recording about where you can buy various things. You will hear a new word: **aspirina** (no need for a translation ...).

'Tu' and 'Lei': a summing up

The polite form of address uses the third person of the verb instead of the second, and the third person feminine pronoun (**Lei**) for the reasons explained in Unit 3: **Che cosa desidera?** (formal) instead of **Che cosa desideri?** In formal situations two or more people may also be addressed in the third person plural (**Che cosa desiderano?**) In recent years, however, with the gradual dismantling of class barriers and the democratization of society, the informal **tu** has been gaining ground, particularly among young people. Longstanding customers often use it when talking to shopkeepers, and it is not uncommon for some shopkeepers or market traders to do the same. If in doubt still use the **Lei** form, and remember that the **tu** form is not normally compatible with a title, like **signore**, **signora**, **dottore**, etc. In southern Italy the 2nd person plural (**voi**) is often used as a singular polite form (**Che cosa desiderate?**), but you need not concern yourself with all the subtleties of a usage which, in theory, admits to nine different gradations of formality.

Comparisons

The following expressions contain the main words you need to make graded judgements. Taking as a model the sentence: **questo profumo è caro** this perfume is expensive:

meno ... di   less ... than
  questo profumo è meno caro di quello

più ... di   more .../...-er than
  questo profumo è più caro di quello

[così] ... come   as ... as
  questo profumo è [così] caro come quello

molto   very
  questo profumo è molto caro

molto più   much more
  questo profumo è molto più caro di quello

molto meno   much less
  questo profumo è molto meno caro di quello

piuttosto   rather
  questo profumo è piuttosto caro

abbastanza   rather, enough
  questo profumo è abbastanza caro

troppo   too (much)
  questo profumo è troppo caro

Così [placed in square brackets] can be omitted. Most of the above expressions can be made negative by placing **non** before the verb: **questo profumo non è meno caro di quello, non è molto caro, non è troppo caro.**

Position of adjectives

Adjectives normally come *after* the noun when they imply a contrast or an opposition: **tavolini esterni** are the tables on the pavement outside as opposed to those inside the bar; **vino rosso** (red wine) is not **vino bianco** (white wine). Adjectives may appear *before* a noun in a non-contrastive sense: if I say **un rosso vino** I am simply highlighting its colour, not contrasting it with a white wine. This rule also applies to words qualified by two adjectives: **Gran Caffè Adriano** (not any other **Gran Caffè**) or **grande città industriale** (not **agricola**).

If the adjectives are both defining and opposable, they both follow the noun in a logical order of priority: **vocabolario scolastico italiano**, **acqua minerale gasata**, etc. (an order, incidentally, which is exactly the reverse of the English order: Italian school dictionary, sparkling mineral water).

Some adjectives, therefore, take slightly different meanings according to their position. **Un uomo povero** is a man who is not rich, but a rich man may be **un povero uomo**, as in emotionally stunted or spiritually deprived. **La mia nuova casa** is a 'new' house because I have not lived in it before, but not necessarily **una casa nuova**, one that has just been built. Adjectives may occupy either place when the specific sense includes the non-specific: **Gran Caffè Adriano** has **una nuova veste**, a new look, because, as its manager puts it a moment later, it is **una veste nuova**, a total renovation.

10 Change the underlined verbs from the 'lei' form to the 'tu' form

a   <u>Ha</u> visto il Gran Caffè Adriano nella sua nuova veste?

    ——————————

b   Mi <u>può</u> dare un'acqua minerale gasata, per favore?

    ——————————

c   Se <u>prende</u> la metropolitana, <u>arriva</u> prima dell'autobus.

    ——————————

d   <u>Si trova</u> bene in questo albergo?

    ——————————

e   Perché non <u>viene</u> a trovarmi domani pomeriggio?

    ——————————

ANSWERS P. 106

11 The following adjectives have contrasting meanings:

forte strong, **leggero** light, mild; **caro** expensive, **economico** cheap; **grande** large, **piccolo** small; **elegante** elegant, **ordinario** ordinary, common. For each of the following sentences write another phrase with the same meaning but with the contrasting adjective, e.g. **Questo albergo è più economico** or **meno caro**.

a   Questo vino rosso è meno leggero. …

  i.   ——————————————

b   Questa camera è molto più cara …

  ii.   ——————————————

c   Questo albergo è meno grande …

  iii.   ——————————————

d   Questo profumo è più forte …

  iv.   ——————————————

e.   La nuova veste del ristorante è meno ordinaria …

  v.   ——————————————

ANSWERS P. 106

12 Each of the underlined nouns in the following sentences is accompanied by two adjectives. Choose a pair that fits from the list below, using each adjective only once, and place the adjectives and the noun in the most appropriate order.

a   Latina è una <u>città</u> …

b   Ho acquistato un <u>vocabolario</u> …

c   Questo è un <u>profumo</u> …

d   Vorrei una bottiglia di <u>acqua</u> …

e   L'albergo è totalmente rinnovato, in una <u>veste</u> …

agricola	eccellente	elegante	francese	italiano
liscia	minerale	nuova	piccola	scolastico

KEY WORDS AND PHRASES

un pane	a loaf
se non ti dispiace,	if you don't mind
se non le dispiace (formal)	
Intero o mezzo?	Whole or a half?
avrei bisogno di ...	I'd need ...
Posso sostituire ...?	May I replace ...?
basta	enough
un decimo	one tenth
venti per cento	20 per cent
intermedia	intermediate, middle
meno costoso	less expensive
molto più piccola di ...	much smaller than ...
molto più a basso livello	at a much lower level, less sophisticated
molto meno elegante	much less elegant
uno dei più eleganti	one of the most elegant
belle giornate	beautiful days
bellissima piazza	most beautiful square
non glie lo so dire	I can't tell you
mi dicono che ...	they tell me that ...
il centro storico	the old (part of the) town
dove si trova ...?	where is ...?
a sessanta chilometri da ...	sixty kilometres from ...

Shops

Like the England of old, Italy is still very much a nation of small shopkeepers, many of whom somehow still manage to resist the onslaught of supermarkets, with their greater purchasing power and consequently lower prices, by giving a really excellent personal service to their regular customers. The owners are often found behind the counter: they have a personal interest in gaining and retaining your custom, and are able to advise you on what best suits your needs. They will also charge you what they think you are prepared to pay which may not necessarily be the lowest possible price: some judicious bargaining is often in order (ask for **uno sconto** a discount). If you want **prezzi fissi**, fixed prices, go to department stores or supermarkets. Some shops will give you a discount if you pay by travellers cheque: make sure their rate of exchange is not less than in the banks. Foreign currencies are rarely accepted except in frontier towns. Personal cheques are hardly ever used, but credit cards are now welcome in most establishments.

Some shop signs, like **Gelateria** or **Profumeria**, name the trade. Others, like **Fornaio**, refer to the shopkeeper. A few, like **Alimentari** or **Tabacchi**, mention what is being sold. Thus a flower shop may be named **Fioreria**, **Fioraio** (**Fiorista**), or simply **Fiori**. Some go by a fancy name or an uninformative trademark if the window display clearly shows what they sell. A few shop signs may be misleading to English speakers. **Confezioni** is not a confectioner's but a clothes shop. In a **Pasticceria** you will find cakes and confectionery, not pasta. Spices (**droghe**), not drugs, were sold in a **Drogheria**, now selling the range of goods you would find at a grocer's. Chemists sell medical drugs in a **Farmacia**, often together with a range of cosmetics and toiletries, but they do not normally develop films. For that you will have to go to a specialized shop (**Foto**, **Fotografia** or **Ottico**), dealing in cameras, films and optical goods (including prescription spectacles). The ubiquitous T-sign for **Tabacchi** indicates a State Monopoly outlet licensed to sell cigarettes and other tobacco goods, often as part of a larger shop (e.g. a coffee bar). You can also buy postage stamps there, without having to go to a post office.

Watch out for sales, advertised by a variety of signs: **Saldi, Svendita, Liquidazione, Occasioni, Ribassi, Prezzi eccezionali**.

AND FINALLY...

13 You are in a baker's shop. Ask for bread, following the instructions on your recording.

▼ **ANSWERS**

EXERCISE 2

(a), (b), (d), (e), (g), (i), (m)

EXERCISE 3

(a), (d) mi dai ... se non ti dispiace; (b), (c) mi dà ... se non le dispiace

EXERCISE 4

(a) il più costoso (b) un terzo (c) intermedio
(d) molto meno (e) dieci per cento (f) la metà

EXERCISE 8

(a) General food store (b) Gift shop (c) Off-licence
(d) Chemist's (e) Ice-cream parlour (f) Fruiterer's
(g) Baker's (h) Patisserie (i) Poulterer's
(j) Perfumery (k) Supermarket

EXERCISE 10

(a) hai (b) puoi (c) prendi, arrivi (d) ti trovi (e) vieni

EXERCISE 11

(a) più forte (b) molto meno economica (c) più piccolo
(d) meno leggero (e) più elegante

EXERCISE 12

(a) piccola città agricola (b) vocabolario italiano scolastico
(c) eccellente profumo francese (d) acqua minerale liscia
(e) elegante veste nuova

8

A VARIETY
OF CHOICES

▶ More about shopping and comparing values
▶ asking for, and acting on, advice
▶ how to say you like or dislike something
▶ about colours

**BEFORE
YOU
BEGIN**

Some languages appear more complex than others because their complexity is differently distributed. What one gains in simplicity, for instance, by a limited number of endings in English, one loses by a less flexible word order which is subject to complex rules. Yet, to keep things in perspective, the order of complexity of all Italian endings is about the same as that of the multiplication table.

POINTS TO REMEMBER FROM UNIT 7

'Tu' and 'Lei' forms:

Mi dai ...? (tu: informal)
Mi dà ...? (Lei: polite) } (Will you) give me ...?

Hai ...? (tu: informal)
Ha ...? (Lei: polite) } Do you have ...?

Comparison words:

più more **meno** less **molto** very **tanto** so (much) **troppo** too (much)
(così) ... come ... (as) ... as ... **piuttosto** rather **abbastanza** rather, enough

Position of adjectives:
una notizia certa a confirmed news item (not uncertain, reliable)
una certa notizia a certain news item (a particular news item)

Pronunciation notes

In all languages consonants are either voiced (accompanied by a vibration of the vocal chords) like *b-* or *d-*, or voiceless (without a vibration) like *p-* or *t-*. Voicing and voicelessness are mostly represented by different letters. Some Italian letters, however, are capable of both pronunciations. One of them is *-s-*, which tends to be voiced (as in the English word ease).

(a) before another voiced consonant: **sbarbato** shaven, **slip**, **smog** (borrowed from English, but with the wrong pronunciation!);

(b) in between vowels (as in **casa** house, **cosa** thing and in adjectives ending in *-oso*, *-osa*, like **dubbioso** dubious, **famoso** famous).

It is voiceless otherwise, as in English bus: **spaghetti** spaghetti, **sera** evening, **insistere** to insist. A stronger voiceless *-s-* is represented by the spelling *-ss-*, as in **cassa** cash desk, box, **assistere** to assist, **basso** low).

At the butcher's

LISTEN FOR...

▶ **questo qua**	this one here
▶ **Vanno bene come grandezza?**	Are they all right for size?
▶ **io ne volevo ...**	I wanted ...
▶ **Le occorreva altro?**	Did you require anything else?
▶ **Arrivederci!**	See you again!

Signora	Spezzatino bianco di vitella.
Macellaio	Io le darei questo qua. Un bel tocchettino magro. Così vanno bene i pezzettini come grandezza?
Signora	Sì.
Macellaio	Perfetto.
Signora	Io ne volevo mezzo chilo.
Macellaio	Così a occhio sono quattrocento trenta grammi. Quattro e venti. Le occorreva altro, va bene così? Perfetto. Tutto per la modica cifra di diecimila cinquecento lire. Prezzo speciale. Le ho rubato solo mille lire.
Signora	Mi ha rubato solo mille lire?
Macellaio	Ecco a Lei. Grazie e una buona giornata, signora. Arrivederci.

> **macellaio** butcher, **macelleria** (butcher's shop), **macello** (abattoir), **Che macello!** (What a mess!)

> **spezzatino bianco di vitella** diced veal (for casserole); **spezzatino** from **spezzare** (to break up); **bianco** white, because it is not red meat; **vitella** or **vitello** mean both calf and veal.

> **io le darei** I would give you: see *Grammar*, p. 118.

▶ **questo qua** this one here; pointing words like **questo** and **quello** are often reinforced by **qua** (here) and **là** or **lì** (there): **mi dia quello là invece** (give me that other one there instead).

> **un bel tocchettino magro** a lovely lean little piece; **tocco** = **pezzo**, **tocchettino** or **pezzettino** (little piece)

▶ **Vanno bene come grandezza?** Are they all right for size? **Va bene/vanno bene come ...** is a useful expression: **Va bene come colore?** Is the colour OK?, **questi rigatoni vanno bene come pasta al forno** these rigatoni are OK for baked pasta.

> **perfetto** perfect, a fashionable sentence filler

▶ **io ne volevo ...** I wanted ... The use of this tense, called imperfect, also found in **Le occorreva altro?** Did you require anything else? will be described later: see *Grammar*, p. 198. **Mi occorre** I need, **che cos'altro ci occorre?** what else do we need? from **occorrere** (to be necessary). So, just as you have to say the equivalent of 'it is pleasant to me' for 'I like' (see Conversations 3 and *Grammar*, pp. 118–19), you say 'it is necessary to me' to say 'I need'. You could also say **ho bisogno di ...** (see Unit 7, p. 93).

così a occhio approximately, roughly (lit. so at eye), said of something that can be estimated visually, at a glance.

grammi grams. A gram is one thousandth of a kilo; 100 grams are **un etto**, about 3½ ounces.

modica cifra moderate figure

Le ho rubato solo mille lire I have robbed you of only one thousand lire, **rubare** (to steal, to rob)

> **una buona giornata** (have) a good day. The ending *-ata*, modifying **giorno**, indicates duration. Likewise, **una mattinata di lavoro** (a morning's work), **una serata a teatro** (an evening at the theatre). **Una nottata** usually indicates a sleepless night.

▶ **arrivederci!** see you!, bye! (lit. **a rivederci**, to see us again)

◗ A grocer's advice on suitable pasta

LISTEN FOR...

▶ **Che tipo di pasta consiglia?**   What type of pasta do you advise?
▶ **dipende da ...**   it depends on ...

Giovanni	Che tipo di pasta consiglia?
Droghiere	Dipende quale ... qualità preferisce, se pasta da minestrone, pasta per fare pastasciutta, o pasta al forno.
Giovanni	Per fare della ... della pastasciutta.
Droghiere	A Milano usan gli spaghetti, però ... va molto bene la pasta un po' più grossa: bucatini, e ... tipo maccheroni, e ... così dipende dal ... dai gusti del cliente.
Giovanni	E come pasta al forno, forse le ...le penne.
Droghiere	Pasta al forno, vanno ... no, la ... lasagne va di più. Le penne devono essere molto grosse.
Giovanni	Hm ... grazie.
Droghiere	Prego.

droghiere, droghiera grocer

▶ **Che tipo di pasta consiglia?** What type of pasta do you advise? from **consigliare**, to advise, **consiglio** (advice, counsel)

▶ **dipende** it depends; **dipende dai gusti del cliente** (it depends on the customer's tastes)

preferisce you prefer, from **preferire** (to prefer). See *Grammar*, p. 118.

Minestrone is thick vegetable soup. **Pasta asciutta** or **pastasciutta** (lit. dry pasta) is the general name for pasta lightly cooked in boiling water, drained and seasoned in many ways. **Pasta al forno** is the general name for all baked pastas, like **lasagne** or **cannelloni**. For further varieties of pasta, see p. 121.

usan(o) gli spaghetti spaghetti is used. Like 'to stop' (Unit 6, p. 84) and other English verbs, **usare** may take an object (**nel minestrone io uso i bucatini** I use bucatini in minestrone) or refer to the subject (**i bucatini [si] usano nel minestrone** bucatini are used in minestrone). In Italian all names of pasta varieties are plural, and require a plural verb.

grosso -a thick, large, big; the opposite in this sense is **sottile** thin.

va di più is preferred (lit. goes more)

1 The first exercise is a pronunciation exercise of words containing the letter **-s-**. First listen to the following sentences on your recording and repeat them, then read them again checking your pronunciation on the recording.

a. La pasta al forno si fa con penne molto grosse.
b. Le lasagne, invece, devono essere sottili.
c. Preferisco gli spaghetti con la salsa rossa, al pomodoro e basilico.
d. Mi passi il sale, per piacere?

2 Read the following recipe and see how much you've understood by answering the questions which follow it.

PASTA AL FORNO

Ingredienti per 6 persone:
penne, rigatoni o maccheroni mezzo chilo
farina 160 g
burro 70 g
latte mezzo litro
formaggio parmigiano grattuggiato 200 g
prosciutto cotto 100 g
mozzarella 200 g
2 uova
noce moscata
sale

MACCHERONI NAPOLETANI

GERARDO DI NOLA

Fate bollire la pasta in abbondante acqua e sale per dieci minuti. Nel mentre, con la farina, 50 grammi di burro, il latte e la noce moscata, preparate una besciamella. Scolate la pasta e mettetela in una pirofila unta di burro. Aggiungete alla pasta il resto del burro, le due uova, il prosciutto e la mozzarella tagliati a pezzetti, e metà del parmigiano. Mescolate bene il tutto alla besciamella. Coprite col resto del parmigiano e mettete in forno moderato per 25 minuti.

---

a The pasta must be boiled in   (i) a little salted water   (ii) a lot of salted water.
b Besciamella is   (i) a white sauce   (ii) a sort of pastry.
c Cooked ham and mozzarella cheese must be   (i) fried with butter and the two eggs   (ii) chopped into little pieces.
d Grated parmesan must be added   (i) all in one go at the end   (ii) in two stages, before and after placing the mixture in a greased ovenproof dish.

ANSWERS P. 122

3 You are at a grocer's, buying some of the ingredients you need for **pasta al forno**. Follow the instructions on your recording.

▶ **Buying jam**

LISTEN FOR...	

▶ **Che tipi ha?**   What kinds have you got?
▶ **c'è di ...**   we have ...

Giovanni	Buongiorno, signora.
Droghiera	Buongiorno.
Giovanni	Ha marmellata?
Droghiera	Sì.
Giovanni	Che tipi ha?
Droghiera	C'è di pesche, c'è di ciliegie, e di marroni: castagne.
Giovanni	Me ne dà una di castagne, per favore?
Droghiera	Subito.

▶ **Che tipi ha?**   What types/kinds have you got?

▶ **c'è di pesche**   there is peach (lit. there is of peaches). A few names of fruit: **castagna** or **marrone** chestnut, **ciliegia** cherry, **fico**   fig, **fragola** strawberry, **lampone** raspberry, **prugna**   plum; generally used in the plural when speaking of jam. **Marmellata** comes usually in a glass jar called **un vasetto** (lit. small vase). A tin is **una scatola** (box) or **una lattina**.

me ne dà una   give me one of them. Remind yourself of this construction using **ne** in Unit 3, pp. 33–4.

subito   immediately, at once

The manager of Danesi Caffè describes the various types of coffee his firm produces

LISTEN FOR...

▶ **mi consiglia per favore ...** advise me please on ...
▶ **quello adatto per ...** the one suitable for ...
▶ **sia ... che ...** both ... and ...
▶ **caffè decaffeinato** decaffeinated coffee

Aldo	Mi consiglia per favore un caffè da fare con la macchinetta espresso. Un buon caffè.
Gestore	Nel nostro negozio abbiamo tanti tipi di caffè. Quello adatto per la macchinetta espresso è il **Danesi Caffè bar.** È macinato più fino proprio per la macchinetta elettrica da casa, ... le viene il caffè come al bar.
Aldo	Be' invece per la macchinetta moka express?
Gestore	Per la moka abbiamo più assortimento. Là c'è il **Danesi Primo Caffè**, che è in confezione sia da duecentocinquanta grammi che da mezzo chilo, a un costo più basso proprio per l'uso giornaliero. Poi abbiamo il **Danesi Oro** che è un caffè di qualità superiore.
Aldo	Avete anche del caffè decaffeinato, per favore?
Gestore	Si sicuramente. Poi oltretutto se lei vuole qui il solubile abbiamo tutta la gamma dei caffè solubili.
Aldo	Bene, grazie.
Gestore	Prego.

▶ **mi consiglia per favore ...** advise me please on ...; unlike to advise, in English, **consigliare** may take a direct object: **mi consiglia un vino bianco?** would you advise me on which white wine to take? (lit. advise me a white wine?), **Le consiglio di comprare questo Orvieto** I advise you to buy this Orvieto.
la macchinetta espresso in this case, clearly a small electrical espresso machine. For other types of coffee machines, see *Did you know?*, p. 121.
▶ **quello adatto per ...** the one suitable for ...
è macinato più fino it's more finely ground, from **macinare** to grind. If you want ground coffee ask for **caffè macinato**; otherwise **caffè in chicchi** or (**caffè in**) **grani** (coffee beans) (lit. in grains). Other varieties: **tostato chiaro** (light roast), **tostato scuro** (dark roast), **solubile** (instant), **macinato fino** (fine ground).
assortimento assortment, stock variety; **più assortimento** (more variety)
confezione (f) packaging; **confezione sotto vuoto** (vacuum packed), both in **pacchetto** (packet) and **lattina** (tin). **Confezionare** has the general meaning of 'preparing things for sale' hence its various possible uses, e.g. ready-made clothes as in **confezioni maschili**, a shop sign corresponding to gentlemen's outfitters, and **confezione regalo** (gift-wrapped).
▶ **sia ... che ...** both ... and ...

---

giornaliero   daily (from **giorno** day. Also: **giornale** daily newspaper). Other periodical adjectives: **orario** hourly, **settimanale** weekly, **mensile** monthly, **annuale** yearly; **proprio per l'uso giornaliero** (especially for daily use). The other translation of **proprio**, as you may remember (Unit 5) is just, right: **proprio di fronte** (just opposite).

oro   gold

▶ **caffè decaffeinato**   decaffeinated coffee

oltretutto   a filler: anyway (lit. besides everything)

gamma   range, gamut

PRACTICE

4 You are in a grocery and wish to buy several things. Fill in the conversation with the missing words jumbled in the box below. This time there are no more than you need.

a. **DROGHIERE**   Buon giorno. Dica.

b. **CLIENTE**   Un _____ di

marmellata, per piacere.

c. **DROGHIERE**   _____ la vuole?

d. **CLIENTE**   Di _____ .

e. **DROGHIERE**   Desidera altro?

f. **CLIENTE**   Sì, due _____

di caffè _____

g. **DROGHIERE**   Abbiamo questa _____ sottovuoto,

da 250 grammi, qualità _____ . Va

bene?

h. **CLIENTE**   Sì, _____ , me

_____ dia un

_____ .

ciliegie   come   confezione   etti   macinato   ne   pacchetto   perfetto superiore   vasetto

ANSWERS P. 122

5 A woman is thinking aloud about buying things at the grocer's. Listen to her on your recording, reading out her shopping list, and see if you can label the groceries in the pictures below with their Italian name.

A _____

B _____

C _____

D _____

E _____

F _____

ANSWERS P. 122

6 Listen to Aldo at the delicatessen counter of a large grocery in Rome. You do not have to understand every single word to answer correctly the following questions:

a How much sheep's milk ricotta does he want?   (i) 250 g   (ii) 150 g
b He then asks for something without chemical additives (**polifosfati**). What is it? (i) chicken breasts   (ii) ham
c Does he want his parmesan cheese   (i) grated or   (ii) whole?
d What is the average weight of a lump of mozzarella made with buffalo milk?
   (i) between 300 and 350 g   (ii) about nine in a kilo, i.e. just over 100 g

Did you understand the useful word **fresco** meaning fresh?

ANSWERS P. 122

CONVERSATIONS 3

In a fashion shop the assistant describes to a customer the colours available in a range of blouses

LISTEN FOR...

▶ **colori**   colours
▶ **modello**   model, pattern
▶ **se non le piace questa tinta qui**   if you don't like this shade

Commessa	Queste esistono anche in altri colori, se non le piace questa tinta qui: giallo, rosa e viola. Sono rimaste soltanto colorate, ma il bianco è finito. Non so se il tessuto le piace più o meno. Ci sono altri colori e altri modelli. In questo qua, signora, no. Il modello è classico e cambia soltanto la tinta.
Signora	Ho capito.
Commessa	Centotrentamila questo.

esistono   exist, from **esistere**   to exist

▶ **colore**   colour; **tinta** (shade or hue). The Italian names for colours fall into two categories. **Azzurro**, **bianco**, **rosso**, **verde**, **giallo** and **nero** change their endings like normal adjectives: **il cielo azzurro** (the blue sky), **le case bianche** (the white houses), **i campi verdi** (the green fields), **le fiamme gialle** (the yellow flames) (see Unit 2, p. 27), **le camicie rosse** (the red shirts), **il gatto nero** (the black cat). Others, originally names of flowers or fruits, are invariable: **rosa** (rose/pink), **viola** (violet), **arancio** (orange), **marrone** (chestnut/brown). **Blu** (blue, a darker shade than **azzurro**) is also invariable like all monosyllables.

▶ **se non le piace questa qui**   if you don't like this one (lit. this one here)

sono rimaste soltanto colorate   only coloured ones are left (i.e. other than white)

▶ **non so se le piace**   I don't know if you like it (lit. I don't know if to you pleases). This construction is further explained in *Grammar*, p. 119.

tessuto   fabric, material, cloth

modelli   styles, patterns also

ho capito   I see (lit. I have understood)

Another undecided customer needs help

LISTEN FOR...

▶ **il colore sta molto bene**   the colour suits you very well

Commessa	È molto bella anche questa. È un classico, insomma.
Cliente	Gonna e …
Commessa	Gonna e camicetta; quindi è come un abito. Il colore sta molto bene, eh?

commessa   shop assistant
insomma   a very common filler, translatable as 'really' in this context
gonna   skirt
camicetta   blouse

quindi   therefore
è come un abito   it's like a dress. Note the various translations of **come**: **non so come** (I don't know how), **bianco come la neve** (white as snow), **come gusto è il migliore** (as regards taste it's the best).

▶ **il colore sta molto bene**   the colour suits you very well; also **le sta molto bene. Mi sta bene?** (Does it suit me?, Does it fit me?), **stanno benissimo l'una e l'altra** (they both fit you perfectly)

Cologne or lavender water?

LISTEN FOR...

▶ **non è nemmeno una colonia**   it is not even a cologne
▶ **a me piace più la colonia della lavanda**   I like cologne better than lavender

Commessa	Questa è una lavanda, non è nemmeno una colonia, è una lavanda. Senta un attimo, eh? Questa è più leggera come profumazione, eh? … A me come profumo piace più la colonia della lavanda: è meno persistente, meno noioso … Altrimenti qualcosa di più dolce, anche, meno classico, più profumo. Può andare, guardi, questo. Questo è un pochino più dolce.

▶ **non è nemmeno una colonia**   it is not even a cologne. Other examples of this phrase: **non è nemmeno caro** (it's not even expensive); **non mi sta nemmeno bene** (it doesn't even fit/suit me); **non voglio nemmeno questo** (I don't want this either).

senta from **sentire**. This verb has three meanings: to listen (**senta**, listen); to smell (**senta questo profumo**, smell this perfume) and feel (**Come ti senti?** How do you feel?)
leggero   light
profumazione (f)   type of scent

▶ **a me piace più la colonia della lavanda**   I like cologne better than lavender. The shop assistant says **a me piace** for emphasis: she could have simply said **mi piace più la colonia della lavanda**.

persistente   long-lasting, persistent
noioso   annoying, boring
altrimenti   otherwise
dolce   sweet
più profumo,   **più** followed by a noun may be translated as more of a... (perfume)
guardi   look, from **guardare** (to look at)

PRACTICE

7   Write the appropriate colour or colours for each of the following:

a.   La salsa di pomodoro è _____

b.   Le mozzarelle sono _____

c.   Il caffè espresso è _____

d.   La cioccolata al latte è _____

e.   Il basilico è _____

ANSWERS P. 122   f.   Il caffè Danesi Oro è in pacchetti _____

8   Here is a list of items of clothing. Listen to the conversation of the couple on your recording and tick the items they are thinking of buying. You'll hear the words **vestiti** (clothes) and **un paio** (a pair).

a.	**abito**	dress
	– da sera	evening dress
b.	**calzini**	men's socks
c.	**camicetta**	blouse
d.	**camicia**	shirt
e.	**canottiera**	vest
f.	**costume da bagno**	swimsuit
g.	**cravatta**	tie
h.	**giacca**	jacket
i.	**golf**	sweater
j.	**gonna**	skirt
k.	**maglietta**	T-shirt
l.	**mutande**	underwear
m.	**pantaloni, calzoni**	trousers
n.	**scarpe**	shoes

ANSWERS P. 122

9   You are in a department store to buy some perfume as a present. It's quite expensive, so you try to get **uno sconto** (a discount). Follow the instructions on your recording.

GRAMMAR AND EXERCISES

All the grammar notes in this unit concern verbs.

Conditional

You have already met the 'would' form in requests: **vorrei** (I'd like), **avrei bisogno di...** (I'd need), **prenderei** (I'd take), etc. In most cases the conditional can be derived from the infinitive (**dire** ▷ **direi**, **prendere** ▷ **prenderei**; except that the -*a*- of verbs in -*are* turns to -*e*-: **comprare** to buy ▷ **comprerei**, **viaggiare** ▷ **viaggerei**).

There are, however, a few irregularities: **andare** ▷ **andrei**, **avere** ▷ **avrei**, **essere** ▷ **sarei**, **volere** ▷ **vorrei**, **potere** ▷ **potrei**, **dovere** ▷ **dovrei** (this is not a complete list). Once you know the first person, however, you can form all the others. *See table 3.*

Verbs in -*ire*

Unlike **dormire**, **partire**, **sentire** and a few others (Unit 6, p. 86), most verbs in -*ire* put -*isc*- before the singular endings, and in the third person plural of the Present tense. *See table 1.*

If a verb in -*ire* follows this pattern, the ending -*isco* will be shown after the infinitive in the notes and vocabulary: e.g. **preferire** (-*isco*) to prefer.

Table 1

	finire to finish	pulire to clean
I	finisco	pulisco
you	finisci	pulisci
he/she/it <u>or</u> you (polite)	finisce	pulisce
we	finiamo	puliamo
you (pl)	finite	pulite
they	finiscono	puliscono

Past participles

This is the verbal form which, in both Italian and English, may work part-time (hence its name) as an adjective: e.g. **appartamenti mobiliati** (furnished flats), from **mobiliare** (to furnish); **caffè macinato** (ground coffee), from **macinare** (to grind).

Italian participles belong to two groups. Most can be formed by simply replacing the -*re* of verbs in -*are* and -*ire* with -*to*, -*ta*, -*ti*, -*te*. *See table 2.*

Those from -*ere* verbs, and a few from the other groups, cannot be predicted (similarly in English you cannot predict 'flew' from 'to fly' as you can 'cried' from 'to cry'). These verbs will be noted in the text and the vocabulary together with their past participle. A short list of the most common ones will be given in Unit 11, p. 166.

How to say 'I like'

THERE IS NO ITALIAN VERB MEANING 'TO LIKE'. In order to translate the concept you use **piacere** (**piaciuto**), meaning 'to please'. Therefore, in order to say 'I like coffee', you have to say: 'coffee pleases me' **il caffè mi piace**; 'strawberries please me' **le fragole mi piacciono**.

You may place the noun phrase (**il caffè**, **le fragole**) either before or after the verb (**mi piace il caffè**, **mi piacciono le fragole**). Only two persons of this verb, **piace** and **piacciono**, are therefore needed.
NEVER SAY *io piaccio* **unless you wish to say that other people like you!** Here are some further examples:
Ti piace il té? (informal), **Le piace il té?** (formal)
Do you like tea?
Sì, il té mi piace moltissimo Yes, I like tea very much

Table 2

	Infinitive		Past participle			
Verbs in -*are*	**tostare**	to roast, to toast	**tostato**	**caffè tostato**	roasted coffee
	illustrare	to illustrate	**illustrato**	**guide illustrate**	illustrated guidebooks
Verbs in -*ire*	**preferire**	to prefer	**preferito**	**i miei dolci preferiti**	my favourite cakes
	bollire	to boil	**bollito**	**acqua bollita**	boiled water

A variety of choices   *Unit 8*

Table 3

	prendere	comprare	avere	essere	andare
	to take	to buy	to have	to be	to go
I	prenderei	comprerei	avrei	sarei	andrei
you	prenderesti	compreresti	avresti	saresti	andresti
he/she/it <u>or</u> you (polite)	prenderebbe	comprerebbe	avrebbe	sarebbe	andrebbe
we	prenderemmo	compreremmo	avremmo	saremmo	andremmo
you (pl)	prendereste	comprereste	avreste	sareste	andreste
they	prenderebbero	comprerebbero	avrebbero	sarebbero	andrebbero

Vi piace la musica classica?   Do you (pl) like classical music?

No, non ci piace troppo. Preferiamo il rock.   No, we don't like it much. We prefer rock.

'I dislike carrots' is **Le carote non mi piacciono. Mi dispiace,** which you have already come across, does not mean 'I dislike' but 'I am sorry', 'I regret': **Mi dispiace di essere in ritardo**   I'm sorry I'm late (i.e. to be late displeases me). **Non mi dispiace** means 'I don't mind': **se non ti dispiace**   if you don't mind.

10 Test your ability to conjugate a verb from the models provided by working out, in table 4, the present tense of **capire**, **preferire** and **spedire** (conjugated like **finire** in table 1).

ANSWERS P. 122

11 Fill in each gap with the required past participle formed from the verb in square brackets. Remember that the past participle used as an adjective must agree with the noun it refers to, like all adjectives.

a   Vorrei del caffè, ma non tipo espresso: tipo americano, poco ———————— [tostare]

b   La mozzarella è il mio formaggio ——————— [preferire].

c   Compro questa guida di Roma, ———————, [pubblicare] da Verdesi.

d   Abbiamo della marmellata superiore, ———————— [confezionare] in vasetti da mezzo chilo.

e   Il parmigiano come lo vuole, intero o ——————— [grattuggiare]?

ANSWERS P. 122

12 In this exercise two of your friends name a number of things they dislike. You disagree. Use the phrase **A me invece piace** or **piacciono moltissimo** according to the things mentioned.

Table 4

	capire to understand	**preferire** to prefer	**spedire** to send, to post
I			
you			
he/she/it <u>or</u> you (polite)			
we			
you (pl)			
they			

KEY WORDS
AND PHRASES

Arrivederci!	Bye!, See you!
pesca	peach
castagna or **marrone** (m)	chestnut
ciliegia	cherry
fico	fig
fragola	strawberry
lampone (m)	raspberry
prugna	plum
caffè espresso	espresso coffee
decaffeinato	decaffeinated
tostato chiaro	light roast
solubile	instant
macinato fino	fine ground
in grani/in chicchi	coffee beans
Mi consiglia per favore …	Advise me please on …
Che tipo di pasta consiglia?	What type of pasta do you advise?
Che tipi ha?	What kinds have you got?
dipende da …	it depends on …
sia come … che come …	both … and …
Vanno bene come grandezza?	Are they OK for size?
io ne volevo …	I wanted one of …
Le occorreva altro?	Did you require anything else?
quello adatto per …	the one suitable for …
questo qua	this one here
non è nemmeno una colonia	is not even a cologne
a me piace più la colonia della lavanda	I like cologne better than lavender
se non le piace questa tinta qui	if you don't like this shade/hue
colori	colours
arancio	orange
azzurro	light blue, sky blue
bianco	white
blu	blue
giallo	yellow
marrone	brown
nero	black
rosa	pink
rosso	red
verde	green
viola	violet
colorato -a	coloured
il colore sta molto bene	the colour suits you very well

A variety of choices   *Unit 8*

DID YOU KNOW?

Coffee

Italians prefer coffee-makers that work by steam pressure. The most common coffee-maker, which can be used on a normal cooker, is made up of two vessels which, when screwed together, hold ground coffee in a filter in between them. Water is sealed in the bottom half and, as it boils, is forced by steam pressure through the filter into the upper half, from which it can be poured out. This type of coffee-maker was first marketed in the fifties by Bialetti, a foundry in Omegna, with the brand name Moka Express, now loosely applied to other machines of the same type. They come in all shapes and sizes, from one to twelve cups. An earlier type of percolator, based on a similar principle, is still used, particularly in southern Italy. It is called **napoletana** (Neapolitan) because it was probably invented in Naples. The lower vessel is not pressurized and, when water is on the boil, the whole contraption needs to be turned upside down, so that water can slowly seep through the coffee by force of gravity, giving rise to anxious queries: **è passato?, non è ancora passato?** (has it gone through yet?) Modern technology has now produced small electrical espresso makers for the home which can extract all the flavour from finely ground coffee just as efficiently as the larger machines in bars. A steam pipe on the side heats and froths milk to make **cappuccino**. Other varieties of coffee are: **macchiato** (spotted, stained) black with just a spot of milk; **corretto** (corrected) with a tot of your favourite spirit or liqueur; **con panna** with cream; **freddo** ice-cold, short black; **granita di caffè** coffee sorbet.

Pasta

Pasta probably existed in some form in Western Europe even before travellers to the East, like Marco Polo at the end of the 13th century, came into contact with Chinese noodles. **Maccheroni** and **ravioli** cooked in chicken stock and seasoned with parmesan cheese are mentioned in a story by Boccaccio (14th century). Tomatoes, the Aztec 'tomatl', were imported from South America in the 16th century, and called 'golden apples' (**pomodori**) in Italy. Tomato sauce for pasta seems to be an 18th-century development. There are hundreds of different varieties of pasta, of all shapes and sizes. They fall into six main types:
(1) small pasta (**pastina**) as small as rice grains or smaller, shaped like stars, squares, triangles, alphabet letters, etc., to be used in soups or cooked in meat or vegetable stock (**pasta in brodo, pastina in brodo**);
(2) string-shaped pasta, called, in decreasing order of thickness, **vermicelli, spaghetti, spaghettini, capelli d'angelo** (angel's hair);
(3) tube-shaped pasta, of which the basic varieties are **cannelloni, maccheroni** (smooth), **bucatini, rigatoni** (fluted) and **penne** (with a slanted cut);
(4) ribbon-shaped pasta, called, in decreasing order of width, **lasagne, tagliatelle, fettuccine, fresine, bavette**;
(5) frilly and fancy-shaped pasta like **farfalle** and **farfallette** (butterfly-shaped), **fusilli** (coil-shaped), **conchiglie** and **conchigliette** (pasta shells);
(6) stuffed pasta of various shapes, such as **ravioli** (pillow-shaped), **agnolotti** (half-circle), **cappelletti** (hat-shaped) and **tortellini** (ring-shaped).
Pasta can be home-made, freshly made in special shops, or industrially made in factories called **Pastificio**. Be careful when cooking freshly made pasta: it's ready in a flash.

AND FINALLY...

13 State your preferences to room service when ordering breakfast, following the instructions on your recording.

ANSWERS

EXERCISE 2

The point of this exercise is to demonstrate how to go about understanding a text without knowing all the words. Pasta, of course, cannot be baked floating in abundant water, therefore '**scolate la pasta**' is likely to mean 'drain the pasta'. The questions do not require you to know what **noce moscata** is, therefore there is no translation here (if you really want to know look it up in the vocabulary at the end).

(a) pasta must be boiled in a lot of water

(b) six ounces of flour in half a litre of milk and two ounces of butter could hardly solidify into pastry: therefore **besciamella** must be a white sauce (this requires no grammar but some attention to detail)

(c) the word **pezzetti** comes soon after **prosciutto cotto** and **mozzarella**, suggesting cooked ham and mozzarella should be chopped up (**tagliati**, from **tagliare** to cut) into small pieces

(d) parmesan is mentioned twice: **metà del parmigiano** one half of the parmesan and **il resto del parmigiano** the remainder, so it is not added to the mixture in one go.

Note that translations of the words essential to understand the recipe are included in the questions (e.g. **pirofila unta di burro** greased ovenproof dish).

EXERCISE 4

(b) vasetto **(c)** come **(d)** ciliegie **(f)** etti, macinato **(g)** confezione, superiore; **(e)** perfetto, ne, pacchetto

EXERCISE 5

(a) burro **(b)** marmellata di ciliegie **(c)** parmigiano **(d)** biscotti **(e)** pomodori **(f)** spaghetti

EXERCISE 6

(a) ii **(b)** ii **(c)** ii **(d)** i

EXERCISE 7

(a) rossa **(b)** bianche **(c)** nero **(d)** marrone **(e)** verde **(f)** gialli

EXERCISE 8

(m) **(i)** **(a)** **(j)** **(c)** **(n)** **(b)** **(f)** **(k)**

EXERCISE 10

capisco, capisci, capisce, capiamo, capite, capiscono; preferisco, preferisci, preferisce, preferiamo, preferite, preferiscono; spedisco, spedisci, spedisce, spediamo, spedite, spediscono

EXERCISE 11

(a) tostato **(b)** preferito **(c)** pubblicata **(d)** confezionata **(e)** grattuggiato

9 'TWO RETURNS, SECOND CLASS, PLEASE'

WHAT YOU WILL LEARN
- ▶ how to buy railway tickets
- ▶ how to ask for and understand information about train journeys
- ▶ how to say 'one needs …', 'one must …'
- ▶ how to form adverbs from adjectives

BEFORE YOU BEGIN

Languages carry their spoken meanings through distinctive sounds. 'Distinctive' is not the same as 'different'. The two 'l's in 'little' are different; but no English words are distinguished by using one or the other, as they are by using *l*- and -*r* in lot and rot (a distinction perceived by English, but not by Japanese speakers). In Italian the voiced and unvoiced pronunciation of -*z*- (see below) are different but not distinctive. Most Italians use a voiced *z*- to say **zio** (uncle) whereas Tuscans say it with a voiceless initial, but the word remains the same.

POINTS TO REMEMBER FROM UNIT 8
Verbs in -*isco* (**preferire**): **preferisco, preferisci, preferisce, preferiamo, preferite, preferiscono**
Participle as an adjective: **caffè macinato, posti prenotati, la mia musica preferita**
I like … **mi piace il vino bianco; le lasagne mi piacciono; le piace** (formal)/**ti piace** (informal) **la musica classica?**

Pronunciation notes

Like -*s*-, -*z*- has two pronunciations: voiced and unvoiced. They vary considerably according to the education and the regional origin of speakers but do not affect meaning. Reasonably firm guidelines can be given only in the following cases. Double -*z*- is always voiceless (**palazzo** large building, **pezzo** piece, **fazzoletto**

handkerchief) except in **mezzo** -**a** half, and **azzurro** sky blue. Single -*z*- is voiceless in all words ending in -*zione* (**stazione** station, **esagerazione** exaggeration, etc.) and in most other cases; it is voiced at the beginning of words (**zio** uncle, **zucchero** sugar, **zero** nought). You will hear all these words in the recording in Exercise 1.

CONVERSATIONS 1

A traveller buys a one-way ticket

LISTEN FOR...

- **salve** hi
- **andata** one-way

Viaggiatrice	Salve. Un biglietto per Aversa, solo andata.
Impiegato	Per oggi?
Viaggiatrice	Sì grazie.
Impiegato	Quattordicimila quattrocento lire. Sono ventimila. Buongiorno.

- **salve** hi, greetings; a Latin greeting meaning 'may you be in good health!'
- **andata** one-way

sono ventimila the **viaggiatrice** (female traveller) paid with two 10,000 lire notes; the employee says 'that's (lit. they are) 20 thousand' as he hands back 5600 lire in change.

Two travellers buy tickets for Livorno

LISTEN FOR...

- **andata e ritorno** return ticket

Vaggiatore 1	Livorno!
Impiegato	Solo andata?
Viaggiatore 1	Andata e ritorno.
Impiegato	Cento lire le avete, per favore?
Viaggiatore 1	Cento? No.
Viaggiatore 2	Due andata e ritorno Livorno.
Impiegato	Due?
Viaggiatore 2	Sì.

Livorno! You could use a complete sentence, such as **mi dà per favore un biglietto per Livorno**, (give me a ticket for Livorno, please); in fact, many travellers (**viaggiatori**) simply say the name of the station they want to go to.

- **andata e ritorno** return

cento lire le avete? Do you have 100 lire? The ticket cost 100 lire more than a round figure, and the clerk finds it easier to give change if the traveller adds a 100 lire coin to the payment. Note the southern polite form, using the plural **voi** (**avete**) instead of **lei** (**ha**).

due ... Livorno If you want more than one ticket begin your request with the number of persons travelling.

It's simpler to let the booking clerk do all the talking!

	LISTEN FOR...
▶ **valido cinque giorni**	valid for five days

Impiegato	Partenza quando?
Viaggiatrice	Oggi.
Impiegato	Seconda classe?
Viaggiatrice	Sì.
Impiegato	Una persona?
Viaggiatrice	Sì.
Impiegato	Valido cinque giorni. Ordinario. Diciannovemila e duecento.

> ▶ **valido cinque giorni**   valid for five days.
> **ordinario**   normal fare. Other types of tickets are **ridotto** or **biglietto a riduzione** (reduced price, concession) (e.g. for children); **festivo** (issued on Sundays and holidays); **familiare** (for families travelling together); **circolare** (round trip) (i.e. returning through a different route); **chilometrico** (valid for a specified number of kilometres, independently of the number of trips or of travellers).

PRACTICE

1

Practise the pronunciation of words containing **-z-**. Repeat the following sentences after the speakers in your recording. There are two new words: **zafferano**   saffron and **zanzare**   mosquitoes.

a. Questo vestito azzurro costa mezzo milione: è un'esagerazione.
b. Mi dia due mozzarelle, mezzo chilo di zucchero e un po' di zafferano.
c. In questa stanza ci sono troppe zanzare.
d. Zerba è un paesino a poca distanza da Piacenza.

2 Listen to the conversation on your recording between a traveller who wishes to go to Modena and a railway information clerk, and answer the following questions. There is a new phrase: **Me lo puo annotare?** Could you note it down for me?

a. The traveller wishes to arrive (i) before 7 a.m. (ii) on or after 7.30 a.m.
b. He will have to take a berth in a couchette compartment. (i) true (ii) false
c. The train will leave from (i) Roma Termini (ii) Roma Tiburtina.
d. It will leave at (i) half past ten at night (ii) about a quarter to midnight.
e. The latest arrival time he is offered is (i) 4.18 a.m. (ii) 5.42 a.m.

ANSWERS P. 138

3 Select the correct answers to the booking clerk's questions from the phrases below to complete the conversation. As usual, there are more phrases than you will need.

a. Per quando il biglietto?

_____

b. Andata e ritorno?

_____

c. Per quante persone?

_____

d. Che classe?

_____

e. Trentasettemila. Duemila lire le ha?

_____

f. Ecco cinquemila di resto.

_____

i. Alle tre e venti.   ii. Due.   iii. Grazie.   iv. Nessuna.   v. No, solo andata.
vi. Per dopodomani.   vii. Prego.   viii. Seconda.   ix. Sì, certo.

ANSWERS P. 138

▶ *At the information office a woman asks how to get to Susa*

LISTEN FOR...

▶ **cambia a Bussoleno per Susa**   you change at Bussoleno for Susa
▶ **Non si può andare direttamente?**   Can't one go there directly?, Isn't there a through train?

Viaggiatrice	Mi scusi, devo andare a Susa.
Impiegato	Undici e quarantacinque, treno per Modane, binario dodici. Cambia a Bussoleno per Susa.
Viaggiatrice	Mmm … Non si può andare direttamente?
Impiegato	Sì, c'è un treno locale alle dodici e cinquanta.
Viaggiatrice	E che binario?
Impiegato	Binario tredici.
Viaggiatrice	Ah, va bene, binario tredici. Grazie.

Modane   name of a station on the Italian–French border
▶ **cambia a Bussoleno per Susa**   you change at Bussoleno for Susa. If you want to know whether you must change, you can ask **Devo cambiare?** See also the next conversation.
▶ **Non si può andare direttamente?**   Can't one go there directly?; Isn't there a through train?

Giovanni asks the information office clerk how to go to Siena, and whether a surcharge is payable on express trains

LISTEN FOR...

▶ **Ci vuole un supplemento?**   Is a surcharge payable?
▶ **Verso che ora?**   About what time?
▶ **A che ora?**   At what time?
▶ **bisogna cambiare**   one must change
▶ **la coincidenza**   the connection

Giovanni	Vorrei andare a Siena.
Impiegato	Per Siena, verso che ora?
Giovanni	Nel pomeriggio.
Impiegato	Ecco, ci sarebbe un treno alle quattordici e quarantacinque.
Giovanni	A che ora arrivo a Empoli?
Impiegato	A Empoli arriva alle quindici e diciannove.
Giovanni	A Empoli bisogna cambiare: e a che ora ho la coincidenza?
Impiegato	La coincidenza ce l'ha alle quindici e cinquantanove, e a Siena arriva alle diciassette e tredici.
Giovanni	Per viaggiare sui rapidi ci vuole un supplemento?
Impiegato	Per viaggiare sui rapidi ci vuole un supplemento. Ci sono rapidi ordinari dove basta solo il supplemento, e rapidi speciali, dove, oltre al supplemento normale, ci vuole anche la prenotazione del posto.
Giovanni	E questa prenotazione si fa all'atto dell'acquisto del biglietto?
Impiegato	Si fa all'atto dell'acquisto del biglietto. Possibilmente farlo qualche giorno prima.

▶ **Verso che ora?**   About what time? If you want to be precise: **A che ora?** (At what time?); **A che ora parte il treno?** (At what time does the train leave?). **Verso**, indicating a direction in space (**verso sud**   towards the south, **verso casa**   homewards) may also be used to indicate approximate time: **verso le due** (about two o' clock), **verso sera** (towards the evening).

ci sarebbe un treno   lit. there should be a train: of course, the clerk knows that there *is* a train; he merely implies that Giovanni *could* take it. **Sarebbe** is a form of the present conditional of **essere** (Unit 8, *Grammar*, p. 118).

▶ **bisogna cambiare** you/one must change. **Bisognare** (to be necessary) is one of a number of verbs used only in the third person before a verb in the infinitive (see *Grammar*, p. 134). It is equivalent to **si deve**, **è necessario**; e.g. **bisogna partire alle tre** (you/one must leave at three), **bisogna pagare un supplemento** (a surcharge must be paid).

▶ **la coincidenza** the connection. **La coincidenza ce l'ha** (lit. the connection there it you have) is the same as **ci ha la coincidenza** (**ci**, there, at Empoli, becomes **ce** before **la**). The Italian flexible word order allows the object to be placed for emphasis *before* the verb, but the appropriate form of the object pronoun **lo**, **la**, **li**, **le** (Unit 5, p. 70) must be added: **Cento lire le avete? = Avete cento lire?** This is useful to avoid confusion: compare **Maria accompagna Carlo alla stazione** Mary is taking (accompanying) Charles to the station; with **Maria <u>la</u> accompagna Carlo alla stazione** Charles is taking <u>Mary</u> to the station (emphasizing Maria).

rapido fast, through train, a name superseded, to a certain extent, by **Intercity** and **Eurocity**.

▶ **ci vuole un supplemento** a surcharge is payable. Like **bisogna** above, **ci vuole ...**, **ci vogliono ...**, **occorre ...**, **occorrono ...** (Unit 8, p. 108 and **basta ...**, **bastano ...** are used only in the third person: **ci vogliono due ore per andare a Siena** (it takes two hours to go to Siena), **occorre anche prenotare il posto** (one must also book a seat), **basta solo il supplemento** (the surcharge is sufficient). See also *Grammar*, p. 134.

oltre besides

la prenotazione del posto seat reservation; **posti prenotati** (reserved seats)

all'atto dell'acquisto at the time (lit. on the act) of purchase

possibilmente if possible

farlo (one should) do it

qualche giorno prima a few days beforehand. Note that **qualche** has no plural and is always followed by a singular noun: **qualche posto è ancora disponibile** (a few seats are still available).

PRACTICE

4 Listen on your recording to the continuation of the conversation with the passenger who wished to go to Modena and answer the following questions relating to his return journey.

  a. About what time does the man wish to travel from Modena? (i) early morning (ii) afternoon

  b. What is his destination? (i) Bologna (ii) Roma Termini

  c. Is it a through journey? (i) yes (ii) no, he has to change trains

ANSWERS P. 138 **d.** At what time will he reach his destination? (i) 15.48 (ii) 18.55

5 Follow the instructions on your recording to ask for information on how to travel by train from Siena to Milan.

Fill in the gaps in the following conversation. The words you need to fill in the gaps have all been used before, and are hidden in the square below. You will find them by moving from square to square (no jumps) across, down, diagonally from left to right or in a combination of these moves.

a. Vorrei un _____ per Modena.

b. Andata e ritorno?

c. No, solo _____

d. _____ classe?

e. No, _____ Che _____

   prendo?

f. Allora, c'è il _____ Roma–Bologna in _____ alle 12.45

   dal binario _____

g. Devo pagare un _____ ?

h. Sì, e _____ anche _____ posto.

   _____ a Bologna alle 16.05, e ha la

   _____ per Modena alle 16.25.

S	S	E	C	A	R	R	I	A	P	A
R	U	A	D	O	N	D	A	V	A	N
A	U	P	P	I	D	O	E	A	R	D
P	S	G	P	R	I	M	A	T	T	A
I	P	I	T	L	A	N	D	R	E	T
D	O	A	R	T	E	F	O	E	N	A
C	O	I	E	N	O	M	V	O	Z	A
A	O	T	N	C	I	D	E	N	T	O
P	R	E	D	E	V	E	E	N	Z	A
I	N	V	N	O	T	A	R	E	D	S
L	B	I	G	L	I	E	T	T	O	O

ANSWERS P. 138

CONESATIONS 3

 A traveller wishes to change his plans

Viaggiatore	Buongiorno. Senta, io ho un problema, ci ho il Pendolino alle ore diciannove, questa sera, però ho finito i miei lavori prima, ... desidererei prendere un altro treno, magari un rapido, Il Pendolino si può rimborsare? Guardi, qua ho tutti i biglietti.
Impiegata	Sì, infatti, senz'altro.
Viaggiatore	Lei mi potrebbe rimborsare il Pendolino e farmi con quello un supplemento rapido?
Impiegata	Quale rapido vuole prendere? Perché c'è un treno alle undici e quaranta ...
Viaggiatore	E il prossimo rapido a che ora c'è? Per La Spezia?
Impiegata	All'una e quaranta, tredici e quaranta.
Viaggiatore	Allora prendo quello, guardi. Mi faccia per quello.
Impiegata	Allora La Spezia tredici e quaranta, eh? Prima classe, eh? Sempre non fumatori?
Viaggiatore	Sì, è uguale, indifferente.
Impiegata	Ci ha il venti per cento di trattenuta sul rimborso ...
Viaggiatore	Va benissimo, è uguale ... A che ora c'è, scusi, ha detto, alle ... tredici?
Impiegata	Tredici e quaranta, binario diciotto, binario diciotto.
Viaggiatore	Binario diciotto. La ringrazio.
Impiegata	Prego, buongiorno.
Viaggiatore	Buongiorno.

▶ **ho un problema** I've got a problem; **niente problema!** (no problem!). A number of nouns end in *-a* but are masculine and form their plural in *-i*. See *Grammar*, p. 135.

il Pendolino name of a high-speed train

ho finito i miei lavori prima I've finished my work earlier (than I expected). This speaker says **i miei lavori** instead of **il mio lavoro**, probably to hint at the many things he had to do. **Miei** is the plural of **mio**. See the other forms for your(s), her(s), etc., in the *Grammar*, p. 134.

▶ **desidererei prendere un altro treno** I'd like to take another train; **desidererei** is the conditional tense of **desiderare** (to wish).

magari perhaps

▶ **Mi potrebbe rimborsare?** Could you give me a refund? (lit. Me could you reimburse?).

con quello with that (the refund money)

▶ **prossimo** next (from now); next from any other point in time is **seguente** or **successivo**: **c'è un rapido alle 3.20: il seguente/successivo è alle 7.20** (there's an express at 3.20: the next is at 7.20).

mi faccia per quello do me (a ticket) for that one. **Mi faccia** is a polite form of request like **mi dia** (Unit 6, p. 76).

sempre non fumatori? still non-smokers? 'Still' because the ticket seller noticed the non-smoker preference on the tickets she had been handed back for a refund. **è uguale** it's (all) the same, **è indifferente** it does not matter. You can also say: **non importa**.

ci ha il venti per cento di trattenuta sul rimborso there is a deduction of 20% (lit. there you have the 20% of deduction) on your refund.

La ringrazio I thank you, a slightly more emphatic way of saying **grazie**, from **ringraziare** (to thank).

▶ *Two travellers are informed that there may be strike problems*

> ## LISTEN FOR...
>
> | ▶ **c'è uno sciopero** | there is a strike |
> |---|---|
> | ▶ **fino a ...** | until ..., as far as ... |
> | ▶ **lei chiede il rimborso** | you ask for the refund |
> | ▶ **sembra che ...** | it appears that ... |

Viaggiatore 1	Per Reggio Calabria ci abbiamo qualche diretto, qualche rapido?
Impiegato	Abbiamo un problema oggi. C'è uno sciopero nel compartimento di Reggio Calabria. Il treno delle dodici e dieci arriva solo fino a Lamezia. Poi da lì metteranno degli autobus. Io le faccio il biglietto per Reggio Calabria e il supplemento separato. A Lamezia, se questo treno si ferma, Lei chiede il rimborso della differenza tra Lamezia e Reggio Calabria. Sono sessantaseimila lire.
Viaggiatore 1	Partenza ha detto a che ora?
Impiegato	Alle dodici e dieci dal binario dodici.
Viaggiatore 2	Paola, mezzogiorno e dieci, prima.
Impiegato	Ha già il supplemento Lei?
Viaggiatore 2	No, devo fare anche il supplemento.
Impiegato	Sono ottantatremila e quattrocento.
Viaggiatore 2	Ci sono problemi di sciopero?
Impiegato	C'è uno sciopero nel compartimento di Reggio Calabria, ma sembra che il treno lo fanno arrivare fino a Lamezia Terme.
Viaggiatore 2	Grazie.
Impiegato	Buongiorno.

Ci abbiamo qualche diretto ...? Is there (lit. Do we have there) any through train ...? Remember that **qualche** is always followed by a singular noun.

▶ **c'è uno sciopero** there is a strike. **Agitazione sindacale** (something like 'trade-union unrest') is another euphemism for strike (remember, **protesta sindacale** in Unit 6, p. 77).

compartimento one of the administrative districts of the Italian State Railways and not to be confused with **scompartimento** (compartment in a train).

▶ **fino a Lamezia** as far as Lamezia; **fino a ...** refers both to time and space: **fino a domani** (until tomorrow), **fino a qui** (all the way to here), **fino ad ora** (up to now), **fino ai sei anni** (up to six years of age).

da lì metteranno degli autobus from there they will have (lit. put) buses. For the future tense see Unit 10, p. 150.

io le faccio il biglietto I'll issue you with a ticket (lit. I make you the ticket).

▶ **Lei chiede il rimborso** (you) ask for the refund; **rimborsare** (to refund, to reimburse).

la differenza tra the difference between, actually between the Rome–Reggio Calabria and the Rome–Lamezia Terme fares: but what the clerk means is perfectly clear.

Paola, besides being a girl's name, is the name of a town in Calabria.

▶ **sembra che ...** it seems that ...: **sembra che c'è uno sciopero** it seems that there is a strike on, **sembra che non stai bene** you look unwell, **cosa ti sembra?** what do you think?

PRACTICE

7 There are many kinds of railway tickets, of various colours, shapes and sizes: here you have a typical one issued by a computerized ticketing machine. Examine it carefully and see how many of the following questions you can answer.

a. Where was the ticket issued?

b. What was the destination?

c. How many people were travelling?

d. In what class?

ANSWERS P. 138

e. How much did the ticket cost?

8 Listen carefully to the short exchange on your recording and answer the following questions.

a. What is the intending traveller's time of departure?   (i) 17.20   (ii) we are not told

b. What is his destination?   (i) Sant'Eufemia   (ii) Catanzaro   (iii) Crotone

c. How many times will he have to change trains?   (i) once   (ii) twice

d. At what time will he reach his destination?   (i) 20.13   (ii) 20.30   (iii) 21.15

ANSWERS P. 138

9 In this exercise you will be booking tickets, but, unlike previous exercises, you will not be prompted. The correct answer will be on the recording after you have replied. The booking-office clerk will ask you some questions and you will give him the following information:

▶ you're going to Turin

▶ you're going with a friend

▶ you want a return

▶ you want second-class tickets

GRAMMAR AND EXERCISES

My, mine, your(s) etc.

Here is the complete pattern:

	Singular		Plural	
	m	f	m	f
my, mine	mio	mia	miei	mie
your(s)	tuo	tua	tuoi	tue
his/her(s) or your(s) (pol.)	suo	sua	suoi	sue
our(s)	nostro	nostra	nostri	nostre
your(s)	vostro	vostra	vostri	vostre
their(s)	loro	loro	loro	loro

Loro is invariable. Apart from **miei**, **tuoi** and **suoi**, all the other forms follow the usual pattern of four-ending adjectives (see Units 3 and 4, pp. 38 and 54).

Examples: **i miei biglietti** (my tickets), **i tuoi problemi** (your problems), **la sua destinazione** (his/her destination), **il nostro treno** (our train), **le vostre camere** (your rooms), **il loro albergo** (their hotel), **le loro biciclette** (their bicycles), etc.

Third person phrases

The construction of **piacere** (Unit 8, p. 119; **mi piace viaggiare in treno** I like travelling by train; **le piacciono le vacanze al mare** she likes holidays at the seaside) is shared by a number of verbs found only in the third person, singular or plural according to the subject. If a verb follows, it is always in the infinitive.

- **basta** it's enough
- **bisogna** it's necessary
- **occorre** it's necessary
- **ci vuole** it's necessary, it's required

The first three combine with verbs: **basta arrivare prima di sera** (it's enough to arrive before evening), **basta cambiare una volta** (it's enough to change once); **bisogna pagare un supplemento** (it's necessary to pay a surcharge), **bisogna prenotare il**

posto (one must reserve a seat); **occorre pagare un supplemento** (a surcharge is required), **occorre prenotare il posto** (you have to book a seat).

All but **bisogna** combine with nouns or adverbs: **bastano diecimila lire** (10,000 lire is enough), **basta così, grazie** (that's enough, thanks); **occorre un supplemento** (a surcharge is needed), **occorre una prenotazione** (a booking is required), **occorrono tre ore di viaggio** (one needs three hours' travel, three hours are needed); **ci vuole la prenotazione** (a booking is necessary), **ci vogliono tre ore di viaggio** (it – the journey – takes three hours).

Some of these expressions may be used, like **piacere**, with monosyllabic pronouns (**mi, ti, gli/le, ci, vi, si**): **non gli/le basta** it's not enough for him/her; **ci occorre più tempo** we need more time; **Cosa ti ci vuole?** What do you require?

Adverbs

You have already come across several adverbs. They are those invariable words usually linked to adjectives (**molto buono** very good) or verbs (**andare direttament a...** to go directly to...). They belong to two main categories (a few belong to both):
(1) adverbs ending in **-mente**. This ending, having the same function as -ly in English, is added to the feminine (or common) form of the adjective: **certo** ▷ **certamente**, **deciso** ▷ **decisamente**: **arriva certamente domani** he'll/she'll certainly arrive tomorrow, **è decisamente meno caro** it's decidedly less expensive.

Adjectives ending in **-le** or **-re** preceded by a vowel drop their final **-e** before adding **-mente**: **possibile** ▷ **possibilmente**, **singolare** ▷ **singolarmente**: **possibilmente prenotarsi qualche giorno prima** (book a few days early if possible), **è singolarmente dotata** (she is singularly gifted).
(2) adverbs which are, or look like, masculine forms of adjectives ending in **-o**: **molto** (much), **troppo** (too much), **poco** (little), **solo** (only), **certo** (certainly), **piuttosto** (rather), **proprio** (just), etc.

Adjectives may occasionally be used as adverbs (see **quanto** in Unit 6, pp. 86–7) in which case they remain fixed in their **-o** form: **ho bevuto troppo**

I drank too much (as opposed to **ho bevuto troppa birra** I drank too much beer); **parte certo domani** he'll/she'll certainly leave tomorrow (but **la sua partenze è certa** his/her departure is certain).

A few adverbs end in -*i* or -*e*: **quasi** almost, **tard** late, **sempre** always, **bene** well, **male** badly.

Nouns ending in -*a*

Not all nouns ending in -*a* are feminine. Many are masculine, and have a regular masculine plural ending in -*i*, like **il poeta** (the poet), **i poeti**; **il collega** (the colleague), **i colleghi** (not to be confused with **collegio, collegi** college). They include:

(a) some nouns ending in -*ma*, the most common of which are **dramma** (drama), **enigma** (enigma), **pigiama** (pijamas), **poema** (long poem), **problema** (problem), **programma** (programme), (and others ending in -*gramma* like **anagramma, epigramma, telegramma**), **sistema** (system), **tema** (theme), **trauma** (trauma): **i drammi di Shakespeare, i programmi del computer**, etc.

(b) a large number, corresponding to English nouns ending in -*ist*. The singular ending in -*a* is common to both genders, splitting into the two normal endings, -*i* (m) and -*e* (f), in the plural:

	Singular		Plural	
Masculine	-a	**il violinista famoso**	-i	**i violinisti famosi**
Feminine	-a	**la violinista famosa**	-e	**le violiniste famose**

In this group we have already come across **musicista, specialista** and **turista**; and the list could continue with names of musicians (**pianista, arpista, organista**); adherents to political parties or ideologies (**socialista, nazionalista, militarista**); specialists in a particular subject (**italianista, anatomista, economista**); followers of philosophical schools (**idealista, realista, marxista**); and lots of others (**propagandista, finalista, individualista, naturalista**, etc.). Many words in this group are related to abstract nouns in -*ismo* (**idealismo, nazionalismo**) and to adjectives in -*istico* (**idealistico, nazionalistico**). Remember this and you will add, at a stroke, some 250 words to your Italian vocabulary.

10 Complete the following sentences with the appropriate third-person expressions chosen from those in the list below.

a. Nella pasta al forno _____ la besciamella.

   A me la pasta al forno _____ moltissimo.

b. Si può andare da Pisa a Siena senza cambiare ma

   _____ partire la mattina presto.

c. Si può andare da Pisa a Siena senza cambiare:

   _____ partire la mattina presto.

d. I vini italiani _____ molto.

e. Per viaggiare in questo espresso internazionale

   _____ il supplemento e la prenotazione.

f. — Vuole altri indirizzi di alberghi? — No, grazie

   _____ questi.

i	basta	v	mi piacciono
ii	bastano	vi	occorrono
iii	bisogna	vii	piace
iv	ci vuole		

ANSWERS P. 138

11 Fill in the gaps with a suitable adverb formed from the adjectives in the box below.

a. Voglio andare _____ a Siena, senza cambiare.

b. _____ bisogna cambiare a Empoli, ma con questo treno non è necessario.

c. Con questo treno espresso si viaggia più

   _____

d. Il Telegrafo non è un giornale nazionale. Si pubblica

   _____ a Livorno.

e. Il caffè mi piace _____ a colazione.

diretto   locale   ordinario   rapido   speciale

ANSWERS P. 138

KEY WORDS
AND PHRASES

salve	hi
andata	one way
andata e ritorno	return
valido cinque giorni	valid for five days
cambia a Bussoleno per Susa	you change at Bussoleno for Susa
Non si può andare direttamente?	Can't one go there directly?, Isn't there a through train?
Verso che ora …?	About what time …?
A che ora?	At what time?
bisogna cambiare	you need to change
la coincidenza	the connection
ci vuole un supplemento	a surcharge is payable
ho un problema	I've got a problem
desidererei prendere un altro treno	I'd like to take another train
Mi potrebbe rimborsare?	Could you give me a refund?
il prossimo	the next
c'è uno sciopero	there is a strike
lei chiede il rimborso	you ask for the refund
sembra che …	it appears that …

The main tourist centres like Venice, Florence and Rome can become very crowded.

'Two returns, second class, please'   *Unit* 9

DID YOU KNOW?

Where to get information

Before you go to Italy, it's worth consulting a travel agent, but they may not have all the detailed information you need. Locate the address of the nearest ENIT (**Ente Nazionale Italiano del Turismo**, Italian State Tourist Board), which has offices or representatives in London, New York, Chicago, Los Angeles and over 20 other important cities in Europe and the world.

Alternatively, make inquiries about **CIT** (**Compagnia Italiana del Turismo**). Alitalia, the national airline, has representatives and offices in many cities served by an international airport and can provide details of flights and package tours. Italian Consulates and Cultural Institutes in major cities may be useful sources of information on summer courses in Italian language and culture, and educational institutions specializing in other cultural areas (music, art restoration, pottery and other crafts, etc.) and on a number of scholarships granted every year by the Italian Government, through its Ministry for Foreign Affairs, to applicants with a convincing study project in mind.

It is also a good idea to write directly to Italy, where various bodies in every province, co-ordinating accommodation and sightseeing services in their particular area, provide information about staying in the country. They are known as APT (**Azienda di Promozione Turistica**, Tourist Promotion Board), IAT (**Informazioni Accoglienza Turistica**, Tourist Accommodation Information) or AAPIT (**Azienda Autonoma per l'Incremento Turistico**, Autonomous Board for the Development of Tourism). Their location and addresses are available from ENIT. There is a developing 'farm holidays' sector, especially in the regions of Trentino-Alto Adige, Venetia, Toscana and Apulia about which these offices are able to provide information. They will advise you about the opening times of local museums and monuments, dates of pageants, fairs and antique markets, current prices in hotels and boarding houses, even timetables of local bus or boat transport which never seem to find their way to tourist offices and travel agents abroad. You should be able to fax most of these offices or agencies.

In large towns, your hotel will provide you with free weekly handouts detailing the main events (concerts, theatres, cinemas, exhibitions, etc.) Similar information will be displayed on posters and flysheets on street corners, and advertised in the local papers, or in the local edition of the national papers.

When planning to visit Italy, you should seriously consider whether to go for the major tourist centres like Venice, Rome or Florence or go off the beaten track. Some less renowned places (Mantova, Urbino, Orvieto, Todi, Lecce, Agrigento, to name but a few), besides being endowed with marvellous art treasures, are cheaper, less crowded, with less traffic and pollution.

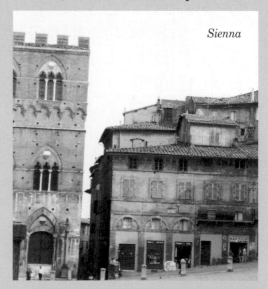

Sienna

AND FINALLY...

12
In this exercise you'll be asking for information on train timetables, connections, etc., for getting from Milan to Salsomaggiore Spa.

ANSWERS

EXERCISE 2
(a) ii **(b)** i **(c)** ii **(d)** ii **(e)** ii

EXERCISE 3
(a) vi **(b)** v **(c)** ii **(d)** viii **(e)** ix **(f)** iii

EXERCISE 4
all ii

EXERCISE 6
.**(a)** biglietto **(c)** andata **(d)** prima (or seconda)
(e) seconda (or prima), treno **(f)** rapido, partenza, tre
(g) supplemento **(h)** deve, prenotare, il, arriva, coincidenza

S	S	E	C	A	R	R	I	A	P	A
R	U	A	D	O	N	D	A	V	A	N
A	U	P	P	I	D	O	E	A	R	D
P	S	G	P	R	I	M	A	T	T	A
I	P	I	T	L	A	N	D	R	E	T
D	O	A	R	T	E	F	O	E	N	A
C	O	I	E	N	O	M	V	O	Z	A
A	O	T	N	C	I	D	E	N	T	O
P	R	E	D	E	V	E	E	N	Z	A
I	N	V	N	O	T	A	R	E	D	S
L	B	I	G	L	I	E	T	T	O	O

EXERCISE 7
(a) Roma Termini **(b)** Bari Centrale **(c)** One **(d)** Second
(e) Lire 37,000

EXERCISE 8
(a) ii: 17.20 is the time the train arrives in
S. Eufemia **(b)** iii **(c)** ii: he will change first at
S. Eufemia then at Catanzaro **(d)** iii

EXERCISE 10
(a) iv, vii **(b)** iii **(c)** i **(d)** v **(e)** vi **(f)** ii

EXERCISE 11
(a) direttamente **(b)** ordinariamente **(c)** rapidamente
(d) localmente **(e)** specialmente

10 'WE HAVE SO MANY SPECIALITIES...'

WHAT YOU WILL LEARN
▶ how to order a meal in a restaurant
▶ the names of the various courses
▶ the way in which they have been prepared

BEFORE YOU BEGIN

Sounds are not consistently represented in writing. The English alphabet uses 26 letters to represent over 40 distinctive sounds. This makes English pronunciation very difficult to learn for Italians who are baffled by words such as cough, bough, though and through. The Italian language, on the other hand, uses 22 letters to represent some 26 distinctive sounds. There are therefore fewer inconsistencies (some have been shown in the pronunciation notes) and on the whole Italian spelling is regular and predictable.

POINTS TO REMEMBER FROM UNIT 9

Verbs used in the third person

bisogna ...	one needs ..., it's necessary ...
basta ...	one needs only ..., it's enough
ci vuole/ci vogliono ...	... is/are required, it takes ...
mi piace/mi piacciono	I like

Adverbs formed from adjectives (English *-ly* = Italian *-mente*)

vero true, **veramente** truly
facile easy, **facilmente** easily

How to book railway tickets:

number of travellers	town	class	single or return
due	**Pisa**	**seconda**	**andata e ritorno**

How many words ending in *-ista* can you remember?

Pronunciation notes

The doubling of consonants is of negligible importance in English: the pronunciation of *-t-* in 'bite' or *-l-* in 'fulfil' is not perceptibly different in 'bitter' and 'fuller'. In Italian, however, various pairs of words are distinguished only by the presence of single or double consonants (e.g. **polo** pole/**pollo** chicken, **fato** fate, destiny/**fatto** fact; **dona** he/she gives, donates/**donna** woman, etc.). To pronounce double consonants correctly you should articulate the consonant for longer if the sound lends itself to this (as in *-m-*, *-n-*, *-l-*), or shorten slightly the preceding vowel if the articulation is brief (as in *-b-*, *-d-*, *-t-*). Some regional varieties of Italian are not sensitive to the difference.

Advice about starters from the inn-keeper of Il Buttero (The Cowboy)

LISTEN FOR...	
▶ **antipasto**	hors d'oeuvres, starters
▶ **un piatto misto**	a mixed plate
▶ **non posso mangiare ...**	I cannot eat ...
▶ **un piatto tipico**	a typical dish
▶ **all'ascolana**	in the Ascoli style

Cini	Che cosa ci consiglia?
Oste	Antipasto, fiori di zucca, olive ascolane, eee, supplì.
Giovanni	Be', ci faccia appunto allora un piatto misto.
Nennella	Anche per me va bene così.
Valerio	Per tutti quanti.
Oste	Va bene.
Marcella	Eee ... no, io non posso mangiare i fritti. Mangerò qualche altra cosa.
Oste	Certo, certo. Va bene.
Aldo	I fiori di zucca sono un piatto tipico romano. Le olive ascolane arrivano da Ascoli, e sono olive ripiene.
Cini	Olive all'ascolana. Sono denocciolate, e ripiene di carne. Tolto il nocciolo e poi impastate e fritte.

oste (m)   inn-keeper (of the same word family as English host, hostel, hotel); **osteria** (inn)

▶ **antipasto**   starters (lit. before the meal). It generally consists of: **piatto misto**   a mixed plate of salami of various kinds, **prosciutto crudo** (Parma ham), **prosciutto cotto** (ham), **sottaceti** pickles (**sotto aceto** = under vinegar), and other **specialità**, such as **fiori di zucca** pumpkin flowers, fried in batter; **olive ascolane** stoned olives with a meat stuffing, also fried in batter; and **supplì** fried rice balls stuffed with mozzarella and ham or other delicacies.

tutti quanti   all of us

▶ **non posso mangiare** ...   I cannot eat ... Marcella finds it difficult to digest **i fritti** fried things (lit. the frieds), from **friggere**, past participle, **fritto**, to fry. Also **frittura di pesce** or **pesce fritto** (fried fish), **patate fritte** (fried potatoes). This is a useful expression you can adapt to suit the things you cannot digest or are unwilling to eat: **non posso mangiare ... cipolle** onions, **aglio** garlic, **frattaglie** offal. **Mangerò** is the future tense of **mangiare** (to eat).

▶ **un piatto tipico**   a typical dish; also **caratteristico**
ripiene di ...   filled with ...

▶ **all'ascolana**   in the Ascoli style. The prepositional article **al**, **alla** is used in a variety of expressions indicating style of preparation: **scaloppine al Marsala** (escaloppes in Marsala sauce); **saltimbocca alla romana** (**salta in bocca** lit. 'jump-in-mouth', a Roman dish made with slices of veal, ham and cheese rolled together and braised in butter); **spaghetti alla carbonara** (spaghetti in the charcoal maker's style, with a sauce made of chopped bacon, raw eggs, butter and cream whisked together and heated for a few moments).

denocciolate   stoned; *de-* indicates (among other things) that something has been removed (as in English declassify, decompress), **nocciolo** is a fruit stone, hence **denocciolare** (to remove the stone).

impastate   in batter (*in-* becomes *im-* before *-p-* and *-b-*: remember **saltimbocca**); **pasta** means also dough, pastry, batter.

▶ *After such a copious antipasto one may well skip the first course ...*

LISTEN FOR...	
▶ **Che cosa ci può offrire di primo?**	What can you offer as a first course?
▶ **sarei tentato da ...**	I'd be tempted by ...
▶ **salterò il primo**	I'll skip the first (course)

Valerio	Che cosa ci può offrire di primo?
Oste	Rigatoni alla buttero.
Valerio	Come sono fatti?
Oste	Con pancetta affumicata, crema di latte, burro, parmigiano.
Aldo	Sì?
Oste	Tonnarelli coi carciofi, spaghetti alle vongole.
Valerio	Bene. Cosa prendi tu, Aldo?
Aldo	Tonnarelli coi carciofi. Sarei tentato dal buttero, ma non posso mangiarlo.
Giovanni	Io penso che salterò il primo.
Nennella	Ma perché, c'è ancora un primo? E questo era soltanto antipasto? Ah, anch'io salterò il primo allora.

▶ **Che cosa ci può offrire di primo?**   What can you offer as a first course? The word for 'course', omitted here, is **piatto**, which also means dish and plate: **primo piatto** (first course, pasta, soup); **secondo piatto** (main, second course).

rigatoni   a type of fluted tube pasta; **alla buttero**, short for **alla maniera del buttero** (in the manner of the cowboy, cowboy style) from the name of the restaurant.

pancetta   the Italian variety of bacon, taken from the pig's belly (**pancia**)

affumicata participle of **affumicare**, to cure food with **fumo** (smoke).

crema di latte (also **panna**) cream (but **crema** = custard)

tonnarelli coi carciofi (egg pasta like spaghetti but square) with artichoke sauce. **Coi** is a combination of **con + i**. Combinations of **con** with other articles (Unit 4, p. 54) are avoided in writing because they would look the same as **collo** neck, **colla** glue, **cogli** you pick.

spaghetti alle vongole   spaghetti with mussels cooked in tomato sauce

▶ **sarei tentato da …**   I'd be tempted by …, **tentare** (to tempt). For instance, **sarei tentato** (or **tentata** if you are a woman) **dalla pasta**, **tentazione** (temptation). **Dal buttero** is shortened for **dai rigatoni alla buttero**.

▶ **salterò il primo**   I'll skip the first (course), **saltare** (to jump, to skip). Note that you can express your wishes both in the present and in the future tense: **prendo/prenderò un sorbetto al limone**   I'll have a lemon sorbet

Ma perché, c'è ancora un primo?   Why, is there still a first course (to come)?

PRACTICE

1 This is a pronunciation exercise on double consonants. Read and repeat the following sentences after the speakers on your recording.

a. Ci faccia un piatto di fiori di zucca fritti, non troppo salati.
b. Poi per me, degli spaghetti alla buttero, con burro e pancetta affumicata.
c. Io prendo tortellini alla panna.
d. Per zia Nennella, dei tonnarelli coi broccoli.
e. Poi scaloppine al Marsala con patate fritte per tutti.

2 The head-waiter of Ristorante Il Balanzone in Milan is describing yet another mouthwatering list of first courses. Tick the statements opposite which you think are true. Before you start, study this list of new words. Do not merely look at them but read them aloud, bearing in mind what you have read earlier about the regularity and predictability of Italian spelling. Listen to the recording with a 'sound picture' of these words in your mind.

fegatini   chicken livers (**fegato** = liver)
fondo dei carciofi   (lit. bottom of the artichokes) artichoke hearts
frutti di mare   (lit. fruits of the sea) shellfish
gnocchi   small flour and mashed potato dumplings, served like pasta; pureed spinach may be added to the dough, turning them **verdi** (green).
in bianco   (lit. in white) plain, without sauce
risotto   risotto (from **riso**, rice), rice cooked in meat or fish stock with various seasonings and ingredients
saltato -a (from **saltare**)   stir-fried, sauté (the participle of French **sauter** = **saltare** to jump)
tortelloni   large ravioli, **raviolini** (small ravioli), **maccheroncini** (small macaroni)

a You can have green gnocchi (i) with tomato sauce and parmesan (ii) with meat sauce.

b. The tortelloni di zucca are served with butter. (i) true (ii) false

c. The raviolini are (i) factory made (ii) home made.

d. Maccheroncini alla carciofara are so called (i) because they used to be the favourite food of artichoke growers (ii) because they are stir-fried with artichoke hearts.

e. Maçcheroncini all'amatriciana are served with bacon and (i) cream (ii) tomato.

f. What type of risotto is served with vegetables (**verdura**)? (i) alla paesana (ii) alla parmigiana

ANSWERS P. 154

3 Do you like or dislike the dishes listed below? The symbol next to their name will tell you what to write. Remember, you use **mi piace** if what appeals to you is singular, and **mi piacciono** if it is plural.

a. I maccheroni all'amatriciana _____

b. Il risotto alla paesana _____

c. Le vongole _____

d. La zucca _____

ANSWERS P. 154 **e.** Le fritture _____

CONVERSATIONS 2

▶ **The party dining at Il Buttero are ready to order main courses**

LISTEN FOR...

▶ **Come lo/la fa?**	How do you prepare it?
Come lo/la cucina?	How do you cook it?
▶ **io niente secondo**	no second/main course for me
▶ **Come contorni che cosa ci dà?**	What have you got for vegetables?
▶ **nessuno**	no one

Giovanni	Io prendo una trippa.
Oste	Sì.
Giovanni	Come la fa, come la cucina la trippa, lei?
Oste	Con sedano, carota, cipolla.
Giovanni	Sì. Ah ecco. Allora prendo una porzione di trippa.
Aldo	Io niente secondo.
Cini	Io prendo delle scaloppine al limone. Grazie.
Oste	Bene, bene.
Aldo	Un'insalata mista, per favore.
Oste	Sì.
Nennella	Anche a me, per favore.
Giovanni	E come contorni che cosa ci dà?
Oste	Carciofi alla romana. Ci sono anche delle puntarelle, un po' amare.
Giovanni	Eh, magari delle … delle puntarelle, allora. Eh? Un po' di carciofi. Chi è che prende carciofi? Nessuno? Allora ci porti delle scaloppine con un po' di puntarelle …

> **una trippa** short for **una porzione di trippa** (a portion of tripe)

▶ **Come la fa?**, **Come la cucina?**   How do you prepare it?, How do you cook it? **La** refers to **trippa**. If the question had been about **carciofi**, it would have been **Come li fa/cucina?**; if about **pollo**, **Come lo fa/cucina?**

> **sedano**   celery; **carota**   carrot; **cipolla**   onion

▶ **io niente secondo**   no second/main course for me (lit. I nothing second). Remember, **niente uova**   no eggs (Unit 4, p. 51), **niente cipolle per me**   no onions for me.

> **insalata mista**   mixed salad

▶ **Come contorni che cosa ci dà?**   What have you got for vegetables? (lit. As surround what thing you give us?). **Contorno** is usually placed on the dish 'around' the meat course and it can be translated as 'vegetables' since that is normally what it is.

> **puntarelle un po' amare**   slightly bitter greens. More about vegetables below.

▶ **nessuno**   no one. See *Grammar*, p. 151.

Next an unusual meat course

LISTEN FOR...

▶ **va condita**   should be dressed
▶ **ai ferri**   grilled

Giovanni	Poi come secondo il … che cos'è il *carpaccio*?
Cameriere	*Carpaccio*. Sì, è un … piatto di carne cruda tagliata sottile. Carne magrissima dev'essere. Possibilmente filetto.
Giovanni	Ah ecco.
Cameriere	Possibilmente. Poi va condita con olio e limone, e pepe, e sopra uno strato di … grana. Sfogliettine di grana, capito?
Giovanni	Ah, di formaggio parmigiano …
Cameriere	Formaggio parmigiano. E poi — euh — ci son delle trotelle da fare ai ferri. Poi c'è la *paillarde*, la costata, la cotoletta, il nodino …
Giovanni	Cos'è la *paillarde*?
Cameriere	La *paillarde* è una bistecca di carne bianca. Dovrebbe essere di vitello, ma molti imbroglioni ci danno anche quella di maiale, perché è più bianca e più saporita. Ah ah! Capito?

carpaccio   tradition has it that this dish of thinly sliced raw fillet (a variation on steak tartare) was first served at a dinner in Venice during the celebrations for the 500th anniversary of the birth of the painter, Vittore Carpaccio (1460? –1525).

carne   translates both as meat and flesh. The same word tends to be used for both the live animal and its meat: **vitello** calf, veal; **manzo** bullock, beef; **maiale** or **porco** pig, pork; **pollo** or **gallina** hen, chicken.

cruda   raw. The opposite of **crudo** is **cotto -a**. If you want your steak well done, ask for **una bistecca ben cotta**; otherwise **poca cotta**. **Bistecca** is an Italinization of beefsteak.

tagliata sottile   thinly sliced (from **tagliare**, to slice, to cut). Note **sottile** instead of **sottilmente**: adjectives may occasionally be used as adverbs; e.g. **il treno corre veloce** the train runs fast (see Unit 9, p. 135).

magrissima   very lean. **Magro**, thin, lean, applies both to steak and to living beings. To slim is **dimagrire**: **sono a dieta perché voglio dimagrire** (I'm on a diet because I want to slim).

filetto   fillet steak

▶ **va condita con olio e limone e pepe**   it should be dressed with (olive) oil and lemon (juice) and pepper: **condire**, to season, to dress (compare with English 'condiment'). A form of **andare** followed by a past participle is a common equivalent of 'must' or 'should': **la pasta va bollita per dieci minuti** (pasta should be boiled for 10 minutes); **il prosciutto va tagliato sottile** (ham must be sliced thinly).

uno strato di grana   a layer of grana (a cheese similar to parmesan)

sfogliettine   small flakes

trotelle   nice little trouts (**trota** + **-ella**); e.g. **gallina** (chicken), **gallinella** (small chicken)

▶ **ai ferri**   grilled (lit. on the irons), also **alla griglia**. The other basic ways of preparing food are: **al forno** baked; **al vapore** steamed (**vapore** steam); **arrosto** roast(ed); **bollito -a** or **lesso -a** boiled; **fritto -a** fried; **saltato -a** stir-fried; **in umido** (lit. in damp) stewed.

paillarde   veal cutlet. Even in Italy some cookery terms are of French origin, or translated from French, like **saltato** (sauté).

costata   rib; **cotoletta** (cutlet); **nodino** (veal loin rolled with fillet)

molti imbroglioni, etc. many crooks also give you pork (lit. that of pork);

   Imbrogliare to deceive. **Ci** 'us' is frequently used in northern Italy to mean 'you'.

saporita   tasty; from **sapore** (m) taste, flavour

capito?   lit. understood, but an equivalent English filler would be 'right?'

PRACTICE

4

Listen to the couple ordering a meal. When you have fully understood what they are saying, answer the following questions:

a. What does the woman choose as a first course? (i) carpaccio (ii) she skips the first course

b. Does she like parmesan? (i) yes (ii) no

c. What does she choose as contorno? (i) carrots (ii) puntarelle

d. How does the man want his gnocchi? (i) with cream sauce (ii) with tomato sauce

e. How does he want his steak? (i) rare (ii) well done

f. What does he choose as contorno? (i) fried potatoes (ii) roast potatoes and green salad

g. What do they drink? (i) white wine and still mineral water (ii) red wine and fizzy mineral water.

ANSWERS P. 154

5

Decide which type of preparation is appropriate to which dish. Some preparations are utterly inappropriate! Write the roman numeral next to the letter you think it matches.

a.   olive ascolane

b.   trote

c.   supplì

d.   spaghetti alla carbonara

e.   carpaccio

f.   risotto alla finanziera

g.   insalata mista

i   a mixture of various greens, tomatoes, chopped onions, capsicum strips, etc., with oil, salt and vinegar dressing

ii   baked in a honey, garlic and caper sauce

iii   dressed with oil, lemon juice and shredded parmesan

iv   fried rice balls stuffed with meat and cheese

v   grilled

vi   seasoned with runny scrambled egg, chopped smoked bacon and cheese

vii   stoned, stuffed with meat and fried in batter

viii   stuffed with anchovies, marinated in white wine and sautéed

ix   with chicken livers

ANSWERS P. 154

6

Order a meal in a restaurant, following the prompts on your recording.

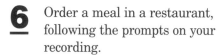

Some more vegetables

Cameriere	Di verdura cotta abbiamo degli spinaci e dei rapini.
Giovanni	Mi fa un misto, spinaci e rapini.
Cameriere	Sì.
Giovanni	Benissimo.
Cameriere	Li vuole già saltati o da condire?
Giovanni	No, da condire.
Cameriere	Con un po' di limone?
Giovanni	Con un po' di olio e limone, sì.
Cameriere	Va be', grazie.

▶ **verdura** vegetables. The word is clearly connected with **verde** (green) and is therefore appropriate to **insalata** (salad), **lattuga** (lettuce), **spinaci** (spinach), **verza** (cabbage) and **rapini** (turnip tops), which are green. It is often used to include non-green vegetables, such as **peperoni** (peppers or capsicums), **carote** (carrots), **cavolfiore** (cauliflower), etc. There is also the word **vegetale**, but it is used to distinguish what grows in the soil from animals (**animali**) and minerals (**minerali**), never in the sense of **verdura**. Other collective nouns for vegetables are: **legumi** pulses (**fagioli** beans, **fave** broad beans, **lenticchi** lentils, **piselli** peas), **cereali** cereals (**grano** wheat, **granturco** corn, **orzo** barley), **tuberi** root vegetables.

▶ **mi fa un misto di ...** will you give me a mixture of ... **Insalata mista** often includes **pomodori, cipolle, peperoni, cuori di sedano** (celery hearts), **finocchio** (fennel), and various kinds of leaf vegetables like **radicchio, rucola** (rocket), **indivia** (endive), which began to find their way into Northern European shops only in recent years.

▶ **da condire** to be dressed. For the uses of **da**, see *Grammar*, p. 150.

va be' = va bene

LISTEN FOR...

▶ **Che cosa ordiniamo?**   What shall we order?

Cameriere	Di dolci abbiamo torta di mandorla, di ricotta e di cioccolato. Anche del gelato, non so, un tiramisù. Tartufo bianco, tartufo nero, una mousse al caffé, al cioccolato, sorbetto al limone, all'arancio, ananas, cocco.
Giovanni	Allora, che cosa ordiniamo …
Aldo	Un sorbetto al limone. Grazie.
Cini	Due!
Cameriere	Per lei un tiramisù?
Giovanni	Un tiramisù. Un altro tiramisù. Allora due tiramisù. E anch'io prenderò un sorbetto al limone.
Cameriere	Tre sorbetti al limone e due tiramisù?
Zia Nennella	Tiramisù, per favore.
Giovanni	Allora, tre sorbetti al limone e tre tiramisù.

Dolci   lit. sweets, is a general term including cakes, pastries, ice creams and all sorts of sweet desserts. **Torta** embraces tarts, cakes and pies and is usually followed by the preposition **di** (**torta di mandorla**   almond cake) when that ingredient is present in substantial quantities; **a** + the appropriate article (**torta al caffè**   coffee cake) when the ingredient is used as flavouring. There would be more chocolate in a **torta di cioccolato** than in a **torta al cioccolato**. Hot sweet pies or puddings are unusual in Italian cookery: the exception is **zabaglione** (m) a thick egg-flip. Crèmes, mousses, jellies and blancmanges belong to the category **budino**, a word related to pudding, but excluding savoury puddings which tend to be called **pasticcio** or **sformato**. **Gelato** is ice cream (the participle of **gelare**, to freeze). **Sorbetto**   sorbet is mostly frozen fruit juice and pulp with sugar, often served in the original fruit peel (**ananas**   pineapple; **cocco** coconut). **Tartufo** (lit. truffle) is a liqueur ice cream enveloped in a chocolate crust. **Tiramisù** (lit. pick me up) is a richer version of **zuppa inglese** (lit. English soup), the Italian name for trifle. Faced with this bewildering choice of sweet courses, the question

▶ **Che cosa ordiniamo**?   What shall we order? is wholly appropriate.

PRACTICE

7 Listen to Zia Nennella explaining how she used to make **zuppa inglese** and tick what you believe is the correct answer to the following questions. You will need a new word: **pan di Spagna** (lit. Spanish bread), a sort of sponge.

a. To obtain the desired effect the ingredients are   (i) layered   (ii) thoroughly mixed.

b. The custard is made with   (i) cornflour or custard powder   (ii) eggs, milk and sugar.

c. Which other ingredients does Zia Nennella add?   (i) chocolate   (ii) rum (iii) bananas

d. Zuppa inglese is best   (i) eaten immediately   (ii) left several hours to develop its full flavour.

ANSWERS P. 154

8 The head waiter of Il Balanzone describes the sweet courses available. Tick off in the following annotated list the TWO that are NOT available.

a. **Crème caramel**, also called **latte alla portoghese** (Portuguese-style milk)

b. **Crostata di ricotta e frutta candita**: a tart (usually latticed) made with a shortcrust pastry base; **ricotta** (lit. re-cooked) is a sort of curd cheese; **frutta candita** is crystallized fruit.

c. **Gelati alla vaniglia, al pistacchio e alla fragola, con panna**: vanilla, pistachio and strawberry dairy-based ice cream, with cream.

d. **Sfogliata alla crema**: a puff pastry cake with egg custard

e. **Torta di cioccolato e noci**: a chocolate and walnut cake

f. **Torta di mele**: apple tart

g. **Zuppa inglese** the Italian name for trifle

9 The two sweets Balanzone did NOT have are available in the restaurant you are dining in now, and you can't make up your mind which one to choose. Complete the following by filling in the missing words.

a. — Che cosa _____come dolce?

b. — Vorrei un _____; un misto di _____, pistacchio e

_____

c. — Con panna?

d. — No _____panna.

e. — Subito.

f. — Scusi, posso cambiare? Invece del _____prendo una

ANSWERS P. 154   _____alla _____

Unit 10   'We have so many specialities …'   149

GRAMMAR AND EXERCISES

Future tense

To form the future tense you take away (as in the conditional, Unit 8, p. 118) the final -*e* of the infinitive (for -*are* verbs, you change -*ar*- to -*er*-), and add the endings shown below, which are the same for all classes of verbs.

Note the stress, and the written accent, on the 1st and 3rd person singular in the table below.

The -*i*- in the infinitive of **mangiare** is there only to show the 'soft' pronunciation of -*g*- before -*a*-. It disappears, therefore, before -*e*-, where it is not required. See Pronunciation notes, Unit 3, p. 29.

The verbs forming their conditional from a shortened stem do so also in the future tense: **andare** (to go) **andrò**; **avere** (to have) **avrò**; **dovere** (must, ought to) **dovrò**; **essere** (to be) **sarò**; **potere** (can, be able to) **potrò**; **rimanere** (to remain) **rimarrò**; **vedere** (to see) **vedrò**; **venire** (to come) **verrò**; **volere** (to want) **vorrò**.

As in English you can use both the present and the future tense to point to a future time. The future tends to express greater deliberation, or a time ahead of some other time expressed in the present, e.g. **oggi mangio carne ma domani mangerò soltanto verdura** today I'll eat meat, but tomorrow I'll eat only vegetables.

Prepositions

Prepositions, first noted in Unit 4, p. 54, in their various combinations with articles, are best treated as links without a specific translation. **Da**, for instance, has various uses in Italian (all except the first one featured in the previous units) which do not correspond to a single English word, or to any word at all:

da + noun

▶ place: **da Luigi** at/to Luigi's place; **i francobolli si comprano dal tabaccaio** stamps can be bought at the tobacconist's; **vado dal dottore** I'm going to the doctor (only with a named person or a noun indicating a person).

▶ origin in space: **vengo dagli Stati Uniti** I come from the United States.

▶ origin in time: **non la vedo dall'ottobre scorso** I haven't seen her since last October.

▶ quantity or rating: **scompartimento da sei posti** six-berth compartment; **confezione da 250 grammi** 250 gram packet; **motore da 3500 cc** 3½ litre engine.

▶ purpose: **carta da lettere** writing paper; **cane da guardia** watchdog; **pasta da minestrone** pasta for minestrone.

▶ agent: **dolci preparati dal Balanzone** cakes prepared by Balanzone (see also Unit 12, p. 182).

Da + infinitive also expresses a purpose or task to be accomplished: **piatto da fare** a dish to be prepared, not on the menu; **mele da cuocere** cooking apples; **verdura da condire** vegetables to be dressed.

	avere	essere	mangiare	prendere	condire
I	av**rò**	sa**rò**	man**gerò**	pren**derò**	con**dirò**
you	av**rai**	sa**rai**	man**gerai**	pren**derai**	con**dirai**
he/she/it, you (polite)	av**rà**	sa**rà**	man**gerà**	pren**derà**	con**dirà**
we	av**remo**	sa**remo**	man**geremo**	pren**deremo**	con**diremo**
you (pl)	av**rete**	sa**rete**	man**gerete**	pren**derete**	con**direte**
they	av**ranno**	sa**ranno**	man**geranno**	pren**deranno**	con**diranno**

Qualche, qualcuno, niente, nessuno

Qualche some, any, a few, is always followed by a singular noun even when the English translation is plural: **solo qualche parola** only a few words; **qualche persona** some people; **Hai qualche mela?** Got any apples? The noun must refer to something that can be counted, otherwise you use **del, dello, della**: **compra del riso, dello zucchero e della panna, per favore** buy some rice, sugar and cream, please.

qualcuno somebody, anybody, is not used before a noun and stands alone as a pronoun: **qualcuno mi dice che ...** somebody tells me that ...; **C'è qualcuno?** Is anybody there?

niente no, nothing, can be followed by a noun or stand alone: **niente pane** no bread; **non costa niente** it costs nothing.

nessuno no, nobody, no one, none, as an adjective inflects like the indefinite article **un, uno, una**: **nessun ristorante** no restaurant, **nessuno studente** no student(s), **nessuna camera** no room(s). As a pronoun: **non c'è nessuno** nobody is there; **non vedo nessuno** I don't see anybody; **non vedo nessuno** I see no one; **nessuno dei miei amici** none of my friends.
None of these words has a plural form.

10 Complete the following phrases inserting the appropriate form of the future tense of the verb between square brackets. The context should tell you which form of the verb to choose.

a. A pranzo prendo un piatto di carne. Questa sera invece [mangiare] _____ verdura.

b. Non so se prendiamo il treno delle sette o delle otto. Ma so che [ritornare] _____ con quello di mezzanotte.

c. Oggi i turisti di questo gruppo cenano in una trattoria tipica. A Trieste, domani sera, [cenare] _____ in un ristorante di prima categoria.

d. Non le consiglio frittura di pesce questa sera. Domani invece ci [essere] _____ pesce fresco.

e. Zia Nennella non ha molta fame. Pensa che [saltare] _____ il primo.

11 Fill in the gaps with the appropriate preposition (**a, con, da, di, in, per**), combined if necessary with the appropriate article. All the phrases below have been used in some form in this unit. Remind yourself by looking back at them.

a. Ci sono delle puntarelle _____ condire. Come le vuole, _____ olio o _____ limone?

b. C'è dell'ottimo manzo _____ umido. Sarei proprio tentato _____ questo piatto.

c. Io prendo _____ tonnarelli _____ carciofi, e la signora tortellini _____ panna.

d. Preferisco la crostata _____ ricotta _____ torta _____ mele.

e. Ci porti del tiramisù e del caffè espresso _____ tutti quanti.

12 Write the opposite of each sentence below, beginning with **Io invece**, on the contrary.
Model: — **Prendo qualche dolce.** — **Io invece non prendo nessun dolce.**

a. Questa sera mangerò qualche cosa.

_____

b. Non vedo nessuno del nostro gruppo in questo ristorante.

_____

c. Ho qualche problema.

_____

d. Domani non voglio visitare nessun museo.

_____

e. Cameriere, per me del tiramisù, per piacere.

_____

ANSWERS P. 154

KEY WORDS
AND PHRASES

Che cosa ordiniamo ?	What shall we order?
Che cosa ci può offrire di …?	What can you offer as …?
antipasto	hors d'oeuvre, appetisers
primo	first course
Come … che cosa ci dà?	What have you got for …?
contorni	vegetables
dolce	sweet course
verdura	(green) vegetables
sarei tentato da …	I'd be tempted by …
salterò il primo	I'll skip the first (course)
io niente secondo	no second/main course for me
non posso mangiare …	I cannot eat …
Come lo/la fa?, Come lo/la cucina?	How do you prepare it?, How do you cook it?
ai ferri	grilled
arrosto	roast(ed)
al vapore	steamed
in umido	stewed
fritto -a	fried
lesso -a	boiled
un piatto tipico	a typical dish
un piatto misto	a mixed plate
mi fa un misto di …	prepare/make for me a mixed plate of …
all'ascolana	in the Ascoli style
una porzione	a portion
nessuno	no one
da condire	to be dressed
va condita	should be dressed

DID YOU KNOW?

Italian Restaurants

You may still find the word **Ristoratore** over the doors of a few railway restaurants, but the most common name is **Ristorante**. Italian **ristoranti** range from the sublime to the average: on the whole it is difficult to blunder into one which is irredeemably bad. Italians are very food-conscious, and standards of preparation are correspondingly high. That also applies to fast food, which can be had from places called **Self Service**, **Snack Bar**, or **Tavola calda** (Hot Table), where chefs miraculously manage to keep large quantities of pasta constantly on the ready in steaming trays — without overcooking it. Sandwiches and all sort of savouries may be had in sandwich bars called **Paninoteca**, a word coined by adding to **panino** (stuffed) bread roll the suffix **-teca** of **biblioteca** (library). Pizza houses, called **pizzeria**, are ubiquitous.

The best reasonably priced food can often be eaten in unpretentious simple establishments, called **Trattoria** or **Osteria**, bearing the name of the chef-owner, e.g. **Da Luigi**, or, occasionally, no sign at all. Their degree of success in pleasing customers may be judged by the number of locals eating there. In these restaurants you may find the owner and his/her family actively involved in cooking and serving the food. **Trattoria** and **Osteria** are names also used by luxury restaurants disguised as country inns: approach cautiously anything sporting the quaint spelling **Hostaria** as you would of something called **Ye Olde Countrie Inne**. Hotel restaurants tend to be more standardized and anonymous, but you may still be pleasantly surprised, and enjoy memorable meals, especially in small country hotels.

Italian waiters often know quite a lot about cooking and are able to give reliable advice: they will sometimes talk you out of a particular choice if they think that one of the **piatti del giorno** (today's specials, lit. dishes of the day) will be equally or more appreciated for whatever reason (quicker service, absence of the cook specializing in what you ordered, better quality of the suggested alternative). Should you want your dish without its particular sauce, or your vegetables prepared differently, variations from the published menu are readily granted. If you can't attract a waiter's attention with the usual '**Senta!**' or '**Scusi!**' you may call out '**cameriere!**' Waitresses are addressed as **signorina** or **signora**, according to their apparent age. At the end of your meal ask for **il conto** (the bill) and check it. Not only for possible mistakes but also to find out whether the service charge (**servizio**) is included or left to your discretion (say 12%). Most bills include a fixed charge (**coperto**) for bread and additional condiments, like olive oil and parmesan cheese.

And so, **buon appetito!** as Italians wish each other before beginning their meals.

AND FINALLY...

13

Practise ordering a meal in Italian. Occasionally you will not be told exactly what to order, but will be given a general prompt (e.g. to order the meat course, or the second choice), so pay attention to what the waitress is telling you.

ANSWERS

EXERCISE 2

(a) i (b) i (c) ii (d) ii (e) ii (f) i

EXERCISE 3

(a) mi piacciono (b) non mi piace (c) mi piacciono
(d) mi piace (e) non mi piacciono

EXERCISE 4

(a) ii (b) ii (c) ii (d) i (e) i (f) ii (g) ii

EXERCISE 5

(a) vii (b) v (c) iv (d) vi (e) iii (f) ix (g) i

EXERCISE 7

(a) i (b) ii (c) ii and iii (d) ii

EXERCISE 8

(c) and (d)

EXERCISE 9

(a) prende (b) gelato, vaniglia, fragola (d) senza
(f) gelato, sfogliata, crema

EXERCISE 10

(a) mangerò (b) ritorneremo (c) ceneranno (d) sarà
(e) salterà

EXERCISE 11

(a) da, coll', col (b) in, da (c) dei, coi, alla (d) di, alla, di
(e) per

EXERCISE 12

(a) Io invece non mangerò niente. (b) Io invece vedo
qualcuno. (c) Io invece non ho nessun problema.
(d) Io invece voglio visitare qualche museo.
(e) Io invece niente tiramisù.

'We have so many specialities ...' *Unit* 10

11 'WHAT DO YOU PREFER?'

WHAT YOU WILL LEARN
- ▶ how to order wine
- ▶ more about food, tastes and flavours
- ▶ more about preferences, likes and dislikes
- ▶ how to talk about things in the past

BEFORE YOU BEGIN

To learn a new language effectively you have to start thinking in that language. You may have in mind an English translation of what you want to say in Italian, but what you say must have an Italian meaning. It won't, if you simply turn English into Italian words. Translation is not transposition (**attualmente** transposes as 'actually' but its translation is 'at present'); and meaning is not translation (**frutti di mare** translates as 'shellfish' but it means 'fruits of the sea'). Even when words have obviously parallel meanings in both languages, the real things they name may be totally different: a cup of coffee is totally unlike **una tazza di caffè** in size, quality and flavour.

PRODUCT OF ITALY

CHIANTI

DENOMINAZIONE DI ORIGINE CONTROLLATA E GARANTITA

1995

NON DISPERDERE IL VETRO NELL'AMBIENTE

150 d e   Imbottigliato da V.I.I.PA. s.r.l.   **PAGNI** Castelnuovo Berardenga - Italia 11,5% vol.

POINTS TO REMEMBER FROM UNIT 10
The structure of an Italian menu:
antipasto misto: prosciutto, salame, olive, sottaceti, altre specialità
primo piatto: pasta asciutta, risotto, minestre varie (choice of soups)
secondo piatto: carne o pesce con contorno di verdure cotte o insalata
dessert: dolci o formaggi; frutta
bevande: vino, acqua minerale, caffè

The future tense: **prenderò, prenderai, prenderà, prenderemo, prenderete, prenderanno**

Nessuno, niente: non c'è nessuno, non capisco niente, niente aglio per me
Qualcuno, qualche: qualcuno mi chiama, vedo qualche membro del nostro gruppo

---

Pronunciation notes

The letter *-u-*, particularly when preceded or followed by *-i-*, causes some confusion in the English-speaking world. The name **Giulio** and the word **prosciutto** can often be seen wrongly spelled as '**Guilio**' and '**proscuitto**'. The confusion arises from the fact that *-u-* in English is often pronounced as two sounds (*-iu-*) as in 'unique' and 'confuse', in Italian it represents only one sound, similar to *-oo-* in boo, root and moon: **unico, confuso**. If the sound *-i-* is combined with *-u-*, then it appears in the spelling: **tranquillo** quiet, **aiuto** help.

▶ A choice of wines

LISTEN FOR...	
▶ **tipo il Trebbiano**	such as Trebbiano
▶ **secco**	dry
▶ **amabile**	medium-dry
▶ **vini sfusi della casa**	house wines

Giovanni	Come vini, avete …
Cameriere	Vini del Piemonte, della Toscana, dell'Emilia, tipo il Trebbiano, il Sangiovese, il Lambrusco secco e il Lambrusco amabile. Euh … poi ci sono tutti gli altri vini. Dei vini bianchi, tipo il pinot grigio, tipo Verdicchio, tipo Soave. Il Soave è buono, secco, *molto* buono. E poi ci sono i vini sfusi della casa.
Giovanni	Vini sfusi. In caraffa …
Cameriere	… in caraffa. Quartino, mezzo litro e un litro.

Piemonte, **Toscana**, **Emilia** are wine-growing regions of Italy.

▶ **tipo il Trebbiano** like Trebbiano. In this idiom the noun **tipo** is used to introduce a type or kind with some characteristic in common: **Trebbiano**, **Sangiovese** and **Lambrusco** are all wines from Emilia. You could translate it as 'like', or 'for instance'.

▶ **secco** dry

▶ **amabile** medium-dry (lit. lovable); also **abboccato**

▶ **vini sfusi della casa** house wines; **sfuso** applies to anything sold unpacked, from dried peas out of a sack, to wine out of a cask. **Un quartino** (a quarter-litre carafe) contains two large glasses. House wines can be very good and are normally much less expensive than bottled wines (**vini in bottiglia**).

▶ *A good wine and a good cheese complement one another*

LISTEN FOR...

▶ **la mozzarella che ti consiglio**	the mozzarella I advise you (to have)
▶ **Che cosa ci ha portato?**	What have you brought us?
▶ **frizzantino**	slightly fizzy

Aldo   La mozzarella che ti consiglio è quella di bufala. E`un pochino più saporita e più buona di quella di fior di latte.

Giovanni   Che cosa ci ha portato? Questi …

Oste   Quello è un formaggio casareccio che portiamo dall'alto Lazio. È molto buono, misto di mucca e di pecora. Potete provare. Le piace? Prego.

Aldo   Il vino è un vino frizzantino, bianco, del Lazio, ben fresco, perché così si può assaporare bene. Serve come aperitivo e anche per accompagnare formaggi e carni bianche, o pesce.

- ▶ **la mozzarella che ti consiglio**   the mozzarella I advise you (to have) (lit. which I advise you); pay attention to the use of **che** meaning which or who (see *Grammar*, p. 166).

  bufala   feminine of **bufalo** (buffalo.) There are a few buffalo herds in southern Italy kept for their milk which is very rich and makes excellent cheese.

  fior di latte   a less creamy type of mozzarella (lit. flower of milk)

- ▶ **Che cosa ci ha portato?**   What have you brought us? The combination of **avere** (or **essere**) + past participle will be explained in the *Grammar*, p. 166.

  che portiamo dall'alto Lazio   which we bring from the hills of Latium (lit. from high Latium)

  mucca   cow, **pecora**   sheep (**latte**   milk, is understood). Latium is famous for its sheep's milk cheese, with a very sharp flavour, called, appropriately, **pecorino romano.**

  potete provare   you may try (it)

- ▶ **frizzantino**   slightly fizzy

  ben fresco   well chilled. In other contexts **fresco -a** means fresh (**frutta fresca**) or uncooked (**verdura fresca**).

  si può assaporare bene   one can taste it well

PRACTICE

1 This exercise features the letter *-u-* and its combination with *-i-*. Read the following sentences and check your pronunciation on the recording.

a. Da Guido abbiamo mangiato del prosciutto come antipasto.
b. Giulia ha ordinato una buona mozzarella di bufala.
c. L'antipasto è piaciuto a tutti.
d. Abbiamo bevuto del Lambrusco della casa, sfuso.
e. Da Guido è chiuso il lunedì, giusto?

2 A small town in Tuscany has given its name to one of the best and most well-known Italian wines. Look at the label below and answer the following questions:

a. Where was the wine produced?   (i) Rosso   (ii) Montalcino
b. In what year was it produced?   (i) 1994   (ii) 1892   (iii) 1870
c. Who bottled the wine?   (i) the producer   (ii) the distributors or shippers
d. Was the production of this wine subjected to any quality controls?   (i) yes   (ii) no

ANSWERS P. 170

e. What degree of alcoholic content does the wine have?   (i) 16.7%   (ii) 13%

MONTALCINO - ITALIA 75 cl. ℮ 13% vol. R.I. 167/SI - ITALIA

ROSSO DI MONTALCINO
DENOMINAZIONE DI ORIGINE CONTROLLATA
IMBOTTIGLIATO DAL VITICOLTORE

Francesco Colombini Gicelli

FATTORIA DEI BARBI

FATTORIA DEI BARBI
proprietà Colombini

viticoltori in Montalcino
Brunello dal 1892
Vinsanto dal 1870

8 008003 939343

NON DISPERDERE NELL'AMBIENTE

3 Order some cheese and wine to round off your meal, as suggested on your recording.

Some comments on English food

LISTEN FOR...	
▶ **più che altro**	rather
▶ **quei sapori tipo agrodolce**	those kind of sour-sweet flavours
▶ **andate matti per ...**	you're crazy about ...

Giovanni	Allora, Enza, ti piace l'Inghilterra?
Enza	Eh, mi piace abbastanza. Unica cosa che non mi piace dell'Inghilterra è il cibo.
Giovanni	Il cibo?
Cesarina	Per noi italiani è un po' un problema, più che altro …
Enza	… quei sapori tipo agrodolce che noi … in Italia non usiamo.
Claudio	I sapori sono molto diversi, anzi sono diversi perché troviamo salato e dolce molte volte assieme. Non si separa il salato dal dolce come in Italia.
Enza	Siamo abituati a un'alimentazione molto diversa, e …
Giovanni	Insomma, non mi pare che andate matti per la cucina inglese, eh?

Ti piace? Giovanni is using the familiar **tu** here; **mi piace abbastanza** (I quite like it).

unica cosa (the) only thing

il cibo the food; what she actually means is **la cucina** (the way it's cooked).

▶ **più che altro** rather (lit. more than anything), but here it is used as a mere filler.

▶ **quei sapori tipo agrodolce** those kind of sour-sweet flavours. The sharp distinction between flavours Claudio mentions later is mirrored in the language, which, as noted in Unit 10, p. 148, has no equivalent of 'pudding' or 'pie', referring to both sweet and savoury foods. The basic flavours in Italian are: **agro** or **aspro** (sour), **acido** (acidic), **amaro** (bitter), **dolce** (sweet), **salato** (salty), **piccante** (hot).

molte volte many times (more on **volta** in Unit 13, p. 190)

assieme (or **insieme**) together

non si separa one doesn't distinguish, from **separare** (to separate, to distinguish)

siamo abituati a … we are used to …

alimentazione (f) way of eating, diet

non mi pare che … it doesn't seem to me that …, I don't think that …

▶ **andate matti per …** you're crazy about … (lit. you go mad about). You can use this phrase to express a strong preference or liking: **Ti piace la cassata? Ne vado matto!** Do you like cassata? (either a rich Sicilian cake or an ice-cream confection) I'm crazy about it.

CONVERSATIONS 2

 Giulio tells Aldo about a restaurant he and his friends should try

LISTEN FOR...

▶ **siamo andati dal Buttero**   we went to Il Buttero
▶ **fare una cena**   to dine
▶ **dietro**   behind

Aldo	Ieri sera siamo andati dal Buttero, fare una cena, una cucina tipica romana. Un piccolo locale in via della Lungaretta.
Giulio	Invece dovreste provare questo ristorante molto carino, che si chiama La Pilotta e sta a Porta Cavalleggeri, dietro il Vaticano, e si mangiano cento tipi di pasta diversi. E ci hanno tutti i tipi di pasta con tutti i tipi di condimento, e è arredato bene, molto cioè elegante, con le spighe di grano attaccate alla parete.

▶ **siamo andati dal Buttero**   we went to Il Buttero. Note the use of **da** meaning to, since Buttero, though the name of a restaurant, refers to a person (Unit 10, p. 150). 'I've been to the chemist' could be both **sono andato in farmacia** (shop) and **sono andato dal farmacista** (person). For **sono andato, siamo andati** see *Grammar*, p. 166.

▶ **fare una cena**   to dine

locale (m)   place, in the sense of venue, internal space, room. In estate agents' jargon it is any subdivision of a house or flat.

dovreste provare   you (pl) should try

molto carino   very nice

▶ **dietro**   behind, the opposite of **davanti** (before): both indicate a location. To indicate a movement use **avanti** (forwards) and **indietro** (backwards): **andare dietro a qualcuno** (to walk behind someone, to follow someone); **andare indietro** (to go backwards). See also Conversations 3.

è arredato bene   it's well fitted out

con le spighe di grano with ears of wheat stuck to the walls

PRACTICE

4 Which of the following words describing flavours applies to the foods listed below?
acido, **amaro**, **aspro**, **dolce**, **salato**, **secco**, **piccante**.

a. caffé espresso senza zucchero _____

b. sugo di limone _____

c. marmellata di fichi _____

d. sottaceti _____

e. vino Soave _____

f. salame _____

g. Bitter Campari _____

h. torta di mele _____

i. prosciutto di Parma

_____

ANSWERS P. 170   k. bistecca al pepe _____

5 Listen to the short conversation about flowers and write against the name of each flower, listed in alphabetical order, who likes what, whether **lui** (he) or **lei** (she). The preference for one of the flowers is not stated, and another flower in the list is not mentioned at all.

a. garofani   carnations _____

b. giacinti   hyacinths _____

c. narcisi   narcissuses _____

d. rosa   rose _____

ANSWERS P. 170   e. violette   violets _____

6 Following the prompts on your recording, give a description of a restaurant you like.

Better to choose a quiet room

LISTEN FOR...

▶ **Preferisce vederle?**   Would you rather see them?
▶ **le preferisce sul dietro**   you would rather have them at the back
▶ **magari**   perhaps

Portiere	Se vuol veder le camere ... preferisce vederle?
Giovanni	No, se può chiamarmi qualcuno che mi aiuti con le valigie.
Portiere	Volentieri. Chiamo subito il facchino così vi mandiamo nelle camere, eh?
Giovanni	Molte grazie.
Portiere	Le camere sono al primo piano, non so ...
Giovanni	Sono al primo piano...
Portiere	... le preferisce sul dietro, perché sono più tranquille ...
Giovanni	Eh, dietro, magari sì, sul dietro sono un po' più tranquille.
Portiere	Ecco, io gli faccio vedere tutt'e due, quale Lei preferisce.

vuol vedere short for **vuole vedere**.
Sometimes the final vowel of a verb is dropped. There is no simple way to explain how and when this happens. You should know that it does, but do not worry about dropping vowels yourself: make sure you pronounce and write all final vowels.

▶ **Preferisce vederle?**   Would you rather see them? (lit. You prefer to see them?)
se può chiamarmi qualcuno che mi aiuti   if you can call me someone to help me (who can help me); **aiutare** (to help), **aiuto** (help), **Aiuto!** (Help!)
il facchino   (luggage) porter
vi mandiamo   we'll send them, from **mandare** (to send)

▶ **le preferisce sul dietro**   you would rather have them at the back (lit. you prefer them). Other possible locations: **sul cortile**   facing onto/overlooking the courtyard; **sul davant**   at the front; **sulla strada**   overlooking the street; **sul giardino**   overlooking the garden; **sul mare**   overlooking the sea; **al primo/secondo**, etc. **piano**   on the first/second, etc. floor; **al piano terreno**   on the ground floor.

▶ **magari**   perhaps, maybe. A different use of this word is to express an unrealized wish, rather like 'if only!' in English. **Non è tranquilla la camera? Magari! è rumorosissima**; Isn't the room quiet? I wish it was: it's extremely noisy (**rumore** noise, **rumoroso -a** noisy)

gli faccio vedere tutt'e due I'll show you both (lit. I make you see). **Fare** followed by another verb in the infinitive is best translated into English as 'let' or 'have': e.g. **gli faccio vedere la camera** I'll let you see the room; **la lampadina è rotta: la fa cambiare?** the electric bulb is gone: can you have it changed? More about this in Unit 14, p. 214. The use of **gli** (lit. to him) instead of polite **li** is fairly frequent when talking to a man.

quale Lei preferisce whichever you prefer. A useful word to express your preferences is **scegliere** to choose: for its conjugation, see *Grammar,* p. 166.

 ## The bedside lamp doesn't work

LISTEN FOR...

▶ **la lampadina**   the light bulb
▶ **Potrebbe farla cambiare, per favore?**   Could you have it changed, please?
▶ **credo che sia fulminata**   I believe it's blown

Giovanni	Signorina, la lampadina vicino al letto a destra non si accende. Potrebbe farla cambiare, per favore?
Receptionist	Ha controllato se è fulminata?
Giovanni	Credo che sia fulminata.
Receptionist	Va bene. Lo segnalerò alle ragazze che si occupano della stanza.
Giovanni	Molte grazie.
Receptionist	Prego.

▶ **la lampadina** the light bulb, a diminutive form of **lampada** (lamp). Other light-emitting objects: **candela** candle; **lanterna** lantern; **pila** torch (also the battery that goes in it: but larger car-size batteries are called **batteria**); **fanale** (m) any light indicating the position of a moving vessel or vehicle; **faro** any light showing its pilot or driver the way, headlamp (of a car), beacon, lighthouse; **luce** (f) light.

non si accende doesn't come on (lit. light up); **accendere**, to light (a fire), to switch on (an electric appliance); the opposite is **spegnere** (**spengo, spegni**, etc., **spento**).

▶ **Potrebbe farla cambiare, per favore?** Could you have it changed, please?
Ha controllato se ...? Did you check whether ...?

▶ **credo che sia fulminata** I believe it's blown. Ignore **sia** (the subjunctive form of **essere**): to say **credo che è fulminata** would be just as acceptable. **Fulminato -a** is also said of a blown fuse (**valvola** or **fusibile**): from **fulmine** (lightning).

lo segnalerò I'll point it out (lit. signal)

▶ **le ragazze che si occupano della stanza** chamber maids (lit. the girls who look after the room). **Occuparsi di** ... (to take care of ...), **occupato** (busy, engaged), **sono occupato** (I'm busy), **il telefono è occupato** (the phone is engaged). **Ragazzo, ragazza** are general words for young people. With a possessive (**il mio ragazzo, la mia ragazza**) it means boy- or girl-friend.

7 Describe the position of the rooms in the hotel illustrated below. Complete the sentences giving first the direction the room faces, and second the floor it's on. The first has been done for you.

a.	Il ristorante è	**sul davanti**	**al piano terreno**
b.	La camera 101 è	_____	_____
c.	La camera 206 è	_____	_____
d.	La camera 320 è	_____	_____
e.	La camera 231 è	_____	_____
f.	La camera 110 è	_____	_____

ANSWERS P. 170

8 Listen to some hotel customers phoning reception about things that do not work. What is it they are complaining about? Write the number of their complaint next to the number of their room: some complaints are not mentioned on your recording.

a. Room 145 _____

b. Room 207 _____

c. Room 310 _____

d. Room 432 _____

i.   The room gives onto the road and it is too noisy.
ii.   The hot water is not working.
iii. There is neither toilet paper nor soap in the bathroom.
iv.   The room does not overlook the garden as requested.
v.   The television set does not work.
vi.   The beds are uncomfortable.

ANSWERS P. 170

9 Ask the receptionist whether she can change your room, following the prompts on your recording.

GRAMMAR AND EXERCISES

How to talk about things in the past (1)

You understood phrases like **Ha visto il Gran Caffè Adriano nella sua nuova veste?** Have you seen …? (Unit 7, p. 96); **le ho rubato solo mille lire** I have cheated you … (Unit 8, p. 109); **ho finito i miei lavori** I have finished my work (Unit 9, p. 131), because the Italian structure was similar to the corresponding English one (to have + past participle).

There are two different types of past tense in Italian. In this Unit you will study the Perfect tense, used when talking about specific events at a definite time in the past (for the Imperfect see Unit 13, p. 198).

The Perfect translates both the English Perfect (I have seen) and the Past Simple or Past Definite (I saw). There is also a Past Simple in Italian (**passato remoto**) which is used like the Perfect and may nearly always be replaced by it.

Perfect tense

The Perfect tense makes use of the past participle. You will remember from Unit 8 that this is formed in Italian from verbs in **-are** and **-ire** by replacing the **-re** with **-to**, etc. (**tostato, bollito**). Here as promised is a short list of the most common exceptions to this rule:

avere	to have	**avuto**	had
decidere	to decide	**deciso**	decided
fare	to do, make	**fatto**	done, made
prendere	to take	**preso**	taken
aprire	to open	**aperto**	open(ed)
chiudere	to close	**chiuso**	closed
essere	to be	**stato**	been
rimanere	to stay	**rimasto**	stayed
scendere	to descend	**sceso**	descended
venire	to come	**venuto**	come
vivere	to live	**vissuto**	lived

The Italian Perfect combines the past participle not only with **avere** (to have) as in English but also with **essere**.

(a) The past participle combines with **avere** if the verb takes or could take a direct object. Then it is always in the **-o** form: **Che cosa hai fatto?** What have you done?; **ho deciso di partire** I have decided to leave; **Maria ha avuto un regalo** Mary has had a gift; **ho preso un tiramisù** I had a tiramisù; **Hai cambiato la camera?** Have you changed/Did you change your room?; **Hanno controllato se …?** Did they check whether …?

(b) The past participle combines with **essere** and agrees with the subject if:

(i) the verb takes a reflexive object (see Unit 6, p. 86: **l'autobus si è fermato** the bus stopped; **l'auto si è fermata** the car stopped (even if the same verb takes **avere** in non-reflexive phrases such as **ho fermato l'autobus** I stopped the bus).

(ii) the verb cannot take a direct object: **Quando sei arrivato-a?** When did you arrive?; **siamo andati-e in Italia** we went to Italy; **il treno è partito in orario** the train left on time; **non è stata bene** she hasn't been well; **è sceso dall'autobus** he got out of the bus.

A few verbs in group (ii), however, take **avere** (e.g. **camminare** (to walk): **abbiamo camminato molto** we walked a lot; **dormire** (to sleep): **ho dormito bene** I slept well.

scegliere to choose

The present tense of this verb is irregular (in the first person singular and third person plural). Its past participle is **scelto**: **ho scelto la camera che dà sul giardino. Cogliere** (past part. **colto**) to pick (fruit, flowers) and **togliere** (past part. **tolto**) to remove, to take away are conjugated like **scegliere** (**colgo, tolgo**, etc.).

	scegliere to choose
I	scelgo
you	scegli
he/she/it <u>or</u> you (polite)	sceglie
we	scegliamo
you (pl)	scegliete
they	scelgono

Che

Here are all the uses of **che**:

(a) it is a question word (what, which): **Che cosa prende? Che lavoro fa? Che città è?**

(b) it means 'than' in comparisons between words or phrases of the same type: **una città più industriale che agricola, mi piace più cucinare a casa che andare al ristorante.**

(c) it introduces the second of a pair in **sia … che …** (both … and …): **una città sia industriale che agricola**

(d) it means 'that' in reported speech or opinion.

Note that this conjunction is frequently omitted in English, but must be used in Italian: **dicono che il treno arriva fino a Lamezia**   they say [that] the train will go as far as Lamezia; **mi sembra che è fulminata**   I think [that] it's blown.

(e) it means 'which', 'who' (subject) or 'whom' (object). 'Whom' in English can be omitted: one can say 'the woman I saw at the restaurant' meaning '… whom I saw'. In Italian **che** cannot be omitted: **la donna che ho visto al ristorante, tutto quello che vuole** all you wish, **questo è un formaggio che viene dall'alto Lazio** this is a cheese which comes from the hills of Latium.

10 Fill in the spaces in the following narration with a form of the Perfect tense chosen from the box. There are more items in the box than spaces.

a. Ieri sera Aldo, Gerald, Zia Nennella, e io _____

_____ a cena al Ristorante Il Buttero.

b. Tutti _____ piatti tipici romani.

c. Gerald non _____ cipolle perché è allergico (allergic).

d. Io _____ vino bianco e rosso per tutti.

e. Come dolce Aldo e Gerald _____ sorbetto al limone, mentre a Zia Nennella e a me il cameriere _____ un tiramisù.

f. Poi _____ la cena con una buona tazza di caffè.

abbiamo finito   abbiamo scelto   è mangiato
ha mangiato   ha portato   hanno scelto
ho ordinato   siamo andati   siamo scelti
sono andati   sono scelti

ANSWERS P. 170

11 In the following text the gaps should be filled by either **è** or **ha**.

La signora Greene _____ arrivata a Venezia la sera alle 10. _____ subito andata in albergo dove _____ scelto una camera sul giardino interno e si _____ trovata molto bene. Si _____ trattenuta a Venezia per cinque giorni e _____ visitato i monumenti più importanti della città. _____ partita per Vienna in vagone letto la sera di giovedì.

ANSWERS P. 170

12 First make sure you understand the following sentences, then link them using **che**.

Model: **La signora Greene è una turista. La signora Greene va a Venezia. La signora Greene è una turista che va a Venezia.**

a. Questa è una cabina telefonica. Questa cabina va colla scheda.

_____

b. Ti consiglio questa mozzarella. Questa mozzarella è di bufala.

_____

c. Dovreste andare in un ristorante. Il ristorante si chiama La Pilotta.

_____

d. Provate questo formaggio. Lo abbiamo portato dall'alto Lazio.

_____

e. Scelgo questa camera. Questa camera dà sul giardino.

_____

ANSWERS P. 170

Unit 11   'What do you prefer?'   167

KEY WORDS AND PHRASES

tipo il Trebbiano	such as Trebbiano
secco	dry
amabile	medium-dry
frizzantino	slightly fizzy
vini sfusi della casa	house wines
la mozzarella che ti consiglio	the mozzarella I advise you (to have)
Che cosa ci ha portato?	What have you brought us?
più che altro	rather
quei sapori tipo agrodolce	those kind of sour-sweet flavours
agro	sour
acido	acidy
amaro	bitter
dolce	sweet
salato	salty
piccante	(spicy) hot
andate matti per …	you're crazy about …
siamo andati dal Buttero	we went to Il Buttero
fare una cena	to dine
dovreste provare	you (pl) should try
Preferisce vederle?	Would you rather see them?
le preferisce sul dietro	you would rather have them at the back
dietro	behind
indietro	backwards
davanti	before, in front
avanti	forwards
sul cortile	facing onto/overlooking the courtyard
sul davanti	at the front
sulla strada	overlooking the street
sul giardino	overlooking the garden
sul mare	overlooking the sea
al primo/secondo, etc. piano	on the first/second, etc. floor
al piano terreno	on the ground floor
magari	perhaps
la lampadina	the light bulb
Potrebbe farla cambiare?	Could you have it changed?
credo che sia fulminata	I believe it's blown
le ragazze che si occupano della stanza	chamber maids (lit. the girls who look after the room)

'Italian' cuisine?

There is, of course, no such thing as 'Italian cuisine' only regional dishes. 'Italy,' wrote Riccardo Morbelli in 1967, 'is a ham-shaped peninsula surrounded by five seas called Barolo, Chianti, Lambrusco, Frascati and Cirò [a Calabrian wine], and is divided into two main regions: Butter Italy in the North and Oil Italy in the South, otherwise known as Riceland and Pastaland.' He formally warned travellers never to ask for spaghetti in the North or risotto in the South, unless they wanted to be served wallpaper glue in either case.

Greater social mobility and internal migrations have changed a situation where cuisine was, like everything else in Italy, intensely parochial, and regional specialities did not travel at all well. Gifted regional chefs from several regions have opened excellent restaurants in other regions (in one well-known case calling it an 'Embassy'!) Apulian farmers have colonized Milan, and Sicilian pastry-cooks and confectioners have added a creamy layer of meaning to the Roman **dolce vita**.

But the fact that food from any region is now available in any other region has not homogenized the various styles into a national cuisine.

Regional specialities are still well worth tasting in their place of origin. Tourists without much time or money for expensive restaurant food can enjoy something of the regional flavours of Italy simply by buying local cheeses, hams and salamis (far too many to allow even a passing mention), and by visiting the local vegetable market. There they will discover that the common round lettuce is only one, and not the tastiest, among dozens of varieties of salad, and that there are many types of vegetables.

Since most of these specialities have a regional and often a dialectal name,

Italians from other areas are no wiser than you. When it comes to buying they too have to point to the thing and say '**mi dia quella lì**', ask '**come si chiama?**' and even '**come si mangia?**' (how do you eat it?). Italian has only recently become a viable national language, so it still lacks standard names for vegetables other than the most common ones. What in some areas are called **bietole** (beet) and **cavolo** (cabbage) in others are called **coste** and **verza**; and what people actually mean by **cicoria** (chicory?, endives?) varies from place to place.

Names of fish, birds, plants and flowers, except the most common ones, are also local or dialectal. The Italian Romantic poet Giacomo Leopardi (1798–1837) had a girl in one of his poems carry **un mazzolin di rose e di viole** (a posy of roses and violets) which is a practical impossibility but a poetic necessity: **rose** and **viole** do not blossom at the same time but are among the half dozen or so names of flowers which all Italians recognize. This lack of generally understandable and acceptable names for things which are part of one's everyday experience may be one of the causes of the rather widespread ignorance of the average Italian about birdlife and gardening, and the slow development in the country of nature-lovers' societies and 'green' political movements.

AND FINALLY...

13

In this exercise you are ordering in a restaurant and you have to express your preferences. There is a new word **ragù**, meaning 'meat sauce'. You won't be prompted, but when the waiter offers you two choices, refuse the first by saying **non mi piace** or **non mi piacciono** and agree to the second by saying **preferisco** ... Here is an example:

WAITER   **Come antipasto abbiamo prosciutto e salame, oppure paté.**

YOU   **Non mi piacciono il prosciutto e il salame** (or: **il prosciutto e il salame non mi piacciono**)**. Preferisco il paté.**

ANSWERS

EXERCISE 2

(a) Montalcino   **(b)** 1994   **(c)** the producer   **(c)** yes
(e) 13%

EXERCISE 4

(a), (g) amaro   **(b)** aspro   **(c), (h)** dolce   **(d)** acido
(e) secco   **(f), (i)** salato   **(k)** piccante

EXERCISE 5

(a) not mentioned   **(b)** not stated   **(c)** Lui   **(d)** Lei
(e) Lei

EXERCISE 7

(b) 101, sul davanti/sulla strada al primo piano   **(c)** 206, sul giardino, al secondo piano   **(d)** 320, sul mare, al secondo piano   **(e)** 231, sul dietro, al secondo piano   **(f)** 110 sul cortile, al piano terreno.

EXERCISE 8

(a) i   **(b)** iii   **(c)** iv   **(d)** v

EXERCISE 10

(a) Ieri sera Aldo, Gerald, Zia Nennella, e io siamo andati a cena al Ristorante Il Buttero.   **(b)** Tutti abbiamo scelto piatti tipici romani.   **(c)** Gerald non ha mangiato cipolle perché è allergico.   **(d)** Io ho ordinato vino bianco e rosso per tutti. **(e)** Come dolce Aldo e Gerald hanno scelto sorbetto al limone, mentre a Zia Nennella e a me il cameriere ha portato un tiramisù.   **(f)** Poi abbiamo finito la cena con una buona tazza di caffé.

EXERCISE 11

La signora Greene è arrivata a Venezia la sera alle 10. È subito andata in albergo dove ha scelto una camera sul giardino interno e si è trovata molto bene. Si è trattenuta a Venezia per cinque giorni e ha visitato monumenti più importanti della città. È partita per Vienna in vagone letto la sera di giovedì.

EXERCISE 12

(a) Questa è una cabina telefonica che va colla scheda.
(b) Ti consiglio questa mozzarella che è di bufala.
(c) Dovreste andare in un ristorante che si chiama La Pilotta.
(d) Provate questo formaggio che abbiamo portato dall'alto Lazio.
(e) Scelgo questa camera che dà sul giardino.

12 'WHILE YOU'RE AT IT, FILL IT UP!'

WHAT YOU WILL LEARN
▶ how to ask for petrol and basic car maintenance
▶ how to talk about the weather and understand weather forecasts
▶ seasons and months of the year

BEFORE YOU BEGIN

As languages change in time they tend to shed case endings (e.g. the distinction between 'who' and 'whom' in English), irregular plurals (the plural of 'cow' used to be 'kine') and similar oddities. Frequently used words and expressions, however, are relatively more stable: that's why the most common words in any language you are likely to learn are often 'irregular'. Many irregularities are more apparent than real and come in families: for instance, among the verbs having some tenses which cannot be predicted from the infinitive, those ending with the same group of syllables (like **accendere**, **prendere**, **rendere**, **scendere**) tend to have the same conjugation.

POINTS TO REMEMBER FROM UNIT 11
Expressing preferences:
preferisco vedere la camera, mi piace di più il vino bianco, vado matto per il tiramisù

The Perfect tense:
avere + participle – the participle doesn't change: **hanno deciso di partire domani** (all verbs taking a direct object, and a few more)
essere + participle – the participle agrees with the subject: **le ragazze sono rimaste a casa** (all verbs not taking a direct object)

'That' and 'whom' can be omitted in English, but **che** cannot:
Giulio told me [that] he leaves tomorrow   **Giulio mi ha detto che parte domani**
The woman [whom] I saw in the market …   **la donna che ho visto al mercato** …

Pronunciation notes

Many Italian words are stressed on the last vowel: for instance, all first and third persons singular of the future tense (**prenderò/prenderà**, **mangerò/mangerà**, etc.), and many nouns (such as **caffè**, **città**, **giovedì**, **ragù**, **supplì** (rice croquette), **tiramisù**. Several English nouns ending in -*ity* correspond to Italian nouns in -*ità* (**ansietà** anxiety, **eternità** eternity, **necessità** necessity, **sincerità** sincerity, etc.). All the nouns in this category don't change in the plural. It is important to pronounce a stress whenever you see a vowel marked by an accent (it does not matter how it is slanted). Do not put an accent where there is none (many words in -*ita*, like **salita**, **uscita**, are NOT stressed on the last vowel!).

A radio advertisement advises motorists on all the checks they should do in winter

LISTEN FOR...

▶ **è inverno**	it's winter
▶ **funzionamento**	working order
▶ **dimenticavo**	I forgot
▶ **già che ci sei**	while you're at it

Lo speaker della radio

È inverno, amico automobilista. Una ragione in più per salvaguardare il perfetto funzionamento del motore della tua auto. Hai pensato all'antigelo? E alle candele? Hai controllato le condizioni dei pneumatici?

E allora, amico automobilista, per la messa a punto della tua auto, recati alla stazione di servizio Roma, dove del personale altamente specializzato ti consiglierà sulla gradazione giusta del lubrificante invernale e dell'antigelo, e sul tipo di candele adatte alla stagione. E se devi riparare o sostituire le gomme, Roma mette a tua disposizione le migliori marche di pneumatici esistenti sul mercato. E magari di' che ti mando io, lo speaker della radio. Vedrai, rimarrai soddisfatto.

Ah, dimenticavo, già che ci sei, fai anche il pieno.

lo speaker della radio clearly not the radio loudspeaker (**altoparlante**: see Unit 2, p. 19), but the radio presenter or announcer, also called in Italian **annunziatore** (m), **annunziatrice** (f).

▶ **è inverno** it's winter. The adjective 'winter' is **invernale**, as in the phrase which comes later **lubrificante invernale** (winter lubricant). For the names of the remaining seasons and related adjectives, see panel on p. 177.

automobilista (m/f) motorist, from **automobile** (f) (motor car)

una ragione in più one more reason (lit. one reason in more); **una persona in più** one more person

salvaguardare to safeguard

▶ **funzionamento** working order, related to **funzionare** (to function, to work – said of machines only). This verb comes in many phrases you may find useful: **la lampadina non funziona** (the light bulb is not working); **non funziona bene** (it isn't working well); **veda se funziona** (see whether it works),

adesso funziona (now it's working, it's in working order).

auto (f) short for **automobile**). Another shortened word is **moto** (f), from **motocicletta** (motorcycle). Shortened words do not change in the plural because they have lost the final syllable where ending changes would normally take place (e.g. **automobile** ▷ **automobili**; **motocicletta** ▷ **motociclette**; but **l'auto** ▷ **le auto**; **la moto** ▷ **le moto**).

antigelo antifreeze. For more words beginning with *anti-*, see Unit 14, p. 211.

candela spark plug (also candle)

pneumatico tyre (also **gomma**)

messa a punto overhaul, general check-up. **Messo -a** is the past participle of **mettere**: **mettere a punto il motore** (to tune the engine).

recati   go (lit. take yourself), from **recarsi** (to go)

stazione di servizio   service station

personale altamente specializzato   highly qualified (lit. specialized) personnel

lubrificante (m)   lubricant, grease, oil; **lubrificare** (to lubricate, to grease, to oil)

adatto -a +a   suited to, suitable for

mette a tua disposizione   places at your disposal

le migliori marche di pneumatici esistenti sul mercato   the best brands of tyres (existing) on the market. For **migliore** see *Grammar*, p. 183.

di' che ti mando io   tell (them) I'm sending you

vedrai, rimarrai soddisfatto   you'll see, you'll be (lit. remain) satisfied; remind yourself of these 'contracted' futures in Unit 10, p. 150.

▶ **dimenticavo**   I forgot

▶ **già che ci sei**   while you're at it (lit. since you are there: informal); **già che ci sono** (while I'm at it); **già che c'è** (while you're at it: formal, or while he/she is at it); **già che ci siamo** (while we're at it)

fai anche il pieno   fill it up (lit. make also the full). The advertiser is addressing his audience with the informal '**tu**', but you should address the attendant formally: **mi faccia il pieno**; or simply: **il pieno**, **per piacere**. You may ask for a specified quantity of petrol: **venti litri di benzina**   twenty litres of petrol. More car vocabulary in the panel overleaf.

 ## What if you have a breakdown?

LISTEN FOR...	
▶ **in qualsiasi parte**	anywhere
▶ **può rivolgersi a …**	you may apply to …
▶ **autostrada**	motorway
▶ **in funzione ventiquattr'ore su ventiquattro**	on 24-hour duty
▶ **A che distanza sono l'una dall'altra?**	What distance are they from each other?

Giovanni	Un automobilista straniero che ha delle difficoltà a che numero telefonico può rivolgersi?
Sig. Cimaglia	Può rivolgersi al numero telefonico centosedici: uno, uno, sei.
Giovanni	Questo numero può essere chiamato da telefoni normali?
Sig. Cimaglia	Sì, può essere chiamato sia da un telefono normale, diciamo, in qualsiasi parte d'Italia, sia sull'autostrada attraverso delle colonnine cosiddette di salvataggio. C'è un pulsante che viene spinto e s'inoltra la chiamata a questa segreteria telefonica in funzione ventiquattr'ore su ventiquattro.
Giovanni	Queste colonnine telefoniche a che distanza sono l'una dall'altra?
Sig. Cimaglia	A circa due chilometri.

straniero -a   foreign, foreigner

che ha delle difficoltà   who has some problems (lit. difficulties). This phrase is a useful alternative to **ho un problema** (Unit 9, p. 131): **ho una difficoltà**, **ho delle difficoltà**.

numero telefonico telephone number. Remember that in Italian you cannot use a noun as an adjective. You must use either an appropriate adjective or a noun with a preposition: telephone directory **elenco telefonico** or **del telefono**; cherry jam **marmellata di ciliegie**; lemon sorbet **sorbetto al limone**.

▶ **può rivolgersi a …** can apply to … (lit. turn to); **A chi posso rivolgermi?** (Who can I ask?); **si rivolga alla polizia** (go to the police)

può essere chiamato da … may be called from …

sia … sia … both … and …; **sia in Italia che in Francia** both in Italy and in France

▶ **in qualsiasi parte** anywhere (lit. in any part). Note that **qualsiasi** is invariable and always followed by a singular noun: **qualsiasi automobile** any car, **qualsiasi telefono** any telephone.

▶ **autostrada** motorway. In Italy there is a distinction between **autostrada**, which is a toll way (turnpike in the US), and **superstrada** which is a freeway. Both are strictly limited to motorized traffic excluding mopeds.

colonnine cosiddette di salvataggio so-called rescue posts; **colonnina** is a diminutive of **colonna** column, pillar; **cosiddetto** = **così detto** so-called (**detto** is the past participle of **dire** to say); **salvataggio** rescue, from **salvare** to save; **salvatore** (rescuer, saviour). But the word commonly used in notices is **soccorso stradale** road rescue; from **soccorrere** to rescue, and **strada** road.

c'è un pulsante che viene spinto, etc. there is a button that has to be pressed (lit. comes pressed) and the call goes to an answering service. In other contexts **segreteria telefonica** is an answering machine.

▶ **in funzione ventiquattr'ore su ventiquattro** on 24-hour duty (lit. in operation 24 out of 24 hours); **funzione** (f) function

▶ **A che distanza sono l'una dall'altra?** How far are they from each other? (lit. the one from the other?)

YOUR CAR

l'auto(mobile) (f), **la macchina** car	**lo sterzo** steering mechanism, **il servosterzo** power steering
il motore a benzina petrol engine	**il condizionatore d'aria**, **il climatizzatore** air conditioning
il motore diesel diesel engine	
la carrozzeria bodywork	**le gomme, i pneumatici** tyres
il parabrezza windscreen	**i freni** brakes
i tergicristalli a due velocità two-speed windscreen wipers	**le candele** spark plugs
il lavavetro windscreen washer (**lavare** to wash)	**lo spinterogeno** distributor
le sospensioni suspension	**l'iniezione elettronica** electronic injection
l'ammortizzatore shock absorber	**il cambio a cinque marce** five-speed gearbox
il radiatore radiator	
la coppa dell'olio sump (lit. cup of the oil)	**il cambio automatico** automatic gearbox
il tubo di scappamento the exhaust	**le cinture di sicurezza** safety belts
il silenziatore silencer/muffler	**l'airbag** airbag
il volante steering wheel	

---

1 This is a pronunciation exercise for words ending in a stressed vowel. Read the following sentences and match your pronunciation to that of the speakers on your recording.

a. Mi porti due supplì come antipasto, spaghetti al ragù, niente secondo, e caffé.

b. Oggi prenderò una delle specialità locali: il tiramisù.

c. Giovedì andrò in città per necessità di lavoro.

d. La validità del biglietto è fino a venerdì.

2 Complete the following sentences about cars and motoring with a suitable phrase taken from the box below. As usual, there are two phrases which do not fit.

a. La mia auto ha _____ a sei cilindri.

b. Ogni 15 000 chilometri bisogna _____ e fare un

controllo generale.

c. Dove posso rivolgermi per _____ della mia auto?

d. Può rivolgersi alla _____ in piazza del Mercato.

e. D'inverno bisogna mettere _____ nel radiatore.

f. Non ho quasi più benzina. Devo _____ .

ANSWERS P. 186

> l'antigelo   cambiare l'olio   fare il pieno   la messa a punto
> una candela   stazione di servizio   un motore   un pneumatico

3 You are at a service station. Follow the presenter's prompts to ask for the things you need.

◗ Cold weather

LISTEN FOR...

▶ **fa freddo**   it's cold

Corinna	Viterbo è una città molto fredda.
Giovanni	Fa freddo a Viterbo?
Graziella	Molto, molto freddo, sì.
Giovanni	Più freddo che a Roma?
Graziella	Più freddo che a Roma, sì.
Signora 1	Fa freddo questa mattina.
Signora 2	Eh, un pochino.
Signora 1	Eh?
Signora 2	Oggi abbastanza.
Signora 1	Comunque, è tempo suo.
Signora 2	Embè, certo.

freddo -a cold. Think of 'fridge' and don't be misled by the spelling of its opposite, 'hot', which is **caldo -a**. Remember that if a tap in your hotel bathroom is marked C, it is the HOT water tap.

▶ **fa freddo** it's cold; **fa caldo** it's hot. **Fare** is used when there is no subject, but if there is one, then use **essere**: **il clima della Sicilia è caldo** (the climate in Sicily is hot); **Com'è oggi il mare? – È freddo** (How's the sea today? – It's cold). If you feel cold/hot say: **ho freddo/caldo**.

▶ **fa più freddo che a Roma** it's colder than Rome; but **Viterbo** (subject) **è più fredda di Roma**. Names of towns are considered to be feminine, like **città**.

un pochino diminutive of **un poco** (a little)

oggi abbastanza today (it's) quite (cold)

comunque è tempo suo anyway it's seasonal (lit. it's its weather, its = of this season). Remember that tempo means in Italian both time and weather. **Che tempo fa?** (What's the weather like?) Related words are **tempesta** (tempest), **temporale** (storm, thunderstorm), **tempaccio** (foul weather).

embè, certo well, sure (embè = e be', e bene)

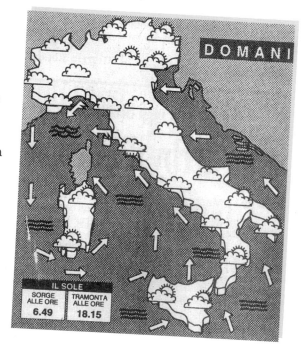

What was the weather like?

LISTEN FOR...

▶ **Com'era il tempo?**   What was the weather like?
▶ **Che bel tempo!**   What fine weather!
▶ **sul serio**   in earnest
▶ **meno male**   thank goodness

Giovanni	Pff! Come fa caldo qui in Italia. E com'era il tempo durante le tue vacanze in Inghilterra?
Aldo	Alcune giornate di sole. Il resto ventoso e nuvoloso.
Giovanni	Questo in che mese?
Aldo	Agosto.
Giovanni	Pioggia?
Aldo	No.
Giovanni	Meno male, perché quando in Inghilterra piove, eh? piove sul serio! Qui, invece, guarda che bel tempo oggi!

come fa caldo   how hot it is; note that **caldo** translates both warm and hot: the gradation must therefore be expressed by adverbs or superlatives: **non molto caldo, piuttosto caldo, molto caldo, caldissimo**. Other possible adjectives: **torrido** torrid; **temperato** temperate, **mite** mild.

▶ **Com'era il tempo?**   What was the weather like? **Era** was and other forms of the imperfect (the other past tense) will be explained in Unit 13, p. 198.

durante during

alcune giornate di sole   a few sunny days; **sole** (m)   sun

ventoso windy, from **vento** (wind); **nuvoloso** cloudy, from **nuvola** (cloud). Other similar adjectives: **piovoso** rainy (**piovere, piovuto** to rain, **pioggia** rain), **tempestoso** stormy, **nevoso** snowy (**neve** (f) snow), **nebbioso** foggy (**nebbia** fog).

In che mese?   In what month?

agosto   August. The names of the other months are in the panel below. Note that they don't have a capital letter in Italian.

▶ **meno male** thank goodness (lit. less badness). This is a very common way of expressing relief in Italian: **non c'è sciopero: meno male!** or **meno male che non c'è sciopero** (thank goodness there's not going to be a strike).

▶ **sul serio** in earnest (lit. on the serious).

▶ **che bel tempo** what fine weather; **che brutto tempo, che tempo orribile** what bad/awful weather; **fa brutto, piove e tira vento** the weather's bad, it's rainy and windy.

NAMES OF THE SEASONS AND RELATED ADJECTIVES

la primavera	spring;	**primaverile**
l'estate	summer;	**estivo -a**
l'autunno	autumn;	**autunnale**
l'inverno	winter;	**invernale**

MONTHS OF THE YEAR

gennaio	January	**luglio**	July
febbraio	February	**agosto**	August
marzo	March	**settembre**	September
aprile	April	**ottobre**	October
maggio	May	**novembre**	November
giugno	June	**dicembre**	December

---

4 Choose the correct caption for each scene from the selection in the box below. There are two extra captions.

a

b

c

d

e

f

| c'è un temporale | piove | c'è il sole | tira vento | è nuvoloso | fa molto caldo | fa molto freddo | c'è neve |

5 You may like to know the jingle Italians use to remember which months of the year have 30 and which 31 days. Listen to it on the recording, then answer the following questions:

a. Which month is hinted at in the third line of the jingle?
b. Which is the third month with 30 days mentioned in it?
c. Is reference made to any 31-day month, and if so which one?
d. Which spring month is mentioned?

ANSWERS AND JINGLE P. 186

6 Listen to the weather forecaster giving yesterday's temperatures for the northern Italian towns (given in degrees Celsius). Write them in the appropriate boxes then answer the following questions:

	MINIMA	MASSIMA
Bolzano		
Torino		
Milano		
Verona		
Venezia		
Trieste		
Bologna		

a. Dove ha fatto più freddo?

_____

b. Dove ha fatto più caldo?

_____

c. Ha fatto meno caldo a Verona o a Venezia?

_____

d. Dove c'è stata la più piccola differenza tra temperatura minima e massima?

_____

CONVERSATIONS 3

 Here's a weather forecast from the radio

| LISTEN FOR... |

▶ **tempo previsto per domani**   tomorrow's weather forecast
▶ **regioni occidentali**   western regions
▶ **durante il pomeriggio**   during the afternoon

Tempo previsto per domani

Sulle regioni occidentali della penisola e sulle sole maggiori, poco nuvoloso durante il pomeriggio. Sul settore nord-occidentale e sul versante adriatico, nuvolosità variabile con locali precipitazioni anche temporalesche, che andranno trasferendosi da nord verso sud. Temperatura in lieve diminuzione sulle regioni orientali della penisola. Senza variazioni su quelle occidentali.

▶ **tempo previsto per domani** tomorrow's weather forecast (lit. weather foreseen for tomorrow); **previsto** is the past participle of **prevedere** (to foresee). Also: **previsioni del tempo per domani**. The 'official' term for weather forecast is **bollettino meteorologico**.

▶ **regioni occidentali** western regions. The four compass points are: **nord** north, **ovest** west, **est** east, **sud** south. They combine as in English: **nord-ovest** (north-west), **sud-est** (south east) etc. They are also called **settentrione** (from the Latin name for the seven stars of the Big Bear), **occidente**, **oriente** and **mezzogiorno**. The related adjectives are **settentrionale** or **nordico** (northern); **occidentale** (western, occidental); **orientale** (eastern, oriental); **meridionale** (southern).

la penisola the peninsula, i.e. Italy; **le isole maggiori** (the larger/major islands, i.e. **Sardegna** Sardinia and **Sicilia** Sicily). Weather forecasts show the general tendency of formal or official Italian to use a noun phrase where a verb phrase would be used in English: e.g. **temperature in lieve diminuzione** (lit. temperatures in slight decline) instead of 'temperatures will fall slightly'; or **prevalenza di cielo sereno** (prevalence of clear sky) instead of 'skies will be mostly clear'.

▶ **durante il pomeriggio** during the afternoon

versante adriatico the Adriatic slope, the side of the Apennines facing the Adriatic sea

nuvolosità cloudiness, i.e. clouds: another trait of official Italian is to prefer abstract to concrete nouns. Likewise **precipitazioni** rainfall.

variabile variable; **senza variazioni** no change (lit. without variation)

temporalesche (f pl) stormy; **temporale** (storm)

andranno trasferendosi will gradually move (lit. will go transferring themselves)

◗ *A road report*

▶ **nebbia**   fog
▶ **visibilità**   visibility
▶ **e per il momento è tutto**   that's all for the time being

Raccomandiamo prudenza per la nebbia presente su gran parte dell'Italia centro-settentrionale. In particolare riduce la visibilità sulla Torino–Savona da Torino a Marene. In questo tratto, in alcuni punti, la visibilità non supera i trenta metri. La nebbia è presente anche su molte zone del centro-sud, tra Lazio e Campania. Sulla A 11 tra Montecatini e la barriera di Pisa-Nord la visibilità non supera i venti metri. E per il momento è tutto. Il prossimo appuntamento con Onda Verde alle 22,57 su Radio Uno.

raccomandiamo prudenza take care (lit. we recommend prudence)

▶ **nebbia** fog; **nebbia fitta** (thick fog); **banchi di nebbia** (fog patches); **nebbioso -a** (foggy)

centro-settentrionale is a combined adjective meaning 'central *and* northern' (not the northern half of central Italy); similarly **centro-meridionale** central and southern.

sulla Torino–Savona on the Torino–Savona motorway (**sulla** because **autostrada** is implicitly understood)

in questo tratto in this segment

▶ **la visibilità non supera i trenta metri** visibility is below (lit. does not exceed) 30 metres

A 11 the code name of a national road

la barriera the toll gate

▶ **e per il momento è tutto** that's all for the time being (lit. and for the moment is all)

il prossimo appuntamento, etc. the next appointment with 'Green Wave', the name of a radio programme for motorists, with information on weather and road conditions

PRACTICE

7 Look at the map on the next page and complete the following sentences with the phrases in the box below. As usual, there are more phrases than you need.

a. Milano è a circa duecento chilometri a _____ di Bologna.

b. Torino è a circa centoquaranta chilometri a _____ di Milano.

c. Milano, Torino e Venezia sono città dell'Italia

_____ .

d. Napoli è a circa duecento chilometri a

_____ di Roma.

e. _____ e _____ sono

città dell'Italia meridionale.

f. Cagliari si trova sulla costa

_____ della Sardegna.

g. Palermo si trova sulla costa

_____ della Sicilia.

ANSWERS P. 186

Napoli   Bari   nord-ovest   meridionale   sud-est   settentrionale   orientale   nord
sud-ovest   a cinquanta chilometri

8

Listen to the weather forecast in your recording, and select the correct statements from those below.

a. The weather is going to be cloudy   (i) in the northern regions (ii) in the central-southern regions and on the Adriatic coast.

b. Rain is   (i) nearly certain   (ii) only possible.

ANSWERS P. 186   c. The weather is   (i) likely to improve   (ii) likely to get worse.

9

Here is a **cruciverba** (crossword puzzle) for you to solve. The clues (**definizioni**) are in Italian and refer to **orizzontali** (across) and **verticali** (down). You will need a new word: **la fine**   the end.

ORIZZONTALI

1 Tre quarti dell'anno sono ____ mesi.
2 Si dice anche occidente.
3 Più di un resto.
4 La fine della primavera

VERTICALI

1 Bologna è a ____ di Firenze.
2 _____ si trova Torino? – Si trova a circa 140 km da Milano.
3 Il Gran Caffè Adriano è aperto in una ____ rinnovata.
4 La direzione contraria a 2 orizzontale.
5 Oggi ____ molto vento.

ANSWERS P. 186

GRAMMAR AND EXERCISES

Sex and gender

When linguists talk about gender, they mean largely arbitrary categories to which nouns are conventionally assigned in some languages *by their form or inflexion* (not merely by choosing different opposing words, as in English, for example, he to she, boar to sow, or stallion to mare).

(a) In Italian the *unmarked* gender is masculine. This means that if the sex of a person is not known or is irrelevant, that person is traditionally referred to in the masculine (the radio announcer and Giovanni referred to their ideal motorist in Conversations 1 as **amico** and **straniero**). The masculine plural is used in speaking of people of mixed sex: **gli studenti** is commonly used when talking about male and female students together.

(b) From a noun referring to a male individual it is often possible to derive another referring to a female by means of a suffix. For instance:
   (i)   masculine in -*o*, feminine in -*a*:
           il gatto (tomcat), **la gatta**
   (ii)   masculine in -*tore*, feminine in -*trice* :
           l'annunziatore (announcer), **l'annunziatrice**, **l'attore** (actor), **l'attrice** (actress)
   (iii)   masculine in -*e*, feminine in -*essa*:
           il leone (lion), **la leonessa**, **lo studente**, **la studentessa**, **l'avvocato** (lawyer), **l'avvocatessa**, **il dottore**, **la dottoressa**

Only in a few cases are masculine and feminine unrelated words: **lo stallone** (stallion), **la giumenta** (mare); **il toro** (bull), **la vacca** (cow) (see the farm animals in Unit 13, p. 196).

Passive construction

There are no differences here between English and Italian. Take a sentence with an object: **l'automobilista** (subject) **può chiamare il numero 116** (object) the motorist may call the number 116. This sentence has a 'reverse' equivalent in which the object becomes the subject: **il numero 116 può essere chiamato da un automobilista**   The number

116 may be called by a motorist. The former subject is preceded by 'by' in English and by an appropriate form of **da** + article in Italian. This is called a passive construction.

Other examples: **il meccanico ha cambiato l'olio** the mechanic changed the oil ▷ **l'olio è stato cambiato dal meccanico**   the oil has been changed by the mechanic; **il Balanzone ha fatto tutti i dolci** Balanzone made all the cakes ▷ **i dolci sono stati tutti fatti dal Balanzone** the cakes have all been made by Balanzone.

Italian, however, has one further option in which **essere** (to be) is replaced by **venire** (to come), but only in simple tenses, i.e. those which are not formed by combining **avere** with a participle: **la lettera sarà spedita domani** = **la lettera verrà spedita domani** (the letter will be posted tomorrow); **il numero 116 può essere/venire chiamato da tutti i telefoni** (The number 116 may be called from every phone); **il pulsante è/viene spinto** (the button is pushed).

Note, in this connection, that **andare** (to go) may be used to replace 'must be': **il pulsante va spinto** = **il pulsante deve essere spinto** (the button must be pushed); **la lettera va spedita domani** (the letter must be posted tomorrow).

Migliore, peggiore

Comparisons are normally expressed in Italian by using **più** or **meno** before an adjective (Unit 7); and only in a few cases by using modified forms (a bit like the -*er* forms in English), which therefore do NOT need **più** or **meno**. Two common modified forms are **migliore** and **peggiore**:

migliore
queste gomme sono migliori di quelle che avevo these tyres are better than the ones I had; **queste gomme sono le migliori**   these tyres are the best. Related words: **meglio, migliorare, miglioramento; d'inverno è meglio fare il cambio dell'olio** in winter it's better to change the oil; **la mia salute migliora**   my health is getting better;

c'è un miglioramente   there's an improvement.
peggiore
oggi il tempo è peggiore/il peggiore
today the weather is worse/the worst
Related words: **peggio, peggiorare, peggioramento;**
il tempo va peggio, **il tempo peggiora**   the weather
is getting worse; **c'è un peggioramento del tempo**
there's a worsening of the weather.

10 Supply the missing masculine or feminine
term in the following pairs.

	M	F
a	**il lavoratore** (worker)	_____
b	**lo studente** (student}	_____
c	_____	**la leonessa** (lion, lioness)
d	_____	**la viaggiatrice** (traveller)
e	**il cugino** (cousin)	_____
f	_____	**la dottoressa** (doctor or GP)
g	**il cavallo** (horse)	_____

ANSWERS P. 186

11 Form the 'reverse' (active or passive) of
the following sentences. You need a new
word: **vendere** to sell (past participle **venduto**).

a. L'orario dei treni è dato dall'ufficio informazioni.

_____

_____

b. Il tabaccaio vende i biglietti dell'autobus.

_____

_____

c. I francobolli sono venduti dal tabaccaio.

_____

_____

d. Zia Nennella preferisce il tiramisù.

_____

_____

e. Il garage 'Roma' mette a disposizione un'auto
durante il servizio.

_____

_____

ANSWERS P. 186

12 Fill in the gaps in the following sentences
choosing from the words in the box.

a. Il caffè Danesi Oro è _____

come qualità del Danesi Primo Caffè.

b. La qualità del servizio è _____

molto.

c. C'è un _____ nella qualità del

servizio.

d. Piove e tira vento. Il tempo da ieri è molto

_____ .

e. Piove e tira vento: è _____

tornare in albergo.

f. Il _____ del tempo non era nelle

previsioni: oggi fa più freddo di ieri.

meglio   miglioramento   migliorare   migliorata
migliore
peggioramento   peggiorare   peggiorato   peggiore

ANSWERS P. 186

KEY WORDS
AND PHRASES

Note also the words in the panels on p. 174 and p. 177.

è inverno	it's winter
Com'era il tempo?	What was the weather like?
fa freddo	it's cold
fa caldo	it's hot
fa più freddo	it's colder
fa meno caldo	it's less hot
piove (piovere, piovuto)	it rains
la pioggia	rain
piovoso	rainy
c'è il sole	it's sunny
tira vento	the wind's blowing, it's windy
Che bel tempo!	What fine weather!
tempo previsto per domani	tomorrow's weather forecast
punti cardinali	points of the compass
nord	north
sud	south
est	east
ovest	west
regioni occidentali	western regions
regioni orientali	eastern regions
regioni settentrionali	northern regions
regioni meridionali	southern regions
nebbia	fog
visibilità	visibility
funzionamento	working order
funzionare	to work
dimenticavo	I forgot (imperfect tense)
già che ci sei	while you're at it (informal)
in qualsiasi parte	anywhere
può rivolgersi a …	you can apply to …
autostrada	motorway
soccorso	rescue
in funzione ventiquattr'ore su ventiquattro	on 24-hour duty
A che distanza sono l'una dall'altra?	How far are they from each other?
meno male	thank goodness
sul serio	in earnest
e per il momento è tutto	that's all for the time being

DID YOU KNOW?

Motoring in Italy

Any good motoring guidebook will give you most of the information you need to know before setting out to Italy by car. Of those traffic signs that give written instructions, you are sure to be able to guess the meaning of **deviazione**, **parcheggio, lavori in corso**. Less obvious signs are **rallentare, strada dissestata, caduta massi** — though it's doubtful you could do much about the last one! (see translations overleaf). On another sign the words **soccorso stradale** precede the telephone number of the emergency rescue service which, with luck, you'll never need.

Here, however, are a few tips you may not find in guidebooks. Traffic and parking conditions in large towns like Milan, Rome, Florence or Naples are so bad that using a car there is a positive inconvenience rather than an asset. Some cities ban private cars from the **centro storico** during periods of particular congestion and pollution (those with an even number plate on even days, the remainder on odd days). In some cities the bans are regular and permanent. Italians not only are allowed to drive at speeds higher than the limits prevailing in English-speaking countries, but they accelerate and manoeuvre faster. They do not watch the tail lights of the car in front, but the traffic lights ahead. As a consequence the whole column of cars stopped at a crossing tends to move forward as the lights change with little or no delay. On some urban ring roads large permanent red lights mark important crossings: their meaning is 'prepare to stop'. To know what you have to do, watch the smaller set of traffic lights underneath. Pedestrian crossings are spots where traffic authorities thought it would be convenient *for motorists* to have crossing pedestrians (**pedoni**) channelled; they are NOT places where pedestrians actually have priority. Beware, therefore, of stopping suddenly to let a pedestrian through at a crossing: the driver behind you may not expect it and may bump into you. Do not use any of the flashing headlight signals you may be familiar with, or expect to recognize any.

Quick flashes in succession usually mean 'get out of my way!' Invisible cyclists still use country roads at night, with only the faintest of lights or no lights at all.

You can now go from one end of Italy to the other on a network of superb motorways some 7000 km long. On all motorways there are frequent service areas open day and night, often connected by large buildings straddling the roadway. These contain toilets, restaurants, public telephones, snack bars, shops, tourist information offices and even banks or automatic tellers. Various by-passes help vehicular flow around other major cities, often providing links with other motorways and airports. Many of these by-passes have lengthy toll-free sections widely used by urban traffic. Milan is skirted west and east by two by-passes (**tangenziale ovest** and **tangenziale est**) converging south onto the A1 motorway to Rome, and linked north by the Turin–Venice motorway. A ring of motorways surrounds Rome (**Grande Raccordo Anulare** lit. great ring-shaped link road).

If you have to use motorways, pay your tolls by **Viacard**, a pre-paid magnetic card operating like a phone card, which you can buy on the motorways at many toll gates, from the offices of the **Automobile Club Italia**, or from many banks. You may, however, spend at least as much on toll fees as you save in fuel costs; and you will certainly miss all the picturesque, interesting and welcoming towns which ordinary roads pass through. Motorways draw a very large proportion of long-distance traffic, and so they are often as crowded as a main street during the rush hour: the difference is that the rush goes on at speeds significantly in excess of the upper limit, which is 130 km per hour. Motorways, particularly the northern ones, are best avoided in bad weather, or when fog is forecast. Many Italian drivers are so supremely confident in their and their fellow drivers' ability, that they think nothing of speeding in thick fog or severe frost. The resulting pile-ups of hundreds of vehicles with correspondingly high levels of casualties unfortunately also involve many cautious motorists stopping on the hard shoulder to avoid an accident.

13 A friend inquires about the weather in your part of the world. Answer as prompted in your recording.

ANSWERS

EXERCISE 2

(a) un motore **(b)** cambiare l'olio **(c)** la messa a punto **(d)** stazione di servizio **(e)** l'antigelo **(f)** fare il pieno or c'è neve

EXERCISE 4

(a) c'è il sole **(b)** c'è un temporale **(c)** è nuvoloso **(d)** fa molto caldo **(e)** piove **(f)** fa molto freddo <u>or</u> c'è neve

EXERCISE 5

(a) February **(b)** June **(c)** No 31-day month is specifically mentioned **(d)** April (in the Northern hemisphere; November (in the Southern hemisphere). The jingle is:

Trenta giorni ha novembre
con april, giugno e settembre; [april = aprile]
di ventotto ce n'è uno,
tutti gli altri ne han trentuno. [han = hanno]

	MINIMA	MASSIMA
Bolzano	-2	5
Torino	-3	4
Milano	1	14
Verona	3	7
Venezia	2	11
Trieste	-2	3
Bologna	4	15

EXERCISE 6

(a) A Torino **(b)** A Bologna **(c)** A Verona **(d)** A Verona

EXERCISE 7

(a) nord-ovest **(b)** sud-ovest **(c)** settentrionale **(d)** sud-est **e)** Napoli, Bari **(f)** meridionale **(g)** nord

EXERCISE 8

(a) ii **(b)** ii **(c)** i Did you guess that **miglioramento** is connected with **migliore** meaning better?

EXERCISE 9

		²D			
¹N	O	V	³E	⁴V	E
²O	V	E	S	⁵T	
³R	E	S	T	I	
D		T		R	
		⁴V	E	R	A

EXERCISE 10

(a) la lavoratrice **(b)** la studentessa **(c)** il leone **(d)** il viaggiatore **(e)** la cugina **(f)** il dottore **(g)** la cavalla

EXERCISE 11

(a) L'ufficio informazioni dà l'orario dei treni. **(b)** I biglietti dell'autobus sono venduti dal tabaccaio. **(c)** Il tabaccaio vende i francobolli. **(d)** Il tiramisù è preferito da Zia Nennella. **(e)** Un'auto è messa a disposizione dal garage 'Roma' durante il servizio.

EXERCISE 12

(a) migliore **(b)** migliorata **(c)** miglioramento **(d)** peggiorato **(e)** meglio **(f)** peggioramento

What the signs mean ...
Deviation, Parking, Road Works Ahead, Slow, Uneven Road Surface, Falling Stones

MANY YEARS AGO...

WHAT YOU WILL LEARN
▶ more about how to talk about things in the past
▶ more expressions of time
▶ how to give information about your personal history
▶ how to request this information from others
▶ the names of farmyard animals

BEFORE YOU BEGIN
The written word lacks a large amount of significant information present in speech: unintentional features (like voice tone and pitch, distinguishing one speaker from another; traits like speed of delivery and loudness, conveying something of the speaker's emotions; the use of 'fillers' or 'tags' covering up for hesitation), together with deliberate elements of linguistic meaning like repetition, emphasis and intonation. People will often allow grammatical irregularities in their speech which they would notice and correct in writing (there are examples in Conversations 1 and 2 in this Unit).

POINTS TO REMEMBER FROM UNIT 12
Che tempo fa? Fa freddo/caldo; oggi fa più freddo di ieri

Parco di Pinocchio

Passive construction: **il meccanico mette a punto l'auto** ▷
l'auto è messa a punto dal meccanico

Comparatives: **meglio, migliore, migliorare, miglioramento; peggio, peggiore, peggiorare, peggioramento**

Pronunciation notes

Most Italian words are stressed on the penultimate (last but one) syllable, as in the last example above. The others bear no visible indication of how they should be stressed except when the stress falls on the last syllable (**città, martedì, tiramisù**: see Unit 12); or when one writes an accent to distinguish words with different meanings (e.g. **dà** he/she gives, **da** from; **prìncipi** princes, **princìpi** principles). There are, however, definite stress patterns grouping words with similar endings. For instance, most verbs ending in *-ere* are stressed on the vowel before the ending: **accendere, chiudere, prendere, rendere, scendere, vivere.** All 'they' forms of verbs ending in *-ano* or *-ono* are stressed in the same way (**accendono, chiudono, prendono, rendono, scendono, vivono,** etc.): and that will be the subject of the first exercise.

CONSERVATIONS

Giovanni asks two Tourist Office employees about their visit to England

LISTEN FOR...

- **È mai stata ...?** Have you ever been ...?
- **vent'anni fa** twenty years ago
- **qualche volta** sometimes
- **per conto suo** on your own

Giovanni	È mai stata in Inghilterra?
Signorina 1	Ma, in Inghilterra sono stata esattamente vent'anni fa!
Giovanni	Dov'è stata?
Signorina 1	Proprio a Londra. Ho soggiornato un anno circa a Londra.
Giovanni	Le è piaciuto?
Signorina 1	Allora sì. A me piaceva tanto.
Giovanni	È rimasta a Londra per imparare l'inglese?
Signorina 1	Sì, sì, esatto.
Giovanni	(*turning to the second speaker*) E Lei fa la turista qualche volta per conto suo?
Signorina 2	Sì, ma cerco di non fare il turista. Sono stata a Londra — euh — ho chiesto il materiale d'informazione, poi ho cercato di scoprirla un po' da sola, di conoscer la città personalmente.

▶ **È mai stata ... ?** Have you ever been ...? (referring to a male: **È mai stato?**) **Mai** means 'ever' and **non ... mai** means 'never', e.g. **non sono mai stata in Francia** I've never been to France. **Mai** by itself or at the beginning of a sentence means 'never': **— Sei mai stata in Germania? — Mai**. 'Have you ever been to Germany?' 'Never'.

esattamente exactly

▶ **vent'anni fa** twenty years ago; **una settimana fa** (a week ago); **due giorni fa** (two days ago). Note also: **l'anno/il mese scorso** last year/month; **l'anno/ il mese prossimo** next year/month; **la settimana scorsa/prossima** last/next week.

proprio a Londra right in London

soggiornare to stay, to sojourn; **imposta di soggiorno** (tourist tax)

Le è piaciuto? Did you like it? (i.e. staying in London); if 'it' meant London, **Londra**, it would be **Le è piaciuta?** because names of cities and towns are considered feminine (Unit 12, p. 176). **Piaciuto** is the past participle of **piacere** (to please).

Allora sì. A me piaceva tanto. At the time, yes. I liked it a lot. **Piaceva** is a form of the other past tense called the Imperfect. For the moment, note how it occurs in this and the following Conversations, particularly contrasting it with the perfect tense, then look at the explanations in the *Grammar*, p. 198.

È rimasta ...? Did you stay ...? from **rimanere** (to stay, to remain, to be somewhere)

imparare to learn

▶ **qualche volta** sometimes; **volta** is one of a series of times, e.g. **una volta** (once), **la prima volta** (the first time), **ogni volta** (each time), **tutte le volte** (every time), **una volta alla settimana** (once every week), **una o due volte al mese** (once or twice a month).

▶ **per conto suo** on your (polite) own, by yourself. Also: **per conto mio preferisco vivere in Italia** (as far as I'm concerned I prefer living in Italy); **pago anche per conto del mio amico** (I'm paying also on my friend's behalf).

fare il turista to act the tourist

ho chiesto perfect tense of **chiedere** (to ask for)

ho cercato di scoprirla I tried to discover it. Note how the pronoun **la** (feminine because **città** is understood) is added to the infinitive which drops its final *-e*. That is also true of the remaining forms **lo, li, le. Cercare** (to look for, to try) is used in several common phrases: **cerca di arrivare puntuale** try to be on time; **ti ho cercato questo pomeriggio** I looked for you this afternoon.

da sola by myself, on my own

conoscere to know, to get to know, to become acquainted

personalmente personally, in person, by myself

◗ *Signor Ramenghi reminisces about his travels*

LISTEN FOR...	
▶ **mi è sempre rimasto impresso**	it always stuck in my memory
▶ **una volta**	once
▶ **se non sbaglio**	if I'm not mistaken

Sig. Ramenghi Ricordo un fatto che mi è sempre rimasto impresso sull'Australia: noi facevamo la linea Singapore–Sydney e una volta partendo da Singapore per Sydney abbiamo avuto un cattivo tempo prima di raggiungere l'Australia, ai limiti dell'Australia, e abbiamo dovuto fare un atterraggio di emergenza a Alice Spring[s], che, se non sbaglio, rimane nel deserto australiano.

Giovanni Proprio nel centro, sì.

Sig. Ramenghi Fu una cosa da poco, [in]somma, non fu una grande emergenza. L'atterraggio avvenne di notte, e avevamo l'aereo molto pieno, però la cosa che mi ha impressionato di più è stato che quando abbiamo aperto le porte l'invasione delle mosche. E poi la grande accoglienza de ... del personale di quel piccolo aeroporto, che per esser così piccolo, era attrezzato veramente in modo fantastico. L'emergenza fu risolta e ci portammo via un po' di mosche dell'Australia.

ricordo un fatto I remember a fact. **Ricordare** means both to remember and to remind. It is therefore also possible to say: **mi ricordo di un fatto** (lit. I remind myself of a fact).

▶ **mi è sempre rimasto impresso** it always stuck in my mind (lit. to me it has always remained impressed)

sull'Australia about Australia

noi facevamo la linea Singapore–Sydney we were doing the Singapore–Sydney route. This is another example of the imperfect tense, from **fare**.

The characteristic of this tense is a **-v-** before the ending: further on **avevamo** (we had), from **avere**. To see how it works see the box on p. 198.

▶ **una volta**   once, **due volte** (twice), **tre volte** (three times), etc.

partendo   leaving, from **partire**; for these forms in **-ando**, **-endo** see Unit 7, Conversations 2.

raggiungere   to reach

ai limiti   on the boundary

abbiamo dovuto ...   we had to ...: **ho dovuto** is the perfect tense of **dovere**. More examples in subsequent conversations and notes.

un atterraggio di emergenza   an emergency landing (**atterrare** to land, **terra** land). Often **-nza** or **-nzia** = -nce or -ncy: no need to give you the English equivalent of **adolescenza**, **ambulanza**, **decenza**, **distanza**, **finanza**, **infanzia**, **licenza**, **presidenza**, **temperanza**, **tendenza**, **vigilanza**, etc.

▶ **se non sbaglio**   if I'm not mistaken; **sbagliare** (to make a mistake), **sbaglio** (mistake)

rimane nel deserto australiano   is (lit. remains) in the Australian desert

fu   it was; this is a form of the past simple or past definite (**passato remoto**) of **essere**.

▶ **una cosa da poco**   a thing of no consequence, something unimportant

avvenne di notte   it happened at night; past definite of **avvenire** (to happen)

▶ **la cosa che mi ha impressionato di più è stato che ...** (the thing which impressed me the most was that ...) should be followed by a verb phrase like **siamo stati invasi dalle mosche** (we were invaded by flies), but the speaker uses a noun phrase which does not require **che**. It is as if he had said in English 'what impressed me most was that, when we opened the doors, the invasion of flies'. Such lack of grammatical precision is frequent in spoken language, whatever the language (see *Before You Begin*, p. 187).

la grande accoglienza   the great welcome

per esser così piccolo era attrezzato, etc.   was truly magnificently equipped for such a small airport

fu risolta   was resolved

ci portammo via   we took away; past definite of **portare**, to carry

Singapore

PRACTICE

1 This exercise is on the stress pattern common to many 'they' forms of verbs. Complete the sentences with a third person form according to the model:

Cue: **io mangio ma loro non ...**
completed sentence: **io mangio ma loro non mangiano**

Read each sentence aloud and check your pronunciation with the recording.

a. Io entro, ma loro non _____.

b. Io vedo, ma loro non _____.

c. Io leggo, ma loro non _____.

d. Io compro, ma loro non _____.

e. Io capisco, ma loro non _____.

f. Io pago, ma loro non _____.

2 Listen to Signor Ramenghi telling Giovanni about his early career and tick what you believe to be the correct answers to the following questions:

a. What did Mr Ramenghi do soon after working on ships?　(i) he worked for Alitalia　(ii) he worked in the hotel business

b. Which countries did he work in during that period? Tick all those he mentions.　(i) Italy　(ii) Germany　(iii) England　(iv) Switzerland (v) France

c. During which period did he work for Alitalia?　(i) 1977–1984　(ii) 1967–1985

ANSWERS P. 202 d. What did he do?　(i) he was a jumbo jet pilot　(ii) he was head steward

3 Imagine that today is Monday 27 January **lunedì ventisette gennaio**. Write in the spaces below the dates corresponding to the following expressions:

a. tre giorni fa _____

b. la settimana scorsa _____

c. esattamente due mesi fa _____

d. dopodomani _____

e. lunedì prossimo _____

ANSWERS P. 202 f. la settimana prossima _____

Dino tells Giovanni about his early life

LISTEN FOR...

▶ **sono nato**	I was born
▶ **i primi dieci anni**	the first ten years
▶ **qualche anno dopo**	a few years later
▶ **mi sono trasferito ...**	I moved ...

Giovanni	Dino, dove sei nato?
Dino	Sono nato in un paesino del Friuli che si chiama Tolmezzo. Ho passato i primi dieci anni della mia vita appunto a Tolmezzo, poi per motivi professionali mio padre ha dovuto trasferirsi a Bolzano in Alto Adige e lo abbiamo seguito qualche anno dopo. Quindi ho passato gli anni dell'infanzia a Tolmezzo, gli anni dell'adolescenza a Bolzano dove ho finito le scuole.
Giovanni	E dove hai fatto i tuoi studi universitari? In che città?
Dino	Per gli studi universitari mi sono trasferito a Pisa.

▶ **sono nato** (Perfect tense of **nascere**) is translated as 'I was born'; but **nato** does not *mean* born. **Nascere** is an active verb, something the baby does, whereas to be born is a *passive* verb, meaning to be given life by the mother.

Friuli, Alto Adige   two regions in north-eastern Italy (see *Did you know?*, p. 201)

▶ **i primi dieci anni della mia vita**   the first 10 years of my life; **gli ultimi dieci anni** (the last ten years)

appunto   precisely, as it happens

per motivi professionali   for professional reasons

ha dovuto trasferirsi   he had to move (lit. to transfer himself)

lo abbiamo seguito   we followed him

▶ **qualche anno dopo**   a few years later; **qualche anno prima** (a few years earlier). Remember that the noun following **qualche** is always singular.

▶ **mi sono trasferito a Pisa**   I moved to Pisa. See *Grammar*, p. 198.

Pisa

◗ *A change of booking*

LISTEN FOR...

▶ **il venticinque gennaio**   the 25th of January
▶ **Me lo può fare?**   Can you do it for me?
▶ **volevo sapere se potevo...**   I wanted to know if I could...

Giovanni   Buongiorno. Io ho una prenotazione Roma–Sydney per il venticinque gennaio. Ma l'agenzia mi aveva già confermato il cambio al ventisette gennaio. Me lo può fare?

Agente di viaggio   Al ventisette gennaio. Certamente, però è una prenotazione che io non posso riprendere dal mio terminale. Ora chiamo l'Alitalia e mi faccio dire se pe ... per questa tariffa possiamo applicare tranquillamente uno sticker. Alitalia buongiorno. È la Playtime. Posso chiederti un favore? Volevo sapere se potevo applicare uno sticker su una prenotazione di un biglietto fatto a Sydney. Perfetto, ti ringrazio. Ciao.

prenotazione   booking

▶ **il venticinque gennaio**   the 25th of January. Remember that in Italian dates are expressed in the order day/number/month/year and the number used is the cardinal (25), not the ordinal (25th).

mi aveva già confermato   had already confirmed; **aveva** is a form of the imperfect of **avere** (see *Grammar*, p. 198).

▶ **Me lo può fare?**   Can you do it for me? When the monosyllabic pronouns **lo**, **la**, **li** and **le** (Unit 5, p. 70) are preceded by **mi**, **ti**, **gli/le**, **ci**, **vi** and **si** (Unit 9, p. 129), these change to **me**, **te**, **glie**, **ce**, **ve** and **se**: **te lo chiedo** I'm asking you for it; **glie li do**

I'm giving them to him/her/them, etc. All personal pronouns, including these, are tabled in the next unit.

non posso riprendere dal mio terminale   I cannot access from my (computer) terminal

mi faccio dire   I'll ask them to tell me (lit. to me I make say). Other common expressions with **fare** followed by an infinitive: **lo faccio entrare** (I let him in); **ti faccio vedere** (I let you see, I show you); **mi hanno fatto cambiare l'ora di partenza** (they made me change the time of departure). More about that in the next unit.

per questa tariffa   for this tariff

applicare uno sticker   apply a sticker: an example, together with the name of the travel agency, Playtime, of the impact of trade English on the Italian language (but note the pronunciation 'steeker').

tranquillamente   happily, with no problem (lit. calmly, quietly).

Posso chiederti un favore?   May I ask you a favour? Note that monosyllabic pronouns (**mi**, **ti**, **gli**, **le**, **lo**, **la**, **li**, **ci**, **vi** and **si**) are attached directly to infinitives, which drop their final -*e*: **devo farlo**   I must do it, **ho cercato di scoprirla da sola** I tried to discover it by myself, etc.

▶ **volevo sapere se potevo ...**   I wanted to know if I could; Imperfect tense of **volere** and **potere**

PRACTICE

4 Fill in the gaps in the sentences below with one of the following forms of **essere**: **sono**, **sono stato** (or **sono stata**), **sarò**. You won't need your recording.

a. _____a Tolmezzo i primi dieci anni.

b. _____a Londra due anni fa.

c. _____a Roma la settimana prossima.

d. _____in Italia da due settimane.

e. _____in Alto Adige per i prossimi due anni.

ANSWERS P. 202 f. _____a casa dopodomani.

5 Using Dino's story and the following questions as a guide, make up some sentences about your past.

a. Dove sei nato/nata?

_____

b. Hai passato l'infanzia lì?

_____

c. Dove sei andato a scuola?

_____

d. Dove abiti adesso?

_____

e. Che tipo di città/paese è?

_____

f. Quanti abitanti ha?

_____

g. Ti trovi bene lì?

ANSWERS P. 202

_____

6 This exercise is about the combinations **me lo**, **te li**, **ce la**, etc., described in the second sound clip. Fill in the gaps in the answers with the appropriate combinations chosen from the box below, then check your answers with your recording.

Model: **Ti hanno spedito i biglietti? — No, me li spediscono domani.**

L'agenzia ti ha cambiato la prenotazione?

No, _____cambia domani.

La banca vi ha dato i travellers cheques?

No, _____dà domani.

Hai mandato a tuo zio una cartolina illustrata?

No, _____mando domani.

Quando ci presenti i tuoi amici italiani? **presentare** = to introduce

_____presento domani.

Hai dato i regali ai tuoi nipotini?

No, _____do domani.

| ce li   glie li   glie la   me la   ve li |

CONVERSATIONS 3

 A student explains why she came to Rome to study

LISTEN FOR...

▶ Come mai ...?	Why ...?
▶ ho deciso di trasferirmi	I decided to move
▶ per studiare	(in order) to study
▶ sono qui da un tre o quattro mesi	I have been here about three or four months

Giovanni E come mai è venuta da Lecce a studiare a Roma?

Marcella Perché la Facoltà d'Architettura non c'è a Lecce. Poi le Facoltà d'Architettura sono tutte a numero chiuso in Italia. Dove si superava il test allora era il caso di entrare. L'ho superato a Roma e ho deciso di trasferirmi qui a Roma per studiare.

Giovanni Ma Lei ha acquistato già un accento romano. Da quanto tempo è a Roma?

Marcella Eh, sono qui da un tre o quattro mesi.

▶ **Come mai ... ?** Why ...? Unlike **perché**, which also means 'because', **come mai** is used only in questions. It also suggests one does not expect an unsatisfactory or debatable answer. Otherwise one tends to ask **perché**: **Perché non hai risposto quando ti ho chiamato?** Why did you not reply when I called you?

la Facoltà d'Architettura the Faculty of Architecture

numero chiuso selective entry (lit. closed number)

dove si superava ... etc. it was advisable to [seek to] be admitted where one [had] passed the [admission] test

▶ **ho deciso di trasferirmi** I decided to move; **Che cosa hai deciso?** What have you decided?

▶ **per studiare** (in order) to study; **per** + infinitive is the standard way to express aim or intended result: **sono qui per imparare l'italiano** I am here to learn Italian; **per accendere, premere il bottone A** to switch on, press button A.

▶ **sono qui da un tre o quattro mesi** I have been here about three or four months. For this construction see *Grammar* on p. 199. Remember that the indefinite article **un** before a number (including a fraction like **mezzo**) indicates approximation: **c'erano un cinque o sei persone** there were about five or six people; **vorrei un mezzo chilo di vitello** I'd like about half a kilo of veal.

Piazza del Pantheon, Rome

Enrico e Cesarina tell Giovanni about the places they come from

LISTEN FOR...

▶ **Che posto è?** What (sort of) place is it?
▶ **Quanti abitanti fa?** How many inhabitants does it have?
▶ **in confronto a ...** in comparison with ...

Giovanni	Che posto è Palombaro?
Enrico	Eh, è un piccolo paesino di collina. Si trova molto vicino alla catena degli Appennini, alla Maiella, no?
Giovanni	Quindi è un paese agricolo.
Enrico	Mmm, sì, però più che agricoltura è l'allevamento.
Giovanni	Bestiame?
Enrico	Sì, bestiame, o ... ovini, suini ...
Giovanni	Mmm, mmm.
Enrico	Bo ... bovini.
Giovanni	Quanti abitanti fa Palombaro più o meno?
Enrico	Molto pochi. Siamo in tut ... in tutto milletrecento abitanti.
Giovanni	(*to Cesarina*) Allora in confronto a Palombaro Suzzara è una città.
Cesarina	Eh, Suzzara non è una città molto grande. È una cittadina dove sono sorte ultimamente alcune industrie. Comunque prevale l'attività agricola.

▶ **Che posto è ?** What (sort of) place is it? Other phrases with **posto**: **che bel posto** what a beautiful place; **un posto di montagna** a mountain resort, **tutto è a posto** everything is OK, **mettere a posto** to tidy up, to put (things, persons) in their place.

collina hill, hillside
catena mountain range (also chain)
Maiella a mountain in the Apennines (**Appennini**)
allevamento animal breeding; **allevare** to raise, to bring up
bestiame (m), from **bestia** (beast, animal), is a general word for cattle and farm animals, excluding poultry which is called **pollame** (**pollo** chicken). It is subdivided into **bovini** cows, heifers, oxen and bulls; **ovini** sheep and goats; and **suini** pigs. The names of the various farm animals are listed in a box below.

▶ **Quanti abitanti fa?** How many inhabitants does it have (lit. make)? Enrico might have replied **fa in tutto 1300 abitanti,** but included himself among them by saying 'we are 1,300 in all'.

FARM ANIMALS

pecora sheep, **agnello** lamb, **ariete** ram
capra goat, **caprone** billy goat, **capretto** kid
maiale (m), **porco** pig, **scrofa** sow
mucca, vacca cow, **toro** bull, **bue** (pl **buoi**) ox, **vitello** calf
cavallo horse, **stallone** stallion, **giumenta** mare
asino donkey, **mulo** mule
gallina chicken, **gallo** rooster, **pulcino** chick
oca goose, **anatra** duck, **tacchino** turkey

▶ **in confronto a ...** in comparison with ...; e.g. **in confronto a me tu sei snello** (compared to me you're slim); **il giapponese è difficile in confronto all'italiano** (Japanese is difficult in comparison with Italian).
sorto past participle of **sorgere** (to arise)
ultimamente recently, lately
prevalere to prevail

7 Replace the infinitives in the square brackets in the following sentences with the appropriate forms of the Imperfect. How the Imperfect works is explained in *Grammar*, p. 198.

a. Io [**volere**] _____ mezzo chilo di vitello. — Sì, signora. Le [**occorrere**] _____ altro? Va bene così?

b. Durante le mie vacanze [**piovere**] _____ sempre e [**tirare**] _____ vento.

c. Una volta le cipolle mi [**piacere**] _____. Adesso non mi piacciono più.

d. Quando [**essere**] _____ giovane, il signor Ramenghi [**lavorare**] _____ come steward sugli aerei dell'Alitalia. Spesso [**fare**] _____ la linea Singapore–Sydney.

e. L'agente di viaggio ha telefonato all'Alitalia perché [**volere**] _____ sapere se [**potere**] _____ applicare uno sticker al mio biglietto.

ANSWERS P. 202

8 Follow the instructions on your recording to construct a simple narrative about past events. You will be guided to answer questions like: Dove abitava? (Abitavo a …), Come si trovava? (Mi trovavo bene …), Aveva amici o parenti? etc.

9 By reference to 15 September, select from the box the Italian expressions identifying the following times. One question may have two correct answers.

a. 15 luglio

b. 15 novembre

c. 15 ottobre, 15 novembre, 15 dicembre, 15 gennaio, etc.

d. 15 e 30 ottobre, 15 e 30 novembre, 15 e 30 dicembre, 15 e 30 gennaio, etc.

e. 15 settembre, 15 novembre, 15 gennaio, 15 marzo, 15 maggio, etc.

ANSWERS P. 202

f. il periodo dal 15 settembre al 15 novembre

due mesi dopo

due mesi prima

due volte al mese

i primi due mesi

ogni due mesi

ogni mese

una volta al mese

GRAMMAR AND EXERCISES

How to talk about things in the past (2)

The Perfect tense together with the Past Definite (not included in this course are used to talk about things which occurred at a specific time or period in the past, and are regarded as completed or finished (which is what 'perfect' means):

Sono stato a Londra la prima volta nel 1980 e ci sono rimasto due anni   I was in London the first time in 1980 and stayed there two years.

Dino's account (Conversations 2) presents a series of stages each of which must be completed before the next one may begin: therefore all the verbs are in the Perfect tense.

The other past tense is called the Imperfect, and is formed by taking the infinitive, replacing the final -*re* with -*v*-, and adding the endings -*o*, -*i*, -*a*, -*amo*, -*ate*, -*ano*, very similar to those of the Present tense. Some verbs form their Imperfect from an 'extended' infinitive: **bere** to drink ▷ **bevevo**; **fare** to do ▷ **facevo**; **dire** to say ▷ **dicevo**. **Essere** has the only irregular Imperfect.

The Imperfect leaves things 'unfinished' and is therefore used to talk about situations or conditions lasting or recurring over an unspecified length of time in the past. It can often be translated into English as 'was -*ing*' or 'used to …':
Quando ero a Londra andavo spesso a teatro. Allora costava poco. When I was in London I used to go often to the theatre. Then it was cheap. **Quando ero bambino …** when I was a child …, **quando**

	essere	parlare	avere	finire
I	ero	parlavo	avevo	finivo
you	eri	parlavi	avevi	finivi
he/she/it you (pol)	era	parlava	aveva	finiva
we	eravamo	parlavamo	avevamo	finivamo
you (pl)	eravate	parlavate	avevate	finivate
they	erano	parlavano	avevano	finivano

avevo dieci anni when I was 10 (see note opposite).

Some verbs, therefore, expressing a completed or instantaneous action, are rarely if ever used in the Imperfect tense: **la posta è arrivata**   the post has arrived; **una bomba è esplosa**   a bomb exploded; **la mia famiglia si è trasferita a Bolzano** my family moved to Bolzano.

The two tenses may be contrasted in the same sentence:
Lavoravo in un grande albergo, e così ho imparato l'inglese. I used to work in a luxury hotel (unspecified duration), that's how I learned English (completed action).
Ho soggiornato un anno circa a Londra. Mi piaceva tanto. I spent about one year in London (completed action). I liked it very much (while I was there, unspecified time).
Facevamo la linea Singapore–Sydney e una volta abbiamo avuto cattivo tempo. We were doing the Singapore–Sydney route (unspecified length of time, or recurrent time) and on one occasion (specific time) we hit bad weather.

The Imperfect is also used to 'tone down' a request:
Volevo sapere se potevo applicare uno sticker
I wanted to know whether I could apply a sticker;
Volevo mezzo chilo di vitello   I'd like half a kilo of veal.

Expressions of time with *da* and *per*

You are familiar with expressions like: **vivo a Roma da tanti anni; faccio l'apicultore da trentacinque anni; sono in Italia da tre o quattro mesi.** Instead of the Present tense and the preposition **da**, their English translation uses a form of Perfect and the preposition 'for': 'I have been living in Rome for many years (and still live there)'; 'I have been a beekeeper for 35 years (and still am)'; 'I have been in Italy for three or four months (and I am still there)'.

Note, however, that the English structure 'Perfect tense + for' in the previous paragraph has a different meaning if transposed into Italian. **Sono vissuto a Roma per molti anni; sono stato un apicultore per trentacinque anni; sono stato in Italia per tre o quattro mesi** mean 'I lived in Italy for many years', 'I was a beekeeper for 35 years', 'I was in Italy for three or four months' but no longer.

Perfect of *dovere, potere, volere*

The past participles of these verbs are: **dovuto, potuto, voluto**.

Like 'must', 'can' and 'will', these verbs are followed by an infinitive without any intervening preposition. To form the Perfect tense of these verbs, you should use the auxiliary, **essere** or **avere**, appropriate to the verb that follows: <u>sono</u> **dovuto venire** I had to come, because you say **sono venuto**; **non <u>ha</u> potuto prendere il treno**, because you say <u>ha</u> **preso il treno**; but Italian speakers often disregard this rule and use **avere** in most cases.

Age

In English you say 'when I was 10 (years old)'. In Italian you say **quando avevo dieci anni**. The question 'How old are you?' is translated as **Quanti anni hai?**

10 Complete the following sentences with the verb forms in the box at the end of the exercise.

a. Quando _____ l'inglese a Londra
   _____ molto andare a teatro.

b. _____ a Londra solo due volte e
   _____ molto.

c. Per cinque anni _____ come
   steward per l'Alitalia, poi _____ un
   caffè-ristorante mio.

d. Quando _____ come steward per
   l'Alitalia, _____ spesso la linea
   Roma–Singapore.

e. _____ dieci anni a Tolmezzo, poi la
   mia famiglia _____ a Bolzano.

f. Durante la mia infanzia _____ a
   Tolmezzo.

> facevo   ho aperto   ho lavorato   ho passato
> lavoravo   mi è piaciuta   mi piaceva
> si è trasferita   sono andato   studiavo   abitavo

ANSWERS P. 202

11 Translate the following passages into Italian. You will have to choose between Perfect and Imperfect tenses. The first sentence is done for you. Can you guess the Italian word for 'promotion'?

When I was a child I went to school in Rochester. Quando ero bambina sono andata a scuola a Rochester. My family moved to Chatham when I was 15.

_____

_____

My father worked for a bank, and got a promotion.

_____

_____

I finished university in 1986, when I lived in London.

_____

_____

12 Fill in the gaps with **da** or **per**.

_____ quanto tempo vivi a Londra?

Vivo a Londra _____ quindici anni. Sto in questa

casa _____ diversi anni. Ma ho abitato la mia

casa di prima solo _____ quattro anni e mezzo.

_____ quanto tempo sei stata a Bologna?

Sono stata a Bologna _____ cinque o sei anni.

ANSWERS P. 202

KEY WORDS
AND PHRASES

Expressions of time:

vent'anni fa	twenty years ago
qualche anno dopo	a few years later
qualche volta	sometimes
i primi dieci anni	the first ten years
una volta	once
il venticinque gennaio	the 25th of January
sono qui da tre o quattro mesi	I have been here three or four months [and still am]
sono stato là per tre o quattro mesi	I was there three or four months [but no longer am]

Asking for information:

È mai stata …?	Have you ever been …?
Come mai …?	Why …? How come …?
Me lo può fare?	Can you do it for me?
Che posto è?	What (sort of) place is it?
Quanti abitanti fa?	How many inhabitants does it have?
Quanti anni ha?	How old is he/she/are you (polite)?
Da quanto tempo è …?	How long has he/she/have you (polite) been … [and still are]?
Per quanto tempo è stato/stata … ?	How long was he/she, were you (polite) … [but no longer]?
volevo sapere se potevo …?	I wanted to know if I could …?
per conto suo	on his/her own, on your own (polite)

Giving information:

sono nato	I was born
mi è sempre rimasto impresso	it always stuck in my mind
se non sbaglio	if I'm not mistaken
ho deciso di trasferirmi	I decided to move
ha dovuto trasferirsi	he had to move
per studiare	(in order) to study
in confronto a …	in comparison with …

Population in Italy

In 1861, according to the census organized by the first united Italian government, the population of Italy was about 26 million people. Today it is over 56 million. Since the mid-1980s, however, Italy's population has shown a tendency to decline, with deaths exceeding births for the first time in several centuries. The largest towns are **Roma**, the capital, with nearly 2.8 million inhabitants; **Milano**, around 1.4 million; **Napoli**, with just over a million; and **Torino**, with just under. There are about 40 towns with over 100,000, and 75 with over 50,000 inhabitants. Italy was divided for most of its history into several independent states and principalities, and therefore nearly every Italian town of some importance was at some time or other a state or regional capital. Probably because of it, Italians tend to underestimate the importance of provincial towns which never achieved capital status: in the next unit you will hear a student describe his home town, Gambettola, with up to 50,000 people in it, as **un paesino**, a small village. Thriving provincial centres with more than 100,000 inhabitants are often described as **cittadine**, small towns.

Government and political structure

Italy is divided into 20 statutory **regioni**, of which five (**Valle d'Aosta**, **Trentino Alto Adige**, **Friuli–Venezia Giulia**, **Sicilia** and **Sardegna**) have a special constitution. All these Regions are subdivided into 103 provinces comprising 8,184 municipalities (**comuni**), each headed by an elected **sindaco**. Local government powers were enhanced by legislation passed in the late 1960s. Foreign visitors also benefited from an increased number of interesting cultural initiatives on a regional level (art exhibitions, concerts, festivals, theatrical events, restoration and preservation of ancient monuments, greater care for the environment, etc.).

A constitutional monarchy from 1861 to the end of World War II, in 1946 Italy became a Republic with a President elected by Parliament. For about 40 years government remained firmly in the hands of the Christian Democrat Party (**Democrazia Cristiana**) whose influence was bolstered by the United States in the interest of making Italy a pillar of NATO's anti-Communist line-up and preventing the second largest party, the Communist Party (**Partito Comunista Italiano**), from gaining power. This aim was achieved not without a large measure of political corruption which tainted the other parties eventually admitted to sharing government, like the Socialists (**Partito Socialista Italiano**). Whatever reason there might have been for propping up or tolerating a corrupt regime in Italy, it disappeared in the late 1980s, when Communism collapsed in the former USSR and in Eastern Europe. The Christian Democrat–Socialist coalition fell from power, and hundreds of politicians and industrialists were indicted by magistrates for taking and giving huge bribes (**tangenti**).

The general shake-up of Italian politics, which was supposed to reduce the number of small parties and factions jostling for power, did not change things much. The victors of the 1994 general elections were a largely nondescript movement conjured up by the wealthiest Italian media entrepreneur (**Forza Italia**), a strengthened right-wing party called **Alleanza Nazionale** (National Alliance) and a Northern separatist league (**Lega Nord**). Lacking a common political programme, the government alliance they formed lasted predictably for a very short time. The former main parties, having renamed themselves **Partito Popolare** (Popular Party) and **Partito Democratico della Sinistra** (Democratic Party of the Left), in turn produced splinter movements. The victory of the **Ulivo** (olive-tree) coalition at the 1996 general elections brought to power for the first time in modern history communist and left-wing politicians, together with social democrats and progressive Catholics.

AND FINALLY...

13 Follow the instructions on your recording for this final speaking exercise. You'll be asked a few questions about your language learning. You will need a new verb: **cominciare**, to commence, to begin.

ANSWERS

EXERCISE 2

(a) ii, 'ho sempre fatto la carriera alberghiera'   **(b)** i, iii, iv,
(c) ii   **(d)** ii

EXERCISE 3

(a) venerdì ventiquattro gennaio   **(b)** dal venti al ventisei
gennaio   **(c)** il ventisette novembre   **(d)** mercoledì
ventinove gennaio   **(e)** il tre febbraio   **(f)** dal tre al nove
febbraio (normally you do not need to write the numbers
in full; this is just to remind you of the Italian numbers).

EXERCISE 4

(a), (b), sono stato/a   **(c), (e), (f)** sarò   **(d)** sono

EXERCISE 5

(a) Sono nato/nata a …
(b) Sì fino a … anni. / No, a … anni mi sono trasferito a …
con la mia famiglia.
(c) Sono andato a scuola nel posto dove sono nato. / Sono
andato a scuola a …
(d) Adesso abito a …; mi sono trasferito a … da … anni.
(e) È una grande città / è un paese piccolo / agricolo / di
campagna / industriale / commerciale.
(f) … abitanti / Non so esattamente: circa …
(g) Sì, mi trovo molto bene. Sono contento. / Non mi piace.
Spero di partire, di andare a …, di trasferirmi a … .

EXERCISE 7

(a) volevo, occorreva   **(b)** pioveva, tirava   **(c)** piacevano
(d) era, lavorava, faceva   **(e)** voleva, poteva.

EXERCISE 9

(a) due mesi prima
(b) due mesi dopo
(c) una volta al mese, ogni mese
(d) due volte al mese
(e) ogni due mesi
(f) i primi due mesi

EXERCISE 10

(a) studiavo, mi piaceva   **(b)** sono andato, mi è piaciuta
(c) ho lavorato, ho aperto
(d) lavoravo, facevo   **(e)** ho passato, si è trasferita
(f) abitavo.

EXERCISE 11

La famiglia si è trasferita a Chatham quando avevo quindici
anni.
Mio padre lavorava per una banca, e ha avuto una
promozione.
Ho finito l'università nel millenovecento ottantasei, quando
vivevo a Londra.

EXERCISE 12

Da quanto tempo vivi a Londra?
Vivo a Londra da quindici anni. Sto in questa casa da diversi
anni. Ma ho abitato la mia casa di prima solo per quattro anni
e mezzo.
Per quanto tempo sei stata a Bologna?
Sono stata a Bologna per cinque o sei anni.

WHAT YOU WILL LEARN
- ▶ how to talk about things you would like to do
- ▶ how to invite people to an evening out
- ▶ how to explain minor health problems to a doctor or a pharmacist
- ▶ the main parts of the human body

BEFORE YOU BEGIN

You can speak a line of print exactly as it is written, but writing does not represent the other features of language found in speech. On the other hand, writing has one feature not found in speech, without which one could not read easily: spaces between words. How do we tell spoken words apart without silent spaces between them? It would be too complicated to explain how it's done. What's important is that the moment you can single out unknown words from a sentence spoken in the language you are studying, you can find out what they mean and how they are used. That is the moment when you turn from a guided student into an autonomous learner.

POINTS TO REMEMBER FROM UNIT 13

Use of the Imperfect to express:
(a) unspecified period of time: **quando ero a scuola ...**   when I was at school ...
(b) repeated occurrences: **ogni volta che la incontravo ...**   every time I met her ...
(c) 'toning down' requests: **volevo delle informazioni`**   I wanted some information
(d) conditions: **se Carlo voleva, veniva**   if Carlo had wanted to he would have come.

Expressions of time:
studio l'italiano da quattro mesi I've been studying Italian for four months [and still am]
ho studiato l'italiano per quattro mesi I studied Italian for four months [and then stopped]

Pronunciation notes

Another group of words bearing the stress on the second syllable before the last one includes a number of nouns/adjectives ending in *-ico*, like **meccanico** and **democratico**, mostly analogous to English words ending in *-ic/-ical* (mechanic, mechanical, democratic). They will be the subject of Practice Exercise 1.

Nennella and Giovanni make plans for the evening

LISTEN FOR...

▶ **Che cosa ti piacerebbe fare?**   What would you like to do?
▶ **si potrebbe ...**   one could ...
▶ **Che cosa danno?**   What's on?
▶ **l'idea mi va**   I like the idea

Nennella	Che cosa ti piacerebbe fare questa sera? Si potrebbe andare al cinema?
Giovanni	Ma, non c'è niente di bello al cinema, niente che vorrei vedere.
Nennella	Se ti piace la musica popolare potremmo andare ad un concerto.
Giovanni	Mmm ... un concerto. Che cosa danno?
Nennella	Musica popolare dell'Italia meridionale. Canti e danze della Basilicata.
Giovanni	Ah ... sì, l'idea mi va. Andiamo a questo concerto.

▶ **Che cosa ti piacerebbe fare?**   What would you like to do? For **piacerebbe, potrebbe, potremmo, vorrei**, see Unit 8, p. 118. These are other ways of asking basically the same question: **Che cosa vogliamo fare questa sera?, Che cosa facciamo questa sera?, Che cosa si fa questa sera?**

▶ **si potrebbe ...**   one could ...: **si potrebbe andare al cinema** (one could go to the cinema); **si potrebbe fare una passeggiata** (one could go for a walk), etc. Alternatively: **potremmo andare al cinema** (we could go to the cinema); **a un concerto** (to a concert).

niente di bello   nothing good. Note the use of **di** after **niente**: **niente di interessante** (nothing interesting); **non c'è niente di male** (there's no harm in it). 'Good' speaking of shows and entertainment is **bello** (lit. beautiful).

niente che vorrei vedere   nothing (that) I'd like to see. Remember that **che** must be used in some cases when 'that' is normally omitted in English (see Unit 11, pp. 166–7).

▶ **Che cosa danno?**   What's on? (lit. What do they give?) You can use **danno** for all sorts of performances and entertainments: **danno un'opera di Puccini a teatro** they're performing an opera by Puccini at the theatre. Remember that the English 'on' speaking of radio and TV is **a** + article, NOT **su**: **questa sera danno un concerto alla radio**   tonight there's a concert on the radio, **c'è *Via col vento* stasera a canale 5**   *Gone with the Wind* is on tonight on channel 5.

musica popolare   folk music; **popolo** (people), in the sense of population, NOT of a group of individuals. This is **la gente** – always singular!; **c'era molta gente** there were many people.

canti e danze   songs and dances; **cantare** (to sing), **danzare** or **ballare** (to dance)

Basilicata   a region in southern Italy

▶ **l'idea mi va**   I like the idea; **Ti va?** (Do you like it?), **non mi va per niente** (I don't like it at all)

◗ *An evening at the opera*

LISTEN FOR...

▶ **se t'interessa**	if you are interested
▶ **sarebbe una buona idea**	it would be a good idea
▶ **pronti per le otto**	ready by eight
▶ **in tempo**	on time

Dino	A te piace l'opera?
Giovanni	Ma, non eccessivamente, devo dir la verità. Perché?
Dino	Siccome stasera danno *La Bohème* al teatro, mi piacerebbe molto andarci. E, se t'interessa, possiamo andare insieme.
Giovanni	Mmm … a che teatro la danno?
Dino	Al Goldoni.
Giovanni	Eh sì, sarebbe una buona idea. Sai a che ora comincia?
Dino	Alle otto e mezzo, e … quindi, se noi siamo pronti per le otto, arriviamo senz'altro in tempo.

non eccessivamente   not very much (lit. not excessively)

devo dir[e] la verità (lit. I must tell the truth), also **per dir la verità**   to tell the truth

siccome   as, since

al teatro   at the theatre. Other examples: **al cinema, alla radio, alla televisione, al circo** (circus), **allo stadio comunale** (city stadium), **al Conservatorio** (Conservatoire).

▶ **se t'interessa**   if you are interested (lit. if it interests you)

Goldoni   name of the theatre (from the 18th-century Venetian playwright)

▶ **sarebbe una buona idea**   it would be a good idea. Or simply, **Buona idea!, Che buona idea!**

▶ **pronti per le otto**   ready by eight

▶ **in tempo**   on time. Note the following expressions: **puntualmente**   punctually; **in ritardo**   late; **In anticipo**   early, in advance.

Unit 14   Going out and staying healthy

1 This is a pronunciation exercise for nouns and adjectives ending in unstressed *-ico*, *-ica*. Remember that the plural of words ending in unstressed *-ico* does not keep the 'hard' *-c-* and ends in *-ici*: **simpatico** nice, likeable ▷ **simpatici**. **Simpatica**, on the other hand, has a normal plural, **simpatiche**. You will hear some new words including **fantastico** fantastic, fabulous and **ascoltato**, past participle of **ascoltare** (to listen).

2 Listen to three people introducing themselves on tape and decide which of the entertainments advertised they would each enjoy.
More than one choice per person is possible.

Carla _____

Luisa _____

Giorgio _____

---

a

TEATRO DELLE MUSE

Stagione internazionale

presenta

la compagnia del Birmingham
Repertory Theatre

in

THE HERETIC

di David Williamson
in lingua originale

---

b

TEATRO LIRICO

Concerto sinfonico Orchestra da
camera della RAI

diretta dal Maestro Bruno Maderna

Musiche di

Albinoni, Purcell, Mozart,

Poulenc, Martinu

---

c

AL CLUB DEL JAZZ

suona il

● NEW AUSTRALIAN JAZZ QUINTET ●

con

Vince Donati .... sax tenore

Ephrem Goldman .... tromba

Nick Papadopoulos .... tastiere

Harry Wright .... contrabbasso

Steve Gulpilil .... percussione

---

d

Al CINEMA ASTORIA

Grande ripresa di
un classico film di
Margarethe von Trotta

Paura e amore

con

FANNY ARDANT

GRETA SCACCHI

VALERIA GOLINO

ANSWERS P. 218

3 Here are the programmes shown by a number of film societies and specialist cinemas in Rome. Read them carefully and answer the following questions. The questions are in Italian but you should have no difficulty in understanding them. **Film**, like all borrowed nouns ending in a consonant (e.g. **sport**, **jeep**, **leader**), does not change in the plural.

CINECLUB
dal 3 all'8 marzo

ARCHIMEDE, Via Archimede 71 (Parioli) Tel. 587 55 67. Chiuso per restauro

AUSONIA, Via Padova 92 (Nomentano) Tel. 742 61 80 Feriali-festivi L. 15.000, ridotti L. 10.000

3 **Il prigioniero di Zenda** di W. Mirisch, con Peter Sellers

4 **Animal House** di J. Landis

5 **The Blues Brothers** di J. Landis

6 **1941: Allarme a Hollywood** di S. Spielberg

7–8 **The Blues Brothers** replica

BOITO, Via A. Boito 12 (Vescovio) Tel. 831 01 98. L. 15.000 Non pervenuto

CENTRE CULTUREL FRANÇAIS
Piazza Campitelli 3, Tel. 679 42 87

3 **Touchez-pas au grisbi** di Jacques Becker

6 **Casque d'or** di Jacques Becker

7 **Vivre sa vie** di Jean-Luc Godard

9 **Au revoir les enfants** di Louis Malle

FARNESE, Piazza Campo de' Fiori 56 Tel. 6 56 43 95. Feriali e festivi L.15.000, Ridotti L.10.000 Rassegna di film interpretati da Greta Garbo, in lingua originale con sottotitoli:

3 **La regina Cristina** di R. Mamoulian

4 **Anna Karenina** di C. Brown

5 **La conquista (Maria Walewska)** di C. Brown

6 **Ninotchka** di E. Lubitsch

FILMSTUDIO, Via Orti d'Alibert 1C (Trastevere). Tel. 865 73 78. Tessera per 4 mesi L. 25.000; ingresso L. 15.000 Rassegna dei film Merchant-Ivory in lingua originale con sottotitoli.

3 **Shakespeare Wallah**

4 **Autobiografia di una principessa**

5 **Quartetto**

6 **Calore e polvere**

7 **Camera con vista**

8 **Howard's End**

---

a. Dove vai, se vuoi vedere film con Greta Garbo? _____

b. Quale cineclub presenta la versione italiana di 'Room with a View' ? _____

c. Dove puoi vedere film francesi nella versione originale? _____

d. Quanto costa un biglietto ordinario in quasi tutti questi cineclub? _____

e. Quale cineclub è chiuso? _____

f. Si possono vedere in questi cinema film italiani con attori italiani? _____

ANSWERS P. 218

Cini and Giovanni plan to have a meal out

LISTEN FOR...

▶ **Perché non facciamo qualcosa insieme?**	Why don't we do something together?
▶ **volentieri**	willingly
▶ **scegliamo un buon ristorante**	let's choose a good restaurant
▶ **magari invitiamo anche lui**	perhaps we could invite him too

Giovanni	Senti, perché non facciamo qualcosa insieme domani sera?
Cini	Volentieri!
Giovanni	Che cosa ti piacerebbe di fare?
Cini	Ma, potremmo mangiare qualche cosa … scegliamo un buon ristorante …
Giovanni	Ce lo facciamo indicare da Aldo.
Cini	Sì.
Giovanni	E magari invitiamo anche lui e la zia.
Cini	Molto bene.

senti, the '**tu**' form of the polite **senta** often used as a sentence opener such as 'well', 'so' (Unit 3, p. 33).

▶ **Perché non facciamo qualcosa insieme?** Why don't we do something together?

domani sera tomorrow night. For this and other expressions of time see Unit 6, p. 81.

▶ **volentieri** willingly, a word connected with **volere** (to want, will)

▶ **scegliamo un buon ristorante** let's choose a good restaurant. The forms in *-iamo* may also be used to mean 'let's …': **andiamo** (let's go); **ascoltiamo** (let's listen); **sentiamo** let's hear (it).

ce lo facciamo indicare da Aldo we'll ask Aldo to suggest one (lit. us it make point out by Aldo). See *Grammar*, p. 214.

▶ **magari invitiamo anche lui** perhaps we could invite him too (lit. perhaps we invite also him)

Gianfranco describes his future work prospects

LISTEN FOR...

▶ **appena ritorno a casa**   as soon as I get back home

Gianfranco	Fino ad ora ho studiato, però appena ritorno a casa inizierò a lavorare in una scuola materna, perché sono anche maestro.
Giovanni	Ah, sei maestro … Una scuola materna: quindi insegnerai a bambini piccoli.
Gianfranco	Dai tre ai sei anni.
Giovanni	Dove insegnerai?
Gianfranco	Insegnerò in un paesino vicino Cesena, che è la mia città natale. Insegnerò a Gambettola, un paesino di circa cinquantamila abitanti.

▶ **appena ritorno a casa …**   as soon as I get back home …; **appena mi ha visto mi ha salutato** (as soon as he/she saw me he/she greeted me); **lo farò appena possibile** (I'll do it as soon as possible). Here **appena** joins two phrases, both with a verb. Otherwise it means 'just', 'hardly', 'barely': **sono appena ritornato a casa** I've just returned home; **mi ha parlato appena** (he/she hardly spoke to me); **la cosa è appena possibile** (the thing is barely possible).

inizierò   future tense of **iniziare**, to begin; used like **cominciare**

maestro -a   nursery and primary schoolteacher

scuola materna   nursery school

bambino -a   child; **bambinaia** (nanny); but the word for childhood is either **infanzia** or **fanciullezza** (another word for child is **fanciullo -a**).

natale   of birth, from **nascere**, to be born, past participle **nato** (Unit 13). **Natale** is also the Italian for Christmas.

4 Listen on your recording to two friends discussing their plans for the evening, and answer the following questions:

   a. What do they decide straight away NOT to do? (i) go to the cinema (ii) stay at home

   b. Does the man like opera? (i) yes (ii) no

   c. Does he want to go to (i) a play? (ii) a concert?

   d. What do they decide to do in the end? (i) go to a symphony concert the following evening (ii) go to a play by Goldoni at the Teatro delle Muse (iii) dine out at a good restaurant

ANSWERS P. 218

5 Your friend doesn't know what to do in her free time. Complete the sentences below with the most likely phrases from those in the box.

   a. Usciamo insieme questa sera? Danno _____

      all'Odeon. Ti piacerebbe vederlo?

   b. Sei stanca? Allora potremmo stare a casa a

      _____ .

   c. Oppure andiamo a _____ . Potremmo

      incontrarci con Anna e Flavia al bar Motta verso le otto.

   d. Se vuoi un po' di cultura, potremmo _____ .

      È aperto domani.

   e. Domani se fa bello, andiamo _____ .

      Comincia già a far caldo.

| al mare | guardare la televisione | prendere un drink | un film di Fellini | visitare il museo |

ANSWERS P. 218

6 And now it's your turn to decide what to do tonight. Follow the instructions on your recording.

At the pharmacy

LISTEN FOR...	
▶ **due tubetti di dentifricio**	two tubes of toothpaste
▶ **mal di testa**	headache
▶ **gocce**	drops
▶ **ci sono diversi prodotti**	there are several products
▶ **effetti collaterali**	side effects

Giovanni	Buongiorno dottore.
Dottore	[*mumbles*] Buongiorno.
Giovanni	Vorrei due tubetti di Iodosan Zambelletti. Due tubetti di dentifricio.
Dottore	Ah, dentifricio?
Giovanni	Di dentifricio. E ha anche dello Iodosan a gocce, come collutorio?
Dottore	Sì.
Giovanni	Allora se me ne dà due.
Dottore	Nient'altro?
Giovanni	Ah, senta, per un mal di testa che cosa lei consiglierebbe?
Dottore	Ma, ci sono diversi prodotti. Un analgesico tranquillo può essere il Moment che non dà grandi effetti collaterali. È un antinfiammatorio.
Giovanni	Ah, un antinfiammatorio.

dottore pharmacists are addressed as **dottore** or **dottoressa**

▶ **due tubetti di dentifricio** two tubes of toothpaste (Iodosan Zambelletti is a brand name).

▶ **gocce** drops. Medicines and drugs also come in **compresse** tablets; **pillole** pills; **pastiglie** lozenges; **bustine** sachets; **iniezioni** injections; **supposte** suppositories; **pomate** ointments; **lozioni** lotions

collutorio gargle, mouthwash

▶ **mal di testa** headache. For other common ailments see the box below.

▶ **ci sono diversi prodotti** there are several products

un analgesico tranquillo a mild painkiller (Moment is a brand name.)

▶ **effetti collaterali** side effects

antinfiammatorio anti-inflammatory Remember **antigelo**? *Anti-*, a prefix meaning 'against', is used, as in English, in many combinations: **antisettico** (antiseptic); **antibatterico** (antibacterial); **antistaminico** (anti-histamine); **antiorario** (anticlockwise), etc. (**antipasto**, however, is related to *ante-* meaning 'before': it's most certainly not meant to put you off your meal!)

COMMON AILMENTS

ho mal di denti	I have a toothache	**mi fa/fanno male ...**	followed by whatever feels painful:
... mal di gola	... sore throat		
... mal di schiena	... backache	**mi fa male il piede destro**	I have a pain in my right foot
... mal di stomaco	... stomach-ache		
ho mal di mare/mal d'auto/mal d'aria		**mi fanno male le gambe**	my legs are aching
I feel sea-sick/car-sick/air-sick		**mi sento male, sto male**	I feel sick
non sto bene, non mi sento bene			
I am not well, I feel unwell			

In a doctor's surgery

LISTEN FOR...

▶ **Ha anche il raffreddore?** Has she also got a cold?
▶ **È alta la febbre?** Is her temperature high?
▶ **un cinque gocce** about five drops

Dottoressa	Ha anche il raffreddore la bambina?
Papà	No.
Dottoressa	Soltanto della temperatura. Ed … è alta la febbre?
Papà	Oh, sì, è alta.
Dottoressa	Mmm … mmm … È alta. Quanti anni ha la bambina?
Papà	Ha due anni.
Dottoressa	[*giving him a prescription*] Ecco.
Papà	Eh … Novalgina?
Dottoressa	Novalgina a gocce. Sì. Le dà un cinque gocce … e tre o quattro volte al giorno. Questo dovrebbe tenere bassa la temperatura e togliere anche un po' il dolore.

dottoressa woman doctor

Dottore and **dottoressa** are titles used in addressing medical people who fall into the following general categories: **medico** general practitioner; **chirurgo** surgeon; **dentista** dental surgeon. Some specializations are indicated by words ending in *-ologo*, *-ologa* or *-iatra* (m/f), such as **radiologo** (radiologist), **oftalmologo** (ophthalmologist) (stress as in English), **pediatra** (paediatrician), **psichiatra** (psychiatrist).

papà daddy, father (note the stress on the end vowel: without it the word means pope).

▶ **Ha anche il raffreddore?** Has she also got a cold? Other common troubles **disturbi**: **influenza** flu, **tosse** cough, **indigestione** indigestion. Various Italian words ending in *-ite* (all feminine) correspond to English words ending in *-itis* referring to inflammatory diseases: **appendicite** appendicitis, **artrite** arthritis, **bronchite** bronchitis, **congiuntivite** conjunctivitis, **epatite** hepatitis, etc.

▶ **È alta la febbre?** Is her temperature high? The words **febbre** and **temperatura** are interchangeable. If you want to measure your temperature ask for a **termometro**, which will be marked in degrees Celsius. Normal temperature is between 36.5° and 37° C.

Novalgina a brand name; prescription is **ricetta**.

▶ **un cinque gocce** about five drops
dovrebbe tenere bassa la temperatura it ought to keep the temperature low
togliere il dolore take away the pain

PARTS OF THE HUMAN BODY
Note the irregular plurals

la testa head	**il petto** chest
l'occhio, gli occhi eye(s)	**la schiena** back
il naso nose	**la gamba, le gambe** leg(s)
l'orecchia, le orecchie (or **l'orecchio, gli orecchi**) ear(s)	**il ginocchio, le ginocchia** knee(s)
la bocca mouth	**il piede, i piedi** foot(feet)
la gola throat	**organi interni** internal organs
il collo neck	
la spalla shoulder	**il cuore** heart
il braccio, le braccia arm(s)	**il polmone, i polmoni** lung(s)
la mano, le mani hand(s)	**lo stomaco** stomach
il dito, le dita finger(s)	**il fegato** liver
il dito del piede toe	**l'intestino** bowel

7 Complete the following sentences with the likely part of the body which is giving trouble, chosen from the box on p. 212. There may be more than one suitable word.

   a. Ho camminato molto oggi, e mi fanno male le _____ e i _____

   b. Ho mangiato troppo, ho l'indigestione e mi fa male lo _____

   c. Ho camminato sotto la pioggia, ho la tosse e ho mal di _____

   d. Questa valigia pesa troppo. Non posso portarla perché mi fa male la _____

   e. Questa sera preferisco non uscire: ho un forte mal di _____ : devo avere un po' d'influenza.

ANSWERS P. 218

8 Rearrange the following conversation between a patient and his doctor. The easiest way to do this might be for you to write the correct order on a separate piece of paper.

   Dottore   Che cos'ha?

   Paziente   Da ieri sera.

   Dottore   Niente di grave. Prenda due di queste compresse adesso, e due dopo cena.

   Paziente   Non mi sento bene.

   Dottore   Ha anche disturbi di stomaco?

   Paziente   Ho mal di testa e anche un po' di febbre.

   Dottore   Da quanto tempo?

   Paziente   Sì, credo di avere fatto indigestione.

ANSWERS P. 218   ***Dottore***   Come si sente?

9 You are in a pharmacy and want something for your sore throat. Follow the instructions on your recording.

IL NASO CHIUSO NON VI LASCIA RESPIRARE?

RINO CALYPTOL®
Libertà di respiro

Con l'azione dell'Ossimetazolina cloridrato e l'effetto balsamico dell'Eucaliptolo apre subito la via al respiro e libera il naso per 6-8 ore.

GOCCE   NEBULIZZATORE   SPRAY

RHÔNE-POULENC RORER

Evitare l'uso per oltre 4 giorni. Leggere attentamente il foglio illustrativo. Aut. Min. San. N° 181

GRAMMAR AND EXERCISES

Personal pronouns

You have been using these pronouns from Unit 1 onwards. Here is a review of their forms, followed by explanations and examples of their use.

1	io	tu/Lei	Lui/lei	noi	voi	loro
2	me	te/Lei	lui/lei	noi	voi	loro
3	mi	ti	lo/la	gli	vi	li/le
4	mi	ti	gli/le	ci	vi	gli
5	mi	ti	si	ci	vi	si

The pronouns in row **1** are used as subjects, like English 'I, he, she, they', etc., but only when emphasis is needed.

Io sono insegnante, e Lei? (Unit 3)
Noi accettiamo le carte di credito (Unit 4)

Those in row **2** are object pronouns, like English 'me, him, her, them', used *after a preposition*, or for direct objects *where emphasis is needed*: e.g. **aspetto lui, non lei** I'm waiting for him, not her; **a me un analcoolico** (Unit 4); **di fronte a Lei** (Unit 5); **niente cipolle per lui** (Unit 10).

The pronouns in rows **3**, **4** and **5** are unstressed pronouns and all come *before* the verb (or after, attached to the verb, if the verb is an infinitive).

Row **3** are direct object pronouns (see Units 5 and 6), e.g. **il prezzo, non lo so, come la vuole (la camera)?**, **(queste albicocche) le prendo, ti vedo domani** I'll see you tomorrow.

Row **4** are indirect object pronouns, replacing nouns preceded by prepositions e.g. **compro un libro per Giorgio** I'm buying a book for Giorgio ▷ **gli compro un libro**; **prenoto dei biglietti per voi** I'm booking some tickets for you ▷ **vi prenoto dei biglietti**; **devo parlare con te** I must speak to you ▷ **devo parlarti**.

Row **5** are reflexive pronouns (Unit 6), e.g. **Come si chiama?**; **l'autobus si ferma qui**; **Quanto ti trattieni?**; **ci troviamo bene in quell'albergo.**

Remember that **mi, ti, ci, vi, si** change to **me, te, glie, ce, ve, se** when followed by **lo, la, li, le**: **me le può fare?** can you do it for me?, **te lo chiedo** I'm asking you for it; **glie li do** I'm giving them to him/her/them, etc. (Unit 13).

Use of *fare* followed by another verb

This is known as the causative construction, in that someone is indirectly causing something to happen. It is useful when asking people to do something for you without implying they should do it themselves. The form of **fare** is followed by an infinitive, e.g.:

Giorgio fa venire un facchino Giorgio calls a porter (lit. makes a porter come); **Giorgio lo fa venire; Mi fa venire un facchino? Me lo fa venire?** Will you call a porter for me?

Giorgio fa chiamare un facchino Giorgio has a porter called (lit. makes [someone] call a porter); **Giorgio lo fa chiamare; Mi fa chiamare un facchino?, Me lo fa chiamare?**

Giorgio fa chiamare un facchino dal tassista Giorgio has a porter called by the taxi driver; **ci facciamo indicare un ristorante da Aldo** we'll have Aldo suggest a restaurant to us (we'll have a restaurant suggested to us by Aldo).

Forms of request

Formal (**Lei**) requests: you'll find some examples throughout the previous units (**mi dia** give me; **mi dica** tell me; **mi faccia il pieno** fill it up, etc.) but they involve the use of the present subjunctive which is outside the scope of this course. This can, in most cases, be replaced by questions in the present tense you have studied (called 'indicative'): **Mi dà un chilo di mele?**, **Mi dice quanto costa?**, **Mi fa il pieno?** etc.

Informal (**tu**) requests: you use the present indicative, except that:
(1) the **tu** form of request for verbs in *-are* ends in

-*a*: **mangia** eat (instead of **mangi**), **entra** come in (not **entri**). The following are irregular: **dà** give, **fa** do, **dì** say, tell.

(2) monosyllabic pronouns are directly attached to the verb, and do NOT change its stress: **questo dolce è squisito: mangialo** this cake is excellent: eat it; **queste mele sono ottime: compratele** these apples are very good: buy them; **scrivimi** write to me; **chiedeteglielo** ask him/her/them for it. With the irregular forms above the initial consonant of the pronoun (except **gli**) is doubled: **dammi** (give me), **dille** (tell her), **fallo** (do it).

(3) In causative expressions (see above) all pronouns are attached to the forms of **fare**, NOT to the infinitive: **fateli entrare** let them in; **fammelo vedere** let me see it.

10 Fill in the spaces with one or, in one case, two appropriate pronouns from the box below.

Questa sera Luisa vorrebbe andare al cinema, ma Giorgio

preferisce il teatro _____ dice che c'è un

ottima commedia al Goldoni, ma _____ non

vuole veder _____ perché all'Odeon danno

l'ultimo film di Greta Scacchi, un'attrice che

_____ piace molto. Giorgio dice che l'Odeon

è molto lontano e ci andrà solo in tassì, se Luisa

_____ paga. Non _____ trovano

proprio d'accordo!

| glie la le lei lo lui si |

11 Your friend thinks that what you ask him to do should be done by the hotel porter.
Model: **Cambia questa lampadina vicino al letto. Facciamola cambiare dal portiere** (Have the porter change it)

a. ___ Compra dei biglietti per il teatro.

_____

b. ___ Porta in camera la valigia.

_____

c. ___ Prenota un biglietto aereo per Palermo.

_____

d. ___ Chiama un tassì.

_____

e. ___ Manda questo fax a tuo fratello.

_____

f. ___ Cambia queste sterline.

_____

12 Replace the infinitives between [square brackets] in the following sentences with the informal request form, both singular and plural.
Model: [**Portare**] in camera la valigia ▷ **Porta/portate in camera la valigia.**

a. [Accendere] la luce, per favore.

_____

b. [Chiedere] a Giorgio se può accompagnare Giulia alla stazione.

_____

c. Per piacere, [accompagnare] Giulia alla stazione.

_____

d. [Chiudere] la finestra: comincia a far freddo.

_____

e. [Controllare] l'olio e l'acqua prima di partire.

_____

f. A Roma [visitare] la zia.

_____

ANSWERS P. 218

KEY WORDS
AND PHRASES

Che cosa ti piacerebbe fare?	What would you like to do?
si potrebbe …	one could …
Che cosa danno?	What's on?
l'idea mi va	I like the idea
se t'interessa	if you are interested
sarebbe una buona idea	it would be a good idea
pronti per le otto	ready by eight
in tempo	on time
Perché non facciamo qualcosa insieme?	Why don't we do something together?
volentieri	willingly
scegliamo un buon ristorante	let's choose a good restaurant
magari invitiamo anche lui	perhaps we could invite him too
appena ritorno a casa	as soon as I get back home
due tubetti di dentifricio	two tubes of toothpaste
mal di testa	headache
gocce	drops
ci sono diversi prodotti	there are several products
effetti collaterali	side effects
Ha anche il raffreddore?	Has she also got a cold?
un cinque gocce	about five drops
È alta la febbre?	Is her temperature high?

Health problems

European Union nationals going to Italy are entitled to free health care subject to appropriate documentation. This should be obtained before leaving home from your local Department of Health office. When in Italy you should show the documents to the **Unità Sanitaria Locale** (Local Health Unit, or USL for short). You will then be issued with a Certificate of Entitlement which you can take to one of the doctors or dentists on the USL panel. The casualty department of a hospital is called **pronto soccorso** (lit. quick aid). The standard of medical care in Italy can be extremely high, though certain areas of the public health service have suffered considerably from decades of bad administration. It is a wise precaution, therefore, to take out private medical insurance which is strongly recommended to those without the safety net of EU reciprocal health agreements.

For minor ailments, most Italians rely on their local chemist. Chemists are all university graduates, chartered members of a national professional organization, with a long training and considerable experience in dispensing medicines. They are allowed to sell a number of proprietary drugs and preparations without prescription, and may even supply you with a prescription medicine you have run out of if they think it is safe to do so. In remote places the chemist may also be willing to give first aid in the case of minor accidents requiring simple medication.

Entertainment

Before you decide what sort of entertainment or show to go to, make a point of getting hold of the local paper, or, if you are staying at a hotel, of a copy of the local 'What's on' (often available in Italian and English). Regional governments, particularly during the tourist season, earmark a proportion of their budget for the sponsorship of free pageants, shows and concerts: look out for those marked **ingresso gratuito** (entry free).

Italians tend to decide what to do in the evenings on the spur of the moment. Only a few very special shows (operas with star performers or pop concerts) may be sold out (**tutto esaurito)** in advance of their performance. It is normally possible to obtain seats for most shows simply by applying on the same day. Shows tend to have much shorter runs than they have on Broadway or the West End — often only a few days.

Theatres are divided (going from dearer to cheaper seats) into **platea** (stalls); **palchi** (boxes); **balconata** (circle); **galleria** (balcony). Opera houses may have a few rows of cheap seats above the top balcony, called **loggione**. Front rows in the stalls and circle are often referred to as **poltronissime** (the superlative - *issimo* attached to **poltrona** arm chair). Cinemas normally make a single charge for all types of seats (**posto unico**). **Prima visione** means the film is being shown for the first time, usually in the more expensive venues.

AND FINALLY...

13 Discuss your holiday plans with a friend.

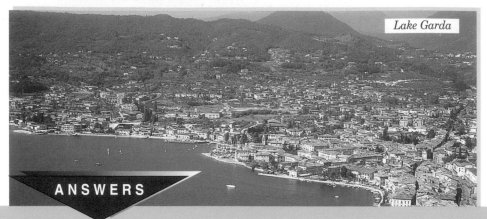

Lake Garda

ANSWERS

EXERCISE 2

Carla **(b)**   Luisa **(a)**, **(b)** and **(c)**   Giorgio **(c)** and **(d)**

EXERCISE 3

(a) al Farnese   **(b)** il Filmstudio   **(c)** al *Centre Culturel Français*   **(d)** 15.000 lire   **(e)** l'Archimede   **(f)** no

EXERCISE 4

M Che cosa si fa questa sera?

F Mmm, non so. Hai già un'idea precisa?

M No, nessuna idea precisa. Non vorrei però andare al cinema perché ci sono già stato ieri sera [**(a)** i].

F D'accordo. Nemmeno io. Guardiamo un po' il giornale. Si potrebbe andare a teatro.

M All'opera? Mmm, non mi piace molto l'opera, per dire la verità [**(b)** ii].

F No, non pensavo all'opera. Pensavo a una commedia. Al Teatro delle Muse danno una commedia di Goldoni, che mi piacerebbe vedere.

M Non c'è nessun concerto sinfonico, da nessuna parte? [**(c)** ii]

F Niente d'interessante questa sera. Domani sera.

M Mmm. Domani sera non posso.

F E allora?

M Allora perché non andiamo a cenare a quel buon ristorante vicino al teatro [**(d)** iii].

F Buona idea.

EXERCISE 5

(a) un film di Fellini   **(b)** guardare la televisione
(c) prendere un drink   **(d)** visitare il museo **(e)** al mare

EXERCISE 7

(a) gambe, piedi   **(b)** stomaco   **(c)** gola <u>or</u> testa   **(d)** mano, schiena, spalla   **(e)** testa <u>or</u> gola

EXERCISE 8

Dottore	Come si sente?
Paziente	Non mi sento bene.
Dottore	Da quanto tempo?
Paziente	Da ieri sera.
Dottore	Che cos'ha?
Paziente	Ho mal di testa e anche un po' di febbre.
Dottore	Ha anche disturbi di stomaco?
Paziente	Sì, credo di avere fatto indigestione.
Dottore	Niente di grave. Prenda due di queste compresse adesso, e due dopo cena.

EXERCISE 10

Questa sera Luisa vorrebbe andare al cinema, ma Giorgio preferisce il teatro. Lui dice che c'è un ottima commedia al Goldoni, ma lei non vuole vederla perché all'Odeon danno l'ultimo film di Greta Scacchi, un'attrice che le piace molto. Giorgio dice che l'Odeon è molto lontano e ci andrà solo in tassì, se Luisa glie lo paga. Non si trovano proprio d'accordo!

EXERCISE 11

(a) Facciamoli comprare dal portiere   **(b)** Facciamola portare …
(c) Facciamolo prenotare …   **(d)** Facciamolo chiamare …
(e) Facciamolo mandare …   **(f)** Facciamole cambiare …

EXERCISE 12

(a) accendi/accendete   **(b)** chiedi/chiedete
(c) accompagna/accompagnate   **(d)** chiudi/chiudete
(e) controlla/controllate   **(f)** visita/visitate

15 HOLIDAY TIME

WHAT YOU WILL LEARN
▶ how to complain about overcharging
▶ more about relating past events

BEFORE YOU BEGIN

Languages change all the time. Sounds change, as can be seen from the difference in many languages between pronunciation and spelling (obviously representing earlier stages of pronunciation). But grammar also changes. Expect to hear Italians producing sentences not conforming to the rules you have learned: one such case is highlighted in Conversations 1.

POINTS TO REMEMBER FROM UNIT 14
Things you would like to do:
facciamo qualcosa insieme, ... si potrebbe andare al cinema, a teatro, al ristorante ...
se t'interessa ..., sarebbe una buona idea ...

Talking about your health:
ho il raffreddore, mal di ... (denti, testa, schiena ...), l'influenza, l'indigestione
mi fa male ...(la testa, la schiena), mi fanno male... (i denti, le gambe)
che cosa mi consiglia?

Combinations of pronouns:
compro un libro per Giorgio ▷ glie lo compro; chiedo una cosa a te ▷ te la chiedo

---

Pronunciation notes

Any stress pattern displayed in the ending of a word tends to be shared by all words having the same ending: e.g. the names of medical and other specialists ending in **-ologo** in the previous unit, all stressed on the first **-o-**; all nouns ending in **-fono** (corresponding to English words ending in **-phone**), also stressed on the vowel before the ending (**microfono, telefono, sassofono**); all adjectives ending in **-ido, -ida** (**lucido**   lucid, **arido**   arid); Note words ending in **-bile** (mostly corresponding to English words ending in **-ble**), where the stress falls on the preceding vowel: **possibile**   possible, **visibile**   visible; and to their antonyms (words with opposite meaning: **impossibile, invisibile**).

▶ A case of internal migration

LISTEN FOR...

▶ **noi siamo tre figlie**   there are three of us daughters
▶ **Si trova bene?**   Are you happy?

Giovanni	Come mai è venuta a Roma?
Paola	Eeh, i miei genitori hanno emigrato qui a Roma, per lavoro, e quindi ...
Giovanni	E da quanto tempo è a Roma?
Paola	Ventisette anni.
Giovanni	Interessante. E quindi la sua famiglia si è spostata a Roma.
Paola	Sì. La mia famiglia è emigrata quando i miei genitori avevano quindici anni, più o meno, sono venuti a Roma e ... noi siamo tre figlie cresciute tutte qui a Roma.
Giovanni	E si trova bene?
Paola	Molto, molto contenta.

i miei genitori hanno emigrato qui a Roma   my parents moved (migrated) to Rome; but note further down **la mia famiglia è emigrata** (my family moved). **Emigrare** does not take a direct object, therefore **essere** is used to form the perfect (Unit 11, p. 166). **Avere**, however, is used with some verbs indicating movement (**camminare**   to walk, **correre, corso**, to run, **viaggiare, viaggiato**, to travel: **ho camminato per tre ore, ho viaggiato da Roma a Palermo, ho corso per prendere l'autobus**); and it is possible that some speakers may feel **emigrare** also belongs to this group. Note that **parenti** in Italian does NOT mean parents but relatives.

si è spostata   moved to; **spostarsi** (from **posto**, place) to change place; **spostamento** (move, displacement)

▶ **noi siamo tre figlie**   there are three of us daughters (lit. we are three daughters) Note also the following expressions relating to the number of people in a group: **In quanti siete?**   How many of you are there? (lit. in how many are you?); **siamo in tre**   there are three of us (lit. we are in three).

cresciute grown up, brought up (past participle of **crescere**, to grow, to bring up)

▶ **Si trova bene?**   Are you happy?

◗ A breakdown in Spain

LISTEN FOR...

▶ in prevalenza   mostly
▶ lì ci sono stati dei problemi   there were problems
▶ se non ...   except ...
▶ essere preparato a ...   to be prepared to ...

Giovanni	Lei ha avuto delle esperienze di viaggio all'estero in automobile?
Sig. Cimaglia	Sì, Io vado all'estero in prevalenza in automo... in automobile.
Giovanni	Dove va?
Sig. Cimaglia	Ma, certamente nei paesi nostri più vicini, in Francia, in Spagna, in Germania, ho usato tranquillamente la mia macchina senza alcun problema. L'unica volta che ho avuto delle difficoltà le ho avute in Spagna perché ho avuto una rottura di un motore, e lì ci sono stati dei problemi. Problemi tra l'altro risolti. Non... non ho avuto, diciamo, delle grosse difficoltà, se non per ... per avere il cambio della moneta, farsi mandare la moneta dall'Italia. Allora sono dei problemi perché uno non può essere preparato a ... sostituire un motore.

esperienze di viaggio all'estero
     foreign travel experiences
▶ **in prevalenza**   mostly
nei paesi nostri più vicini   in the countries nearest to ours (lit. our most near)
ho avuto delle difficoltà ... le ho avute: for the reason why the second past participle agrees with the pronoun **le** which precedes it, see *Grammar*, p. 230.
ho avuto una rottura di un motore I had a breakdown (lit. I had a breakage of an engine). The definite article might also be used: **ho avuto la rottura del motore**. Remember **rompere**, past participle **rotto** (to break).
▶ **e lì ci sono stati dei problemi**   and there were problems there. **Lì** or **là** mean there pointing to a place. **Ci** (or **c'**) before forms of **essere**, like 'there' before forms of 'to be' in English, is an introductory 'there', to warn of a postponed subject: **non c'era nessuno lì**   there was nobody there instead of **nessuno era lì** (nobody was there) (Unit 3).
tra l'altro   among other things, here a meaningless filler, like **diciamo** further on.
▶ **se non ...**   except ... (lit. if not)
per avere, etc.   to have money changed, to have money sent from Italy
▶ **essere preparato a ...**   to be prepared for/to ...
sostituire   to replace

PRACTICE

1

This is a pronunciation exercise on adjectives ending in **-bile**. Confirm the statements below using the adjective with the opposite meaning, formed by the prefix **in-** (**im-** before **-b-** or **-p-**, as in English), as from the following model:
La situazione politica non è stabile. ▷ **È davvero instabile.**

a. La rottura del motore non è tollerabile.

_____

b. Il costo di riparare il motore non è accettabile.

_____

c. Dicono che domani piove, ma non è probabile.

_____

d. Dicono che domani nevica, ma non è possibile.

_____

e. Questa notizia non è credibile.

_____

2 In the following passages replace the verbs between brackets with the appropriate forms of the Perfect tense.

I miei genitori si [conoscere] _____ nel 1969, quando le loro famiglie

[decidere] _____ di spostarsi a Roma. Io e le mie due sorelle

[nascere] _____ e [crescere] _____ a Roma.

Sei mesi fa io [cominciare] _____ a lavorare in questo albergo, e mi

ANSWERS P. 234 [trovare] _____ molto bene.

3 In the following passages replace the verbs between brackets with the appropriate forms of the Imperfect tense.

I miei genitori si [conoscere] _____ già prima di emigrare.

[Andare] _____ a scuola insieme nel paese dove [abitare]

_____ . I loro genitori non [trovare] _____

lavoro perché c'[essere] _____ molta disoccupazione (unemployment)

nella regione. Le due famiglie [avere] _____ parenti che [lavorare]

ANSWERS P. 234 _____ a Roma, e così hanno deciso di spostarsi a Roma.

CONVERSATIONS 2

▶ *Signor Ramenghi remembers his visits to Australia*

<table>
<tr><td colspan="2" align="center">LISTEN FOR...</td></tr>
<tr><td>▶ la maggior parte della mia attività</td><td>most of my work</td></tr>
<tr><td>▶ l'occasione</td><td>the opportunity</td></tr>
<tr><td>▶ avevamo dei periodi di sosta</td><td>we had rest periods</td></tr>
<tr><td>▶ mi piacerebbe visitarlo molto più spesso</td><td>I'd like to visit it much more often</td></tr>
</table>

Sig. Ramenghi	La maggior parte della mia attività l'ho svolta all'Alitalia dal sessantasette all'ottantacinque come capo steward a bordo dei jumbo, eccetera eccetera. E lì fu l'occasione che ebbi di venire in Australia, Melbourne, Sydney, eccetera, eccetera, per voli, diciamo, di linea.
Giovanni	Quindi Lei conosce bene queste due città.
Sig. Ramenghi	Sì, abbastanza perché avevamo dei periodi di sosta di sei, anche sette giorni. Delle due devo dir la verità che mi piaceva molto più Sydney perché c'è il mare, e io sono di Genova, e allora ho sempre apprezzato molto. Melbourne l'ho trovata molto più industriale, più tipo Milano, diciamo.
Giovanni	Sì.
Sig. Ramenghi	Però ho trovato la popolazione australiana fantastica, molto ospitale. È un paese che a me mi dispiace che sia così lontano, perché mi piacerebbe visitarlo molto più spesso, ecco. È un volo un po' lungo.

▶ **la maggior parte della mia attività**   most of my work (lit. the greatest part of my activity)

l'ho svolta   I did it; from **svolgere**, lit. to unfold, to develop, a verb often used speaking of work or activities. See *Grammar*, p. 230.

fu   it was, **ebbi** (I had): forms of the Past simple (**passato remoto**) of **essere** and **avere**

▶ **l'occasione**   the opportunity

Lei conosce bene   you know well. For the difference between **conoscere** and **sapere**, both translating 'to know', see *Grammar*, p. 230.

▶ **avevamo dei periodi di sosta**   we had rest periods; **sosta** (stay), **sostare** (to stay, to rest). Here the Imperfect is used because the verb refers to a repeated or habitual situation. Further on: **mi piaceva ...** implying 'I liked Sydney every time I went there'; whereas **l'ho trovata molto più industriale** refers to Mr Ramenghi's impression of Melbourne once and for all: 'I found Melbourne much more industrialized'. For **l'ho trovata** see *Grammar*, p. 230.

devo dir la verità che...   to tell the truth (lit. I must say the truth that...)

e io sono di Genova, etc. and I am from Genoa, therefore I always much enjoyed (the sea). To understand this remark one should know that many of Sydney's suburbs have views over the bays or the ocean; Port Phillip Bay, on the other hand, is visible only to a minority of Melburnians living along its much flatter coastline.

più tipo Milano   more like Milan (see Unit 11, p. 156)

ospitale   hospitable

che a me mi dispiace, etc.   You would translate it as 'I'm sorry this country is so far away'; but what he says literally is 'It's a country which to me I am sorry that it is so far away'. With constructions like **mi piace** or **mi dispiace**, you don't need another personal pronoun (**a me** is already expressed by **mi**), but many speakers add it for emphasis.

▶ **mi piacerebbe visitarlo molto più spesso**   I'd like to visit it much more often

◗ *Advice to a Travel Agent*

LISTEN FOR...	
▶ **vale la pena**	it's worth it
▶ **appena ne avrò l'occasione**	as soon as I have the opportunity

Agente di viaggio	È una bella città, Sydney?
Giovanni	Molto bella.
Agente di viaggio	Io non l'ho mai vista.
Giovanni	Lei dovrebbe avere dei biglietti a concessione, no? in quanto agente di viaggio. Una volta dovrebbe fare un viaggio fino in Australia.
Agente di viaggio	Dovrei farlo, mi piacerebbe farlo.
Giovanni	Vale la pena. È molto bello.
Agente di viaggio	Eh, appena ne avrò l'occasione … lo farò molto volentieri.

biglietti a concessione concessionary (reduced price) tickets

in quanto agente di viaggio as a travel agent; **in quanto studente** (as a student)

▶ **vale la pena** it's worth it, it's worthwhile (lit. it's worth the pain); **Vale la pena guardare la TV questa sera?** (Is TV worth watching tonight?) **no, non ne vale la pena** (no, it's not worth it); **non vale la pena (di) parlarne** (it's not worth talking about).

▶ **appena ne avrò l'occasione** as soon as I have the opportunity. **Avrò** is the future stense of **avere** (see Unit 10, p. 150).

PRACTICE

4 Listen to the descriptions of four well-known Roman monuments. You do not need to understand everything in order to answer the following questions, but you will need the word **secolo**, century.

The Pantheon

a. Which is the most ancient of the four monuments? i il Pantheon ii le Terme di Caracalla

b. Which is the most recent? (i) il Vittoriano (ii) la Fontana di Trevi

c. Where was King Victor Emmanuel II buried? (i) in the Pantheon (ii) in the Vittoriano

d. How long did it take to build the Trevi Fountain? (i) five years (ii) twenty years (iii) thirty years

e. For how many centuries did the Terme di Caracalla perform their intended function of public baths? (i) two (ii) three (iii) five

f. Two architects are mentioned. Who are they? (i) Virgo and Agrippa (ii) Salvi and Sacconi (iii) Augusto and Adriano

g. Which of the monuments is now used as a summer theatre? (i) il Vittoriano (ii) le Terme di Caracalla

5 Question an Italian acquaintance about her travels, following the instructions on your recording.

6 Fill in the gaps in the sentences below with one of the following verbal expressions:

dobbiamo, dovrebbe, potrai, sono dovuto, sono potuto, vorrei

a. Un anno fa _____ andare a Londra per un mese.

b. _____ andare in Australia appena ne ha l'occasione: le piacerebbe molto.

c. _____ andare in Italia per le vacanze, ma non posso.

d. Mio marito ed io _____ ritornare a casa alla fine di questa settimana.

e. Quando _____ andare nel Canada? Ne vale davvero la pena!

ANSWERS P. 234

f. Non _____ andare in Cina, come avrei voluto.

Dino's last holiday

LISTEN FOR...

▶ **abbiamo fatto una breve vacanza**   we had a short holiday
▶ **una località ideale**   an ideal place
▶ **ci piacciono le passeggiate facili**   we like easy walks

Giovanni	Quando sei stato l'ultima volta dalle tue parti con la famiglia?
Dino	L'estate scorsa. Abbiamo fatto una vacanza, una breve vacanza nelle Dolomiti, che veramente è stata meravigliosa.
Giovanni	In che posto delle Dolomiti sei stato?
Dino	Siamo stati in Val Gardena, in una località che si chiama Ortisei, proprio una località ideale per noi, perché ci piacciono le montagne, ci piacciono le passeggiate facili in montagna.

dalle tue parti   in your part of the country. On the use of **da** to mean 'in', 'to', or 'at' see Unit 10, p. 150.

▶ **abbiamo fatto una breve vacanza** we had a short holiday. Note the expressions **essere** or **andare in vacanza: sarò in vacanza dal 3 al 28 luglio** I'll be on holiday from the 3rd to the 28th of July; **andremo in vacanza in montagna** (we'll go on holiday in the mountains) (lit. in mountain) by analogy with other singular expression like **al mare** (by the seaside); **in campagna** (in the country); **in collina** (in the hills); **all'estero** (abroad).

Dolomiti   Dolomites (mountains in north east Italy)

Val Gardena   Gardena valley (**val** = **valle**)

▶ **una località ideale**   an ideal place

▶ **ci piacciono le passeggiate facili**   we like easy walks; **fare una passeggiata** (to go for a walk); **ieri abbiamo fatto una passeggiata in montagna** (yesterday we went for a walk in the mountains)

The Dolomites

The holiday was wonderful, but the hotelier was not

LISTEN FOR...

▶ **la gente era molto simpatica**   people were very nice
▶ **ci ha imbrogliati sul conto**   he cheated us on the bill
▶ **Ve ne siete accorti al momento?**   Did you realize it at the time?
▶ **ho deciso di lasciar correre**   I decided to let it go

Dino   Il tempo era molto bello, il cibo era molto buono, la gente era molto simpatica. L'unica eccezione è stato il nostro albergatore che ci ha imbrogliati sul conto: un piccolo incidente che non ci ha rovinato la vacanza.

Giovanni   E ve ne siete accorti al momento che vi aveva imbrogliato sul conto o ve ne siete accorti dopo?

Dino   No, me ne sono accorto sul momento, però ho deciso di lasciar correre.

Giovanni   Vi aveva imbrogliato sul costo della stanza o vi aveva fatto pagare di più di quello che dovevate pagare?

Dino   Sì, ci ha aumentato il prezzo di circa il dieci per cento, e io stupidamente non avevo la lettera che comprovava il prezzo, diciamo, originario.

▶ **la gente era molto simpatica**   people were very nice (but remember that **la gente** is always singular!). Like 'nice', **simpatico** is an all-purpose adjective applying to anyone or anything you like or approve of: **com'è simpatica** (how nice she is); **un ristorante molto simpatico** (a very nice restaurant).

▶ **ci ha imbrogliati sul conto**   he cheated us on the bill; **imbrogliare**   to cheat, to con, lit. to tangle, to ravel (**una matassa imbrogliata**   a tangled skein); **Che imbroglio!** What a mess! See *Grammar*, p. 167.
     incidente (m)   accident, contretemps
     rovinato from **rovinare** (to ruin)

▶ **Ve ne siete accorti al momento?** (or **sul momento?**)   Did you realize it at the time? Note that **realizzare** in Italian means 'to make something come true, or real', not 'to become aware of something' which is **accorgersi**, a reflexive verb: **mi sono accorto dell'errore** (I realized the mistake), **mi sono accorto che aveva sbagliato** (I realized he/she had made a mistake), **me ne sono accorto** (I realized it). **Ne** (Unit 3, p. 33) is another pronoun causing the -i in **mi**, **ti**, **ci**, **vi** and **si** to change to **-e** (Units 13, p. 193 and 14, p. 215).

▶ **ho deciso di lasciar correre**   I decided to let it go (lit. run); also **ho deciso di lasciar perdere**. **Lasciamo correre** (let's leave it at that, never mind); **lascia perdere** (don't take any notice). Should you not decide to let it go, you may complain by saying: **mi dispiace ma ...** I'm sorry but ...; **c'è un errore nel conto**   there's a mistake in the bill; **è più di quello che devo pagare**   it's more than I ought to pay; **il totale mi sembra errato/sbagliato**   the total seems wrong to me.
     ci ha aumentato il prezzo   he increased the price; **aumentare** (to increase); **c'è un aumento di prezzo**   there's a price rise
     stupidamente   stupidly
     comprovare   to prove, to vouch for
     originario   original (also **originale**)

---

7 With the help of the captions to the pictures, complete the postcard to a friend who couldn't join you on your holiday on the Italian riviera, by translating the English sentences below.

andare in barca a vela

fare passeggiate in montagna

andare a nuotare

prendere il sole (past part. **preso**)

gente simpatica

andare a ballare

… the people are very nice.
Every day we've been swimming and sunbathing.
Sometimes we went sailing, and on Sunday we went for a walk in the mountains.
Last night we went dancing at the disco.

Bordighera 1° Luglio

Ci è tanto dispiaciuto che non sei potuto venire qui con noi. Siamo qui dal 20 giugno e abbiamo fatto una vacanza meravigliosa. All'albergo…

Oggi purtroppo partiamo!
Cari saluti. Marisa.

Giorgio Ventura,
Via Passetti 12,
ROMA,
Italia.

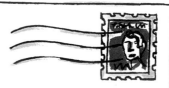

---

purtroppo   unfortunately

ANSWERS P. 234

8 Your hotel bill appears to be incorrect. Complain about it following the instructions on your recording. There's a new expression: **ha ragione** you're right (lit. you have reason).

9 Here is a conversation about a small problem with a bill. Fill in the missing verbs from the box below (which contains two forms which do not fit).

Gina Quando _____ che c'era uno sbaglio nel conto?

Carlo _____ solo dopo essere uscito dal ristorante.

Anzi, _____ mia moglie.

Gina Che cosa _____ allora?

Carlo Quando _____, siamo ritornati al ristorante e

_____ il rimborso di quello che avevamo pagato

in più.

Gina E vi _____?

Carlo Sì, ci _____ ragione senza discussioni.

---

abbiamo chiesto   avete chiesto   avete fatto   ce ne siamo accorti   hanno dato
hanno rimborsato   me ne sono accorto   se n'è accorta   ti sei accorto
ve ne siete accorti

ANSWERS P. 234

GRAMMAR AND EXERCISES

Word order

The normal word order in an Italian sentence is, as in English, subject – verb – object: **Carlo paga il conto** Carlo pays the bill. Sometimes it may be necessary to change this order for emphasis, e.g. **Il conto lo paga Carlo**, in answering the question, 'Who picks up the bill?' **Chi paga il conto?**

When the noun at the beginning of the sentence is the object, it is followed by the appropriate object pronoun (in this case **lo**). Other examples: **il caffè lo prendo senza zucchero** instead of **prendo il caffè senza zucchero**; **la mia attività l'ho svolta all'Alitalia** instead of **ho svolto la mia attività all'Alitalia**; **Melbourne l'ho trovata molto più industriale** instead of **ho trovato Melbourne molto più industriale**. For the agreement of the past participle, see next paragraph.

Agreement of past participle with preceding pronouns

You learned in Unit 11, p. 166, that the past participle preceded by a form of **essere** agrees with the subject (**la mia famiglia si è spostata a Roma; noi tre figlie siamo cresciute a Roma**). When it is preceded by a form of **avere**, it is 'frozen' in its -*o* form (**Carla ha pagato i biglietti, i miei cugini hanno comprato la pizza**). In one case, however, it agrees with the object: when it is preceded by the object pronouns **lo, la, li, le** (shortened to **l'** in the singular):
— **Chi ha pagato i biglietti ?** — **Li ha pagati Carla.**
— **Chi ha comprato la pizza?** — **L'hanno comprata i miei cugini.**

Note also the quotations from Conversations 2 in the preceding paragraph.

Conoscere and sapere

Although they may both be translated into English as 'to know', they have different meanings. **Conoscere** means to be acquainted with someone or something; e.g. **Conosci Maria?** Have you met Mary?, are you acquainted with Mary?; **Conosce benissimo l'Italia** He/She knows Italy very well; **non conosco questo libro** I don't know this book.

Sapere, on the other hand, is possessing an item of information, knowing how to: **sappiamo che ti piace la pizza** we know you like pizza; **Sapete nuotare?** Do you know how to swim?; **non sanno che cosa dire** they don't know what to say. **Non conosco questa poesia** means that I've never read or come across this poem; whereas **non so questa poesia** means that I don't know it by heart. In some cases, the distinction is not relevant, and either verb may be used: **Sai il russo?** Do you know Russian?, Can you speak Russian?; **Conosci il russo?** Have you learned Russian?

Present tense of		
	sapere	**conoscere**
I	**so**	**conosco**
you	**sai**	**conosci**
he/she/it or you (polite)	**sa**	**conosce**
we	**sappiamo**	**conosciamo**
you	**sapete**	**conoscete**
they	**sanno**	**conoscono**

10 Modify the following sentences by putting the object first and confirming it by the appropriate object pronoun.

Model: **prendo il caffè senza zucchero** ▷ **il caffè lo prendo senza zucchero.**

a. Leggerò questo libro durante le vacanze.

_____

b. Claudia ha i biglietti del cinema.

_____

c. Il tabaccaio vende le cartoline illustrate.

_____

d. Questa sera la TV trasmette *Amarcord* di Fellini.

_____

e. Studierò l'italiano a Firenze.

_____

f. Visitiamo la galleria d'arte questo pomeriggio.

_____

ANSWERS P. 234

11 Modify the following sentences, as in the previous exercise, by putting the object first, confirming it by the appropriate object pronoun *and* observing the agreement of the past participle with the pronoun/object.

Model: **ho spedito la cartolina senza francobollo** ▷ **la cartolina l'ho spedita senza francobollo.**

a. Ho letto queste poesie durante le vacanze.

_____

b. Claudia ha comprato i biglietti del cinema.

_____

c. I miei genitori hanno ricevuto ieri le tue fotografie.

_____

d. Ieri sera la TV ha trasmesso *Amarcord* di Fellini.

_____

e. Ho studiato la storia dell'arte a Firenze.

_____

f. Abbiamo visitato la galleria d'arte sabato pomeriggio.

_____

ANSWERS P. 234

12 Complete the following sentences with the appropriate form of **sapere** or **conoscere**.

a. Ho _____Maria l'anno scorso.

b. Hai _____che Maria ha avuto un incidente?

c. Noi non _____bene le strade di questa regione.

d. Io non _____davvero come ringraziarti.

e. Giocherei volentieri a bridge con voi ma non _____le regole.

f. Il mio amico è rimasto sulla spiaggia (beach) perché non _____nuotare.

ANSWERS P. 234

KEY WORDS
AND PHRASES

noi siamo tre figlie	there are three of us daughters
Si trova bene?	Are you happy?
lì ci sono stati dei problemi	there were problems there
essere preparato a …	to be prepared for/to …
la maggior parte della mia attività	most of my work
l'occasione	the opportunity
avevamo dei periodi di sosta	we had rest periods
mi piacerebbe visitarlo molto più spesso	I'd like to visit it much more often
appena ne avrò l'occasione	as soon as I have the opportunity
abbiamo fatto una breve vacanza	we had a short holiday
una località ideale	an ideal place
ci piacciono le passeggiate facili	we like easy walks
la gente era molto simpatica	people were very nice
ci ha imbrogliati sul conto	he cheated us on the bill
Ve ne siete accorti al momento?	Did you realize it at the time?
ho deciso di lasciar correre	I decided to let it go
vale la pena	it's worth it
in prevalenza	mostly
se non …	except …

The media

In Italy there are a few national and several fairly important regional or local newspapers. The distinction is mostly one of circulation and prestige, rather than coverage, as good local dailies, like *La Nazione* (Florence) or *Il Mattino* (Naples) will give nearly as much space to national and international news as the best-known national papers, like *La Repubblica* (Rome) or *Il Corriere della Sera* (Milan: despite its name, a morning and not an evening paper). National dailies, on the other hand, will also carry crime stories and other items of local interest: the layout of some papers is electronically transmitted to regional editors in several towns, who add local news on separate pages before having the whole printed and distributed.

In spite of the fact that many dailies subtitle themselves **quotidiano indipendente**, they are far from being independent of powerful commercial and political interests: the links between *La Stampa* (Turin) and FIAT are a well-known example. In this respect they are not much different from party dailies like *L'Unità*, mouthpiece of the **Partito Democratico della Sinistra** (Democratic Party of the Left, formerly the Communist party) which at least do not make a mystery of their allegiance. There are no Sunday papers: only Sunday issues of everyday papers. The national papers, however, publish one magazine section and various specialized inserts on set days of the week, and are often paired with interesting optional videos, CDs or CD-ROMs (Italian film classics, classical music and jazz, special series on history, history of art, etc.) at much reduced prices. Sports fans can buy a few dailies and weeklies exclusively devoted to sports news. Most Italian morning papers aspire to a 'quality' image which is reflected in a fairly conservative layout.

It is possible to see some difference between 'quality' and 'popular' press only at the level of the illustrated weeklies: usually the larger their format, the greater their gossip, scandal and soft porn contents. There are many illustrated periodicals, some of very high quality, catering for all interests, from photography and interior design to rock climbing and scuba diving. Comics are very popular among adults too, particularly those with interesting off-beat stories and excellent graphics which made the reputation of Guido Crepax, Milo Manara and Hugo Pratt.

The electronic media have developed exponentially from the days when three radio programmes and two TV channels were a monopoly of the State-controlled RAI-TV. The breakdown of this monopoly in the early seventies produced a huge rash of local FM and TV stations, broadcasting a continuous stream of pop, rock and disco music, interspersed with badly presented and incoherently structured phone-ins (radio); or screening lots of old B-movies and soft porn (TV), both surviving on home-made locally-sponsored advertisements. Many of these stations predictably came to grief and were bought up cheaply by shrewd entrepreneurs who gradually built up regional and national networks. In some cases their rapid expansion was more intended to broaden their financial catchment area than aimed at sound economic management. The impact of Silvio Berlusconi's network on Italian political life has certainly been one of the most interesting, some would say dispiriting, social phenomena of the early nineties. The protagonists of the next decade will no doubt be cable distribution and satellite communications, dominated by powerful transnational corporations, and the increasingly commercialized Net. The question is whether 250 TV channels or 25,000 home pages will offer real choice (how long will it take to choose?) or merely more of the same, with little or no space left for autonomous local initiatives.

AND FINALLY...

13 You think there may be some mistake in your hotel bill. Ask the receptionist to check it. You will query an item totalling 57,350 lire, and will need to remember that **pensione completa** means full board (Unit 3, p. 41).

ANSWERS

EXERCISE 2

I miei genitori si sono conosciuti nel 1969, quando le loro famiglie hanno deciso di spostarsi a Roma. Io e le mie due sorelle siamo nate e siamo cresciute a Roma. Sei mesi fa io ho cominciato a lavorare in questo albergo, e mi sono trovata molto bene.

EXERCISE 3

I miei genitori si conoscevano già prima di emigrare. Andavano a scuola insieme nel paese dove abitavano. I loro genitori non trovavano lavoro perché c'era molta disoccupazione nella regione. Le due famiglie avevano parenti che lavoravano a Roma, e così hanno deciso di spostarsi a Roma.

EXERCISE 4

(a) i **(b)** i **(c)** i **(d)** iii **(e)** ii **(f)** ii **(g)** ii

EXERCISE 6

(a) sono dovuto **(b)** Dovrebbe **(c)** Vorrei **(d)** dobbiamo **(e)** potrai **(f)** sono potuto. [Many Italians would say 'ho dovuto' and 'ho potuto': see Unit 13, p. 199.]

EXERCISE 7

... la gente è molto simpatica. Ogni giorno siamo andati a nuotare e abbiamo preso il sole. Qualche volta siamo andati in barca a vela e domenica abbiamo fatto una passeggiata in montagna. Ieri sera siamo andati a ballare in discoteca.

EXERCISE 9

Gina Quando ti sei accorto che c'era uno sbaglio nel conto?
Carlo Me ne sono accorto solo dopo essere uscito dal ristorante. Anzi, se n'è accorta mia moglie.
Gina Che cosa avete fatto allora?
Carlo Quando ce ne siamo accorti, siamo ritornati al ristorante e abbiamo chiesto il rimborso di quello che avevamo pagato in più.
Gina E vi hanno rimborsato?
Carlo Sì, ci hanno dato ragione senza discussioni.

EXERCISE 10

(a) Questo libro lo leggerò durante le vacanze.
(b) I biglietti del cinema li ha Claudia.
(c) Le cartoline illustrate le vende il tabaccaio.
(d) *Amarcord* di Fellini lo trasmette la TV questa sera.
(e) L'italiano lo studierò a Firenze.
(f) La galleria d'arte la visitiamo questo pomeriggio.

EXERCISE 11

(Different word orders may be possible)

(a) Queste poesie le ho lette durante le vacanze.
(b) I biglietti del cinema li ha comprati Claudia.
(c) Le tue fotografie i miei genitori le hanno ricevute ieri.
(d) *Amarcord* di Fellini l'ha trasmesso la TV ieri sera.
(e) La storia dell'arte l'ho studiata a Firenze.
(f) La galleria d'arte l'abbiamo visitata sabato pomeriggio.

EXERCISE 12

(a) conosciuto **(b)** saputo **(c)** conosciamo **(d)** so **(e)** conosco **(f)** sa

REVIEW SECTION

You have covered a great deal of ground in working through this course: it would be very surprising if you could remember everything you have learned! To help you review and consolidate the language you have met, there are fifteen extra speaking exercises – one corresponding to each unit – at the end of the last cassette.

Before you tackle each of these exercises, go back and test yourself on the Key Words and Phrases from the relevant unit. Then repeat aloud any that you had forgotten until you are confident that you know them.

EXERCISE 1
Listen to a man and a woman introducing themselves. Then follow the instructions of the presenter in your recording and introduce yourself. You will need the words **studente** if you are male and **studentessa** if you are female.

EXERCISE 2
In this exercise you will be using questions and statements based on Key Words and Phrases in Unit 2.

EXERCISE 3
You are booking a room in a hotel. The presenter will suggest what you should say.

EXERCISE 4
You'll practise ordering breakfast for yourself and a friend at your hotel. Follow the prompts on your recording.

EXERCISE 5
You've just found out about transport in the area. You are standing at a bus stop and a man approaches you. Follow the prompts on your recording.

EXERCISE 6
Explain to your Italian friend your holiday programme for the coming week.

EXERCISE 7
In this exercise you will be prompted to make comparisons between wines and their prices.

EXERCISE 8
You are doing some shopping at the local grocer's. Follow the instructions on your recording.

EXERCISE 9
You have heard that there is a train drivers' strike today, and want to make sure it does not affect your travel plans.

EXERCISE 10

The waitress approaches you after the second course and offers you a choice of desserts. You are worried about your cholesterol and choose something light. **Composta di frutta cotta** is fruit compôte.

EXERCISE 11

Express your dislikes and preferences following the instructions on your recording.

EXERCISE 12

You are motoring in Italy and need petrol and a few other things.

EXERCISE 13

You have met an interesting Italian and wish to know more about him.

EXERCISE 14

This exercise is complementary to Exercise 11 in Unit 14, but works, so to speak, in the opposite direction. Your travelling companion is very lazy, and wants various people to do things he could well do himself. Tell him so, according to the instructions on your recording.

EXERCISE 15

Give your Italian acquaintance some advice about her holidays. You'll need the word **foresta**   forest.

GRAMMAR SUMMARY

This section on grammar contains a few general concepts and definitions applicable to both English and Italian, a summary of points covered in the course, and some ideas you may find useful for further study. You should refer to the notes and grammar sections of individual units for specific details.

The noun phrase

Nouns are words that can be preceded by articles ('the' or 'a' in English). 'Elephant' and 'city' are nouns because you can say 'the elephant' and 'a city'. So are 'goods', 'writing' and 'who' in contexts such as 'the goods were despatched yesterday', 'the writing on the wall', or 'The Who' (name of a famous pop group). Nouns name living things (like **albero** tree, **segretaria** secretary, **elefante** elephant), objects or abstract notions (**città** city, **partenza** departure).

Nouns can be described or qualified by adjectives (as in 'the city garden' **il giardino cittadino**) or by other nouns ('the garden city' **la città giardino**). In English the qualifier normally comes first: in Italian it is is normally the second word. Italian adjectives tend to have a distinct form (**cittadino** from **città**, **centrale** from **centro**). To build up your vocabulary pay attention to the way in which Italian adjectives relate to nouns or verbs (to use a few examples not needing translation: **normale/norma, famoso/fama, economico/economia, persistente/persistere**). Most English noun qualifiers may be best translated into Italian by a phrase with a preposition (defined further on): the silk tie ▷ **la cravatta di seta**; a fruit tree ▷ **un albero da frutto**; this cheese roll ▷ **questo panino al formaggio**. All the phrases above are noun phrases.

Gender and number

All Italian nouns must be of either masculine (m) or feminine (f) gender. Only in some cases does gender go with sex: **uomo** man is m and **donna** woman is f. That, however, does not hold for the vast majority of nouns denoting inanimate objects, or even for a few nouns denoting sexed beings: **elefante** is m and **tigre** tiger f regardless of their sex. Number can be singular (one) and plural (more than one). This is shown in Italian by changes in the ending of articles, nouns and adjectives. When these words 'go together' they must have the same gender and number.

There are two basic patterns for nouns and adjectives:

		Pattern 1 (four endings)		Pattern 2 (two endings)
	M	F		M / F
Singular	-o	-a	bagno piccolo camera piccola	-e	grande ristorante abile assistente (able assistant)
Plural	-i	-e	bagni piccoli camere piccole	-i	grandi ristoranti abili assistenti (able assistants)

A number of nouns (mostly ending in -*ista* or -*amma*) have a masculine form in -*a*: **l'artista famoso**; **il poeta italiano**; **il nuovo programma**.

Note that nouns and adjectives that 'agree' or go together may not have the same endings if they belong to different patterns: e.g. **la grande camera**, **le grandi camere**; **il piccolo ristorante**; **le nuove assistenti** (new female assistants).

There are some nouns that do not change their ending: nouns ending in a stressed vowel like **caffè** (m) coffee or **città** (f) city, nouns of one syllable like **re** king, nearly all those ending in -*ie* and -*si* like **serie** series and **crisi** crisis, and words ending in a consonant, mostly borrowed from other languages, like **bar** or **sport**. Adjectives that 'agree' with these nouns still do change: **la città italiana**, **le città italiane** (f); **un bar elegante**, **dei bar eleganti** (m).

The verb phrase

In any instance of speaking or writing one can distinguish between:

- the speaker or writer who appears as 'I' or 'we' (1st person);
- the addressee(s) who appear(s) as 'you' (2nd person);
- the person(s) or thing(s) mentioned in the act as 'he', 'she', 'it', or 'they' (3rd person).

Verbs are words that refer to these six distinct persons (three for each number, singular and plural). In English the reference is signalled by a personal pronoun (I, you, etc.) and sometimes by an -*s* (writes), in Italian by distinct endings (**scrivo** I write, **scrivi** you write, **scrive** he/she/it writes, etc.).

Some forms, however, do not refer to any specific 'grammatical person'. One is the entry word in the dictionary (to write **scrivere**), called the infinitive. Other forms are called participles because they 'partake' of both the verb and the noun–adjective role (as in I have written **ho scritto**; the writing on the wall **la scritta sul muro**; the written words **le parole scritte**).

Verbs change not only according to person and number, but also to tense, the relationship between the time of speaking or writing and the time of what is being said or written (present, past, future, etc.). The connection between tense and time, however, is very loose: for instance, most future events, both in Italian and English, are spoken about in the present tense: e.g. tomorrow I'm going to Rome **domani vado a Roma**. Verbs may combine to form various tenses, as in 'I might have written' **avrei potuto scrivere**, or 'it should have been written' **si sarebbe dovuto scrivere**. **Essere** and **avere** are called auxiliary verbs when they enter into combination with participles (**ho scritto**, **sono arrivato**, etc.). Both simple and combined forms, together with their objects (see below), constitute verb phrases.

The number of Italian verb forms may seem daunting but it is in fact reducible to a small number of predictable changes mostly based on the infinitive. ALL 'we' forms, for instance, end in -*mo* (**siamo**, **parliamo**, **finiamo**); and all 'you' plural forms end in -*te* (**siete**, **parlate**, **finite**). Some forms, however, are not predictable from the infinitive (just as in English 'wrote' and 'written' do not follow from 'to write' as 'excited' follows from 'to excite'). In these cases it is usually enough to know the past definite and the past participle: e.g. in English rang, rung (to ring); in Italian **scrissi**, **scritto**, **scrivere** (to write). In all languages the most commonly used verbs are 'irregular'; but some of these irregularities come in groups (e.g. to sing belongs to the same group as to ring).

The Italian past definite (**passato remoto**) is not included in the teaching plan of this course since it can be replaced by the perfect (**ho scritto** I have written) in most cases.

The sentence

Sentences are made up of at least one noun phrase and one verb phrase. A sentence may be extremely simple, e.g. 'she writes', which in Italian may consist of only one word, **scrive**, since the pronoun 'she' (the noun phrase in English) can be dispensed with. Usually sentences come in a less basic shape, as in **Il turista inglese seduto al tavolino del bar scrive molte lettere agli amici lontani** The English tourist sitting at the coffee-bar table is writing many letters to his distant friends. The first eight words in both the English and the Italian example are the noun phrase, the remainder the verb phrase.

The noun phrase may include a verb phrase (sitting **seduto** in the example above); and the verb phrase may include a noun phrase (in the example the verb phrase beginning with 'is writing' **scrive** contains two noun phrases: many letters, to his distant friends). This shows a very important property of language: the ability to combine simple recurring elements into more complex structures. All you need to communicate is just over two dozen sounds — in Italian; more in English — an adequate vocabulary and two basic types of phrase!

The noun, pronoun (see below) or noun phrase denoting the 'person' of the verb is called the subject, regardless of whether it is a real person or does anything at all. In **La tua lettera è stata letta da tutti** Your letter has been read by all, **La tua lettera** is the subject because it determines the form of the verb, **è stata letta** as opposed to **è stato letto** or **sono stati letti**. Any other noun, pronoun or noun phrase connected with the verb by meaning, but distinct from the subject, is called the object. In **Il turista scrive delle lettere agli amici**, **delle lettere** is what the tourist is writing, i.e. the 'direct' object of the verb. The object, unlike the subject, does not affect the form of the verb (**delle lettere** is plural, **scrive** is singular like the subject). **Agli amici** to (his) friends follows from the object, but it is preceded by the preposition **agli**, so it is conventionally called the indirect object.

Verbs which may take a direct object (such as **chiamare**, **scrivere**, etc.) take **avere** as an auxiliary: **ho scritto una lettera**. Most (but not all) verbs which may not take a direct object (such as **venire**, **andare**, **ritornare**, etc.) take **essere**: **Giorgio è ritornato a casa**.

In English the role words have in a sentence is mostly indicated by their order. 'The Italians like to cook pasta' is not the same as 'To cook pasta like the Italians' or 'Pasta the Italians like to cook'. In Italian, on the other hand, word order is relatively flexible and the relationship of words to each other is indicated not by position but by ending: **la pasta piace agli italiani**; **agli italiani piace la pasta**; **agli italiani la pasta piace**; **piace la pasta agli italiani**; **piace agli italiani la pasta**, all mean, admittedly with slightly different emphasis, Italians like pasta.

Other sentence elements

Adverbs are words modifying or qualifying verbs, adjectives or phrases, like 'deeply' in 'thinking deeply', 'deeply resentful' and 'deeply in love'. Most of them (but by no means all) are characterized in English by the ending -*ly*; in Italian by the ending **-mente** added to the feminine or common ending of the corresponding adjective: **profondo** ▷ **profondamente**   deeply; **veloce** ▷ **velocemente**   quickly. The remainder consist of forms with no special ending, such as **bene**   well; **presto**   soon; **tardi**   late; or in 'invariable' masculine singular adjectives like **molto**   much; **troppo**   too much; **poco**   little.

Remember that, as we have seen when talking about nouns and adjectives, the same word may be put to different grammatical uses. **Troppo** is an adjective agreeing with **sale** in **c'è troppo sale nella minestra**   there's too much salt in the soup, and an adverb in **abbiamo mangiato troppo**   we've eaten too much.

Pronouns stand for nouns. Some display not only gender and number like nouns, but also person, like verbs: **lui** (he/him) is a masculine 3rd person singular personal pronoun. In English the verb remains largely the same apart from an -*s* in some cases (I stay, you stay, he/she stays, we stay, you stay, they stay,) and what changes is the pronoun before the verb. In Italian what changes is the ending of the verb (**sto**, **stai**, **sta**, **stiamo**, **state**, **stanno**): that's why subject pronouns are not needed to distinguish between verbal forms and are used only when they are emphatic or contrasting (e.g. **io leggo ma lui scrive**   I read but he writes). **Io** (I) and **tu** (you sing.) can only function as subjects: the forms found after prepositions are **me** and **te** (**È per me?**   Is it for me?, **fallo da te**   do it yourself). Some forms, reviewed in Units 14 and 15, precede the verb: **mi chiamo Giorgio**; **Ti piace?**; **lo prende**; **ci andiamo**, etc. Relative pronouns stand for subjects (or objects) of related verb phrases: as objects they are mostly omitted in English (the room [which] I have free is on the first floor, the girl [whom] you saw is my cousin) but must be expressed in Italian (**la camera che ho libera è al primo piano, la ragazza che hai visto è mia cugina**). 'Pointing' or 'showing' pronouns are called demonstrative (such as **questo**   this, **quello**   that).

Possessives in English change according to the possessor (his car, her car); in Italian they agree with the thing owned (**la sua automobile**, because **automobile** is feminine singular). They tend to be omitted in Italian when the possessor is obvious: **con le mani in tasca** with his/her hands in his/her pocket, **metti il cappello** put on your hat (you are unlikely to place your hands in somebody else's pocket or be told to put on somebody else's hat!).

Prepositions are words indicating the relationship between nouns, such as 'in the room', 'on the table', 'from my uncle', etc. In Italian they often combine with the definite article (see table in Unit 4, p. 54): **nella stanza**, **sulla tavola**, **dallo zio**, etc., in which case they change like the definite article. The preposition **del**, **dello**, **della**, etc, is used as a translation of 'some' or as a sort of article corresponding to the plural of **un**, **uno**, **una**: **compra dello zucchero**   buy some sugar, **c'erano delle nuvole**   there were a few clouds. Think of prepositions merely as links and not as words having a translation or a meaning (see Unit 10, p. 150).

Conjunctions link together parts of the phrase and/or of the sentence, and connect sentences together: e.g. **e**   and, **o**   or, **ma**   but, **quando**   when, **dove**   where, **perché**   why/because, **che**   that, **sebbene**   although, **nonostante**   notwithstanding, etc.

Prepositions, adverbs and conjunctions do not change their form and do not agree with other words in the sentence.

Numbers

For numbers beyond 20 follow the pattern of **venti**: *keep the final vowel except with one and eight.*

0	zero	31	trentuno
1	uno	35	trentacinque
2	due	38	trentotto
3	tre	40	quaranta
4	quattro	41	quarantuno
5	cinque	45	quarantacinque
6	sei	48	quarantotto
7	sette	50	cinquanta
8	otto	55	cinquantacinque
9	nove	60	sessanta
10	dieci	65	sessantacinque
11	undici	70	settanta
12	dodici	80	ottanta
13	tredici	90	novanta
14	quattordici	100	cento
15	quindici	101	centouno
16	sedici	102	centodue
17	diciassette	125	centoventicinque
18	diciotto	150	centocinquanta
19	diciannove	175	centosettantacinque
20	venti	200	duecento
21	ventuno	300	trecento
22	ventidue	400	quattrocento
23	ventitré	500	cinquecento
24	ventiquattro	1000	mille
25	venticinque	1500	millecinquecento
26	ventisei	2000	duemila
27	ventisette	5000	cinquemila
28	ventotto	10,000	diecimila
29	ventinove	100,000	centomila
30	trenta	1,000,000	un milione

1st primo (1°)
2nd secondo (2°)
3rd terzo (3°)
4th quarto (4°)
5th quinto (5°)
6th sesto (6°)
7th settimo (7°)
8th ottavo (°)
9th nono (9°)
10th decimo (10°)
11th undicesimo (11°)
12th dodicesimo (12°)

VOCABULARY

This vocabulary includes only words used in the conversations and related exercises. It does not include words which have been borrowed into English (e.g. pizza). When using it, bear in mind the following conventions:

1   Assume that words ending in *-o* are masculine nouns (m), and those ending in *-a* are feminine nouns (f). The gender is indicated in all other cases.

2   Entries with a double ending (e.g. **studente -essa**, **italiano -a**) are nouns or adjectives with separate masculine and feminine endings. Entries ending in *-e* (e.g. **sottile**) are adjectives with a common ending for both masculine and feminine. Nouns ending in *-e* are followed by (m) or (f) to indicate gender.

3   Entries ending in *-are*, *-ere* and *-ire* are verb infinitives. Any 'irregular' forms are noted (e.g. **fare**, **faccio**, **fatto**). Verbs in *-ire* that have a present in *-isco* show this ending after the infinitive entry. Entries in *-rsi* are reflexive verbs.

4   The English translation given refers exclusively to the contexts in which the word appears, and MUST NOT be taken as its 'meaning' in all cases.

5   The following abbreviations are used: (m) masculine, (f) feminine, (s) singular, (pl) plural, (inv) invariable, (adj) adjective, (adv) adverb, (conj) conjunction.

A

abbastanza   rather, enough, quite
abitante   inhabitant
abito   dress, suit
  abito da sera   evening dress
abituarsi a…   to get used to
abitudine (f)   habit, custom
abruzzese   from Abruzzo
accendere, **acceso**   to light, to switch on
accento   accent
accettabile   acceptable
accettare   to accept
accompagnare   to accompany, to take
accordo   agreement, musical chord
accorgersi di (**accorto**)   to realize
acido -a   acid
acqua   water
acqua minerale   mineral water
  gasata   fizzy
  liscia   still
acquedotto   aqueduct
acquistare   to purchase, to acquire
adesso   now, by now
adolescenza   adolescence, teens
aereo   aircraft
aeroporto   airport
affumicare   to smoke (food)

aglio   garlic
agosto   August
agricolo   agricultural
agricoltore (m)   farmer
agrodolce   sour-sweet
aiutare   to help
aiuto   help
albergatore, albergatrice   hotel-keeper
albergo   hotel
albicocca   apricot
alcool (m)   alcohol
alcuni -e   some
alimentare   to nourish; (adj) alimentary
  (**generi**) **alimentari**   foodstuffs
alimentazione (f)   way of eating, diet
allergico -a a …   allergic to …
allevamento   breeding
alto -a   high, tall
altrimenti   otherwise
altro -e   other
amabile   (of wine) medium sweet
amaro -a   bitter
amico -a   friend
analcoolico -a   alcohol-free
analgesico   analgesic
ananas (m inv)   pineapple
anche   also, too
andare (**vado, vai, va … vanno**)   to go

andata e ritorno   return (ticket)
andata   one way (ticket)
angolo   corner, angle
anno   year
annuncio   announcement
anticipare   to anticipate, to put forward in time
anticipo   advance
  in anticipo   early
antigelo   antifreeze
antinfiammatorio   anti-inflammatory
antipasto   hors d'oeuvre, appetizer
ape (f)   bee
aperitivo   aperitif
apicultore (m)   beekeeper
apicultura   beekeeping
appartamento   flat, apartment
appena (adv)   hardly, (conj) as soon as
applicare   to apply, to stick on
appuntamento   appointment, date
aprile (m)   April
aprire (**apro, aperto**)   to open
aranciata   orangeade, orange drink
arancio   orange
arido -a   arid, dry
armadio   wardrobe
arredare   to decorate, to outfit
arricchire (**-isco**)   to enrich
arrivare   to arrive

arrivederci good bye, see you
arrivo arrival
articolo article, item
ascoltare to listen (to)
aspro -a sour
assaporare to savour, to taste
assieme together
assortimento assortment, stock variety
atterraggio landing (of a plane)
atterrare to land
attimo moment, instant
attore (m) actor
attraversare to cross
attraverso across
attrice (f) actress
aumentare to increase
autobus (m) bus
auto[mobile] (f) car
automobilista (m/f) motorist
autostrada motorway, turnpike
autunno autumn
avanti further on
avere to have
azzurro -a light blue, sky blue

B

bagno bath, bathroom
ballare to dance
bambino -a child
barocco baroque
barriera barrier, gate, toll gate
basilico basil
basso -a low
basta enough, that's enough
bastare to be sufficient
bastone stick, bread stick
batteria car battery
bello -a beautiful, fine
bene well
besciamella béchamel, white sauce
bestiame (m) cattle
bianco -a white
  in bianco plain, without tomato sauce
binario platform, rails
birra beer
bisogna one must, one needs
bisogno need
  avere bisogno to need
bistecca beef steak, steak
blu (inv) blue, navy blue
bocca mouth
bollire to boil
borsa briefcase, bag
bottiglia bottle

bottiglieria off-licence
bravo good, clever, fine
breve short, brief
bufalo -a buffalo
buono -a good
  buongiorno good day, good morning
  buonasera good evening, good night
burro butter
bustina sachet

C

cabina booth, cabin
caduta massi falling stones
caffè (m) coffee
caldo -a warm, hot
calza stocking
calzini (m pl) men's socks
calzoni (m pl) trousers
cambiare to change, to exchange
cambio exchange
camera room
cameriere -a waiter, waitress; room cleaner (in a hotel)
camicetta blouse
camicia shirt
camminare to walk
canale (m) TV channel
candela candle, spark plug
canottiera singlet
capire (-isco) to understand
capitale (f) capital city; (m) financial capital
capolinea (m) terminus
caraffa carafe
caratteristico -a typical
carciofo artichoke
carino -a nice, pleasant, pretty
caro -a dear, expensive
carota carrot
carrello portavaligie luggage trolley
carta paper, chart, document, card
  carta d'identità ID card
  carta geografica/topografica map
  carta igienica/o toilet paper
cartella briefcase, document case
cartolina postcard
casa house
casareccio homemade
castagna chestnut
catena (mountain) chain, ridge
cattivo -a bad
causa cause
cavolfiore (m) cauliflower
cena evening meal, dinner
centrale central

certo certain(ly), (adj and adv) sure
certosa chartreuse
che who, whom, which, that, than
chi who (in questions), whoever
chiamare to call
chiamarsi to be called
  mi chiamo ... my name is ...
chiaro -a clear, light coloured
chicchi di caffè coffee beans
chiedere (chiesto) to ask for
chiesa church
chilo kilo
chilometro kilometre
chirurgo surgeon
chiudere (chiuso) to close
ciao hi, hello
cibo food
cifra figure
ciliegia cherry
cineclub (m) film society
cinema (m) cinema, movie house
cioccolato -a chocolate
cipolla onion
circa about
circuito circuit, network
città (f) town, city
cittadina small town, also citizen (f)
classe (f) class
classico -a classical
clima (m) climate
cocco coconut
cogliere (colgo, colto) to gather, to pick
cognome (m) family name
coincidenza coincidence, connection
colazione (f) **prima colazione** breakfast
  seconda colazione lunch
collutorio gargle, mouthwash
colonia cologne
colonnina pillar, post
colore (m) colour
come how, as, like
  come mai ...? why ...?
commerciante (m/f) business person, dealer
commercio business, trade
commesso -a shop assistant
comodo -a comfortable, convenient
  con comodo at your convenience
compartimento district, compartment
comprare to buy
comprendere (compreso) to understand, to comprehend, to include
compressa tablet
comprovare to prove, to vouch for
comunque anyway, anyhow
concerto concert

concessione (f) concession

condimento condiment, seasoning

condire (-isco) to dress, to season

condizione (f) condition

condizioni meteorologiche weather conditions

confermare to confirm

confezione (f) packaging, packaged product

   confezione regalo gift-wrapped

   confezione sotto vuoto vacuum packed

confrontare to compare

confronto comparison

congresso conference

conoscere (conosciuto) to know, to get to know, to become acquainted

consentire to allow, to consent

conservatorio conservatory, conservatoire

consigliare to advise

consiglio advice

conto count, account

   per conto mio on my account, by myself

contorno vegetables served with main course

contrario -a contrary, opposite

controllare to check, to control

coppia couple

cornetto croissant

correre (corso) to run

   lasciar(e) correre to let it go, not to take notice

corso main street

cortile (m) courtyard

cosiddetto -a so-called

costare to cost

costa rib

costata roast

costo cost, price

costoso -a costly, expensive

costume da bagno (m) swimsuit

cotoletta cutlet

cravatta tie

credibile credible

crescere (cresciuto) to grow up, to bring up

crostata tart

cuccetta sleeping berth, couchette

D

da from, by, at, to, for

data date

davanti before

decaffeinato decaffeinated

decidere (deciso) to decide

decimo -a tenth

dedicare to dedicate

degustare to taste, to sample

degustazione (f) taste, tasting

dio, dei (pl) god

democratico democratic

denocciolato -a stoned

dentifricio toothpaste

dentista (m/f) dentist

deserto desert

desiderare to wish, to desire

destinazione (f) destination

destra right

deviazione (f) deviation

di fronte opposite

dicembre (m) December

dietro behind

differenza difference

dimenticare to forget

diminuzione (f) lessening, fall

dintorni environs, surroundings

dipendere [da] (dipeso) to depend on

dire (dico) to say, to tell

diretto -a direct, straight, non-stop

diritto -a straight

direzione (f) direction

discesa way out (bus, train, tram)

discoteca disco

dispiacersi (dispiaciuto) to feel sorry

   mi dispiace I'm sorry

   ti dispiace ...? would you mind ...?

disponibile available

ditta firm

diverso -a different

dizionario dictionary

doccia shower, shower room

docente (m/f) university teacher

documento document

dolce sweet

   i dolci cakes

dolore (m) pain

domani tomorrow

domenica Sunday

dopo after, next

doppio -a double, twice as much

dormire to sleep

dottore, dottoressa doctor, general practitioner

dove where

dovere (devo, dovuto) must, ought to, to have to

dritto -a straight

drogheria grocery

droghiere, droghiera grocer

duomo cathedral

E

eccedenza excess quantity, surplus

economico -a cheap, economical

effetto collaterale side effect

elegante elegant

elettrico -a electrical

emergenza emergency

emigrare to migrate

Ente del Turismo Tourist Office

entrare to enter

entrata entrance, entry

errore (m) error

esatto -a exact

   esattamente exactly

escursione (f) excursion

esperienza experience

espresso express, espresso

essere to be

est (m) east

estate (f) summer

esterno -a external

estero foreign parts

   all'estero abroad

estero -a foreign, imported

estremo extremity, (adj) extreme

F

fa ago

facchino luggage porter

facile easy

fagiolo bean

famoso -a famous

fare (faccio, facciamo, fatto) to do, to make

farmacia chemist's, pharmacy

fato destiny

fava broad bean

favore (m) favour, service

fazzoletto handkerchief

febbraio February

febbre (f) temperature, fever

fegato liver

   fegatini chicken livers

fermare, fermarsi to stop

fermata stop

ferro iron

   ai ferri grilled

festivo -a holiday, weekend (fare etc.)

fico fig, fig tree

figlio -a son, daughter

filone (m), **filoncino** bread stick

finestra window

finire (-isco) to finish, to end

fiore (m) flower

formaggio cheese
forse perhaps
forte strong
fragola strawberry
francobollo postage stamp
fratello brother
frattaglie (f pl) offal
freddo -a cold
frequente frequent
frequenza frequency
fresco -a fresh, uncooked, chilled
friggere to fry
fritto -a fried
frittura fried food
frizzante fizzy
   frizzantino -a slightly fizzy
frutta fruit
frutti di mare (m pl) shellfish
fulminato -a blown (light)
fulmine (m) lightning
fumare to smoke
fumatore, fumatrice smoker
fumo smoke, fume
funzionamento working order
funzionare to work (of machinery), to function
fuori outside

G

gabinetto toilet
galleria gallery, arcade
garofano carnation
gastronomia gastronomy, cuisine
gelateria ice-cream parlour, ice cream
gelato ice cream
genere (m) gender, kind
generi alimentari (m pl) foodstuffs
genero son-in-law
gennaio January
gestione (f) management
gestire (-isco) to manage
gestore (m) manager
giacca jacket, coat
giacinto hyacinth
giallo -a yellow
giardino garden
gioco play
   carte da gioco playing cards
giornale (m) daily newspaper
giornaliero -a daily
giorno day, daytime
giovedì (m inv) Thursday
giugno June
giusto -a right
goccia drop
golf (m inv) sweater
gonna skirt

grammo gram
gran(o) turco corn, maize
grana (m) a type of cheese
grande, gran large, big, grand
grano grain, wheat
   grani di caffè coffee beans
grattuggiare to grate
grazie thanks, thank you
grosso -a large, thick, big
guardare to look at
guidare to guide, to lead
gusto taste

I

idea idea
identità identity
illustrare to illustrate
illustre illustrious, eminent, famous
illustrazione (f) illustration
imbarco embarkation, boarding
imbevuto soaked, steeped
imbrogliare to swindle, to cheat
imbroglione (m) crook, con man
immediato -a immediate
imparare to learn
impastato -a in batter, wrapped in pastry
impiegato -a employee
imperatore (m) emperor
impressionare to make an impression
impresso impressed
in in, at, to
incidente (m) accident, contretemps
indicare to indicate, to point out
indifferente indifferent
indigestione (f) indigestion
indirizzo address
industriale industrial
infanzia infancy, babyhood
ingresso entrance, entry
iniezione (f) injection
iniziare to begin, to initiate
insalata salad
insegnante (m/f) teacher
insieme together
intenzione (f) intention
interessare to interest
intermedio -a middle, intermediate
intero -a whole
interregionale interregional
intervallo interval, break
intreccio plot
invasione (f) invasion
invece instead
inverno winter
invisibile invisible

L

laboratorio laboratory, workshop
lampada lamp
lampadina electric bulb
lampone (m) raspberry
lattina tin, can
lavanda lavender, lavender water
lavorare to work
lavori in corso road works
lavoro work
leggere (**letto**) to read
leggero -a light, mild
lenticchia lentil
lesso -a, **lessato** -a boiled
letto bed
   letto matrimoniale double bed
libero -a free
libraio -a bookseller
libreria bookshop
libro book
lieve slight
limite (m) limit, boundary
linea line, route
liofilizzato -a freeze-dried
livello level
locale (m) venue, space, room
località locality, place
lozione (f) lotion
lucido -a shiny, lucid
luglio July
lunedì (m inv) Monday
luogo place

M

macchina fotografica camera
macchinetta small machine
macchinetta del caffè coffee-maker
macellaio butcher
macelleria butcher's shop
macello abattoir
macinare to grind
madre (f) mother
maestro -a primary schoolteacher
magari perhaps
magazzino store, depot
   grande magazzino department store
maggio May
maglietta T-shirt
magro -a lean, thin, meagre
mal di ... ...ache
   mal di schiena backache
   mal di gola sore throat
mancare to be missing, to lack
mandare to send
mangiare to eat

manzo beef
marca brand, trademark
marciapiede (m) pavement, sidewalk
mare (m) sea, seaside
marito husband
marmellata jam
marmo marble
marrone (m inv) chestnut, brown
martedì (m inv) Tuesday
marzo March
matto -a mad, go crazy
  andar matto per qualcosa to be crazy about something
meccanico mechanic, mechanical
meglio (adv) better
mela apple
meno less
meno male thank goodness
mercoledì (m inv) Wednesday
meridionale southern
messa a punto check up, overhaul
metro (m/f inv), **metropolitana** underground railway
metro metre
mettere (**messo**) to place, to put
  mettere a disposizione di qualcuno to place at someone's disposal
  mettere a punto to check over, to tune (an engine)
mezzo di trasporto transport
mezzo -a half
michetta round bread roll
microfono microphone
miglioramento improvement
migliorare to improve
migliore (adj) better
  il migliore the best
mio -a my, mine
misto -a mixed
mobile (m) piece of furniture
mobiliato -a furnished
modello model, style, pattern
modico -a moderate
moglie (f) wife
molto very, much
montagna mountain
monumento monument
mosca fly
motivo motive, reason
motore (m) engine
mucca cow
museo museum
musica popolare folk music
musicista (m/f) musician
mutande (f pl) underwear

N

narciso narcissus
nascere (**nato**) to be born
nascita birth
natale of birth
  Natale Christmas
nazionale national
nazionalità nationality
ne of it/him/her/them
nebbia fog
nebbioso foggy
necessario -a necessary
negozio shop
nero -a black
nevoso -a snowy
niente nothing
nipotino little grandson, little nephew
no no
nocciolo fruit stone
noce (f) walnut
  noce moscata nutmeg
noioso annoying, boring
nome (m) name, noun
non not
nono -a ninth
nord (m) north
notizia item of news
notte (f) night
novembre November
numero number
nuotare to swim
nuovo -a new
nuvola cloud
nuvolosità cloud cover
nuvoloso -a cloudy

O

o, oppure or
o ... o ... either ... or ...
occasione (f) opportunity
occhio eye
  a occhio roughly
occidentale western, occidental
occorre it is necessary
occorrere to be required
occupare to occupy
  occuparsi di ... to look after ...
occupato -a busy, engaged (of telephone)
oftalmologo ophthalmologist
oggi today
ogni every
  ogni tanto every now and then
olio oil

oliva olive
oltretutto anyway, besides
opera opera
ora hour, ... o'clock
orario time, timetable
ordinario -a ordinary, normal, full-rate
orientale eastern, oriental
originale original
originario -a original
origine (f) origin
orzo barley
ospitale hospitable
ottavo -a eighth
ottico optician, optical
ottobre (m) October
ovest (m) west

P

padre (m) father
paese (m) village, country
pagamento payment
pagare to pay
paio (m), pl **paia** (f) pair
palazzo large building, palace
pancetta a sort of bacon
pane (m) bread, loaf of bread
panettone (m) Italian Christmas cake
panino bread roll, stuffed roll
paninoteca sandwich bar
pantaloni (m pl) trousers
parcheggio car park, parking
parente (m/f) relative
parere, mi pare it seems to me
parete (f) wall
parmigiano parmesan cheese
partenza departure
partire (**parto**) to leave, to depart
passaggio passage, stroll, people walking
passaporto passport
passeggiare to take a walk, to stroll
passeggiata walk, stroll
pasticceria confectionery, cakes
pastiglia lozenge
pecora sheep
pecorino sheep's milk cheese
pediatra (m/f) paediatrician
peggio (adv) worse
peggioramento worsening
peggiorare to worsen
peggiore (adj) worse
penisola peninsula
pensare to think
pensione (f) boarding house

pensione completa full board
mezza pensione half board
pepe (m) pepper
peperone (m) capsicum, pepper
per for, to
per piacere please
pera pear
perché why, because
perfetto -a perfect
periodo period, time
però however
persistente persistent, long-lasting
persistere (**persistito**) to persist, to last
persona person
personale (m) staff, personnel;
  (adj) personal
pesare to weigh
pesce (m) fish
peso weight
pezzettino small piece
pezzo piece
piacere (m) pleasure
piacere (**piaciuto**) to please
piano floor
piatto dish, plate, course
piazza public square
piazzale (m) small square, place
piccante hot, spicy
piccolo small
piede (m) foot
  a piedi on foot
pieno -a full
  fare il pieno to fill up
pila small battery
pillola pill
piovoso -a rainy
pirofila oven-proof dish
pisello pea
pistacchio pistachio
più more
piuttosto rather
pneumatico tyre
poco little
  un poco, un po' a little
poeta (m) poet
polizia police
pollame (m) poultry
pollo chicken
polo pole
pomata ointment
pomeriggio afternoon
pomodoro tomato
portabiti (m inv) suit holder, wardrobe
  suitcase
portare to carry, to bring
  portare via to take away
portiere (m) doorman, concierge
possibile possible

Posta Centrale General Post Office
posto place
potere (**posso, potuto**) can, to be
  able to
pranzo lunch, dinner
precipitazione (f) precipitation, rainfall
preferire (**-isco**) to prefer
prego don't mention it, please
prelevare to withdraw, to cash
prendere (**preso**) to take
prenotare to book, to reserve
prenotazione (f) reservation
preparare to prepare
prevalere (**prevalso**) to prevail
prezzo price
prima before, earlier
prima colazione (f) breakfast
primavera spring
primitivo -a primitive
primo -a first
principale main, principal
probabile probable
problema (m) problem
prodotto produce
produzione (f) production, produce
professionale (adj) professional
professionista (m/f) professional
professore, professoressa secondary
  schoolteacher, professor
profumazione (f) scent
profumeria perfumery
profumo perfume
progettare to plan, to design, to
  project
progetto project
promontorio promontory
pronto ready, hello (on the phone)
proprio just, right, especially
prosciutto cotto cooked ham
prossimo -a next (from now)
protesta sindacale industrial action,
  strike
protettore protector, patron saint
provare to try
proveniente da coming from
provenienza origin, point of departure
provenire (**provengo, provenuto**) to
  come from
provincia province
prugna plum
psichiatra (m/f) psychiatrist
pubblicare to publish
pubblicazione (f) publication
pullman (m) long-distance bus, coach
pulsante (m) push button
punto di vista viewpoint
puntualmente punctually
purtroppo unfortunately

Q

qualche some, a few (always followed
  by a singular noun)
quale -i which
qualsiasi (inv) any, whatever
quando when
quanto -a how much
quartino quarter litre, quarter-litre
  bottle
quarto -a fourth, quarter
quasi nearly, almost
quello that
questo this
qui here
qui vicino nearby
quindi therefore, that is
quinto -a fifth

R

raccomandare to recommend
radiologo radiologist
raffreddore (m) cold (ailment)
raggiungere (**raggiunto**) to reach
ragione (f) reason
  avere ragione to be (in the) right
ragù (m inv) meat sauce
rallentare to slow down
rapini (m pl) turnip tops
recarsi a … to go to …
regalare to give as a present
regalo gift
regione (f) region
regolare regular
resto change, rest, remainder
ridotto -a reduced, concessionary
  (fare)
rientrare to re-enter, to go back
rifare (**rifatto**) to re-do, to remake
rimanere (**rimango, rimasto**) to remain,
  to stay behind
rimborsare to refund, to reimburse
rimborso refund
ringraziare to thank
riparare to repair
ripieno -a stuffed
  il ripieno stuffing
riprendere (**ripreso**) to pick up again
  to access
ristorante (m) restaurant
ristrutturare to restructure, to
  refurbish
ritardare to delay
ritardo delay
  in ritardo late
ritornare to return
ritorno return

riviera   seaside promenade, riviera
rivolgersi a ...   to apply to ...
rompere (rotto)   to break
rosa   (n) rose, (inv adj) pink
rosetta   a type of bread roll
rosso -a   red
rotondo -a   round
rottura   breakage, breakdown, mechanical failure
rovinare   to ruin
rubare   to steal
rumore (m)   noise
rumoroso -a   noisy

S

sabato   Saturday
sale (m)   salt
  salato -a   salty
salire (salgo)   to climb, to go up
salita   way in (bus, train, tram)
salsa   sauce
saltare   to jump, to skip over, to sauté
salvaguardare   to safeguard
salvataggio   rescue
salve   hi
santuario   sanctuary
sapere (so, sai, sa, saputo)   to know
sapone (m)   soap
sapore (m)   taste, flavour
sassofono   saxophone
sbagliare, sbagliarsi   to err, to make a mistake
sbaglio   mistake
scala   ladder, step ladder, staircase
scalo   landing stage
scaloppe (f) scaloppine (f pl)   escalopes
scarpa   shoe
scatola   box, tin, can
scegliere (scelgo, scelto)   to choose
scendere (sceso)   to get off, to step down
scheda   card (magnetic, index)
sciopero   strike
scolare   to drain
scolastico -a   (pertaining to) school
scompartimento   compartment
scoprire (scoperto)   to discover, to uncover
scorrevole   flowing, smooth
scorso -a   past, last
scrivere (scritto)   to write
scuola materna   nursery school
scusare   to excuse
secco -a   dry
secolo   century
secondo -a   second
sedano   celery

sedersi   to sit down
sedia   chair
segnalare   to signal, to point out
segretario -a   secretary
seguente   next (from a time other than now), following
seguire   to follow
semaforo   traffic lights
sembrare   to seem, to appear
sempre   always, still
sentire   to listen, to feel, to smell
senza   without
  senz'altro   absolutely
separare   to separate, to tell apart
sesto -a   sixth
settembre (m)   September
settentrionale   northern
settimana   week
settimo -a   seventh
settore (m)   sector, area
sfuso -a   sold unpacked or unbottled
sì   yes
siccome   as, since, given that
simpatico -a   nice, pleasant to know
sinistra   left
soccorso   rescue
soddisfatto -a   satisfied
soggiornare   to sojourn, to stay
soltanto   only
solubile   soluble, instant (e.g. coffee)
somma   sum, amount
sorbetto   sorbet
sorella   sister
sorgere (sorto)   to arise
sosta   stay, rest
sostanza   substance
sostituire (-isco)   to replace, to substitute
sottaceti (m pl)   pickles
sottotitoli (m pl)   subtitles
speciale   special
specializzato -a   specialized, qualified
spedire (-isco)   to send, to post
spezzatino   diced meat, casserole
spiga   ear of wheat
spinaci (m pl)   spinach
spingere (spinto)   to push, to press
spostarsi   to change place
stagione (f)   season
stanza   room
stare   to be, to stay
stazione di servizio (f)   service station
strada   street, road
  strada dissestata   uneven road surface
studente, studentessa   student
studiare   to study

studio   study
stupido   stupid
stupidamente   stupidly
subito   immediately, at once
succo, sugo   juice
sud (m)   south
suo -a   his, her(s), its, your(s)
supermercato   supermarket
superstrada   freeway (motorway)
supplemento   surcharge, supplement
supplì (m inv)   savoury rice ball
supposta   suppository
svolgere (svolto)   to unfold, to develop, to do

T

tabaccaio   tobacconist
tariffa   tariff
tartufo   truffle, a variety of choc-ice
tassì (m inv)   taxicab
tastiera   keyboard
tavolino   table, small table
teatro   theatre
telefono   telephone
tempaccio   foul weather
temperatura   temperature
tempesta   tempest
temporale (m)   storm, thunderstorm
temporalesco -a   stormy
terme (f pl)   spa
termometro   thermometer
terzo -a   third
tessere (tessuto)   to weave
tessuto   fabric, material
tinta   hue, shade of colour
tipico -a   typical
tipo   type, kind
tocchettino   small piece
togliere (tolto)   to take away, to remove
tollerabile   tolerable
tomba   grave, tomb
tornare   to return
torta   tart, cake
tostare   to toast, to roast
trafficato -a   congested with traffic
tram (m inv)   tram
tranquillamente   positively, happily, quietly
tranquillo -a   quiet
transitare   to transit
trasferire (-isco)   to move, to transfer; trasferirsi   to move
trasmettere (trasmesso)   to broadcast
trattenuta   deduction
treno   train
trippa   tripe

troppo too much
trota, trotella trout
trovare to find
  trovarsi to be, to meet
tubero root vegetable
tubetto tube, small tube
tuo -a your(s) (informal)
turista (m/f) tourist
tutto -a all

U

uguale equal, the same
ultimamente recently, lately
umido -a damp
  in umido stewed
un po' a little
universitario -a (adj) university
uovo (m), pl **uova** (f) egg
usare to use, to be in use
uscire, esco to go out
uscita exit, airport gate
uva (f pl) grapes

V

vacanza holiday
  essere in vacanza to be on holiday
  fare una vacanza to have a
  holiday

valere (**valgo, valso**) to be worth
  vale la pena di + inf it's worth
  + -ing
valido -a valid
valigia suitcase
valle (f) valley
valuta currency
vaniglia vanilla
vapore (m) steam
  al vapore steamed
variazione (f) variation
vasetto jar, jamjar, small vase
vecchio -a old, elderly
vedere (**visto** or **veduto**) to see
vendere (**venduto**) to sell
venerdì (m inv) Friday
venire (**vengo, venuto**) to come
vento wind
ventoso -a windy
verde (inv) green
veramente truly
vero -a true
versante (m) slope
verso towards, about, around
veste (f) dress, robe, appearance
via way, street, away
viaggiare to travel
viaggiatore, viaggiatrice traveller
viale (m) avenue
vicino -a near, nearby
viola violet, purple (inv adj)

violetta violet
violinista (m/f) violinist
visibile visible
visibilità visibility
visitare to visit
vita life
vitello, vitella calf, veal
vivere (**vissuto**) to live, to dwell
vocabolario vocabulary
volare to fly
volentieri willingly
volere (**voglio, voluto**) to want, will
volo flight
vongole (f pl) clams

Z

zafferano saffron
zanzara mosquito
zero nought
zio uncle
zia aunt
zucca pumpkin
zucchero sugar
zuppa soup
  zuppa inglese trifle

INDEX